The History of
The American Aircraft Industry
An Anthology

The History of
The American Aircraft Industry
An Anthology
G. R. Simonson, Editor

The M.I.T. Press
Massachusetts Institute of Technology
Cambridge, Massachusetts, and London, England

Copyright © 1968 by
The Massachusetts Institute of Technology

Set in Linotype Times Roman and printed
by The Heffernan Press, Inc., Worcester, Mass.
Bound in the United States of America by
The Colonial Press Inc., Clinton, Mass.

All rights reserved. No part of this book may be
reproduced or utilized in any form or by any means,
electronic or mechanical, including photocopying,
recording, or by any information storage and retrieval
system, without permission in writing from the
publisher.

Library of Congress catalog card number: 68-18241

Preface

A book on the United States aircraft industry necessarily deals with a subject that is very important for several reasons. First, the aircraft industry today is one of the nation's largest manufacturing employers. Second, and even more important, the aircraft industry plays a vital role in providing the necessary products for national defense and the defense of the free world. Third, the industry provides transport media upon which the United States economic system is becoming increasingly dependent for efficient operation. Despite the significance of the aircraft industry, at this writing there is no other recent book that deals primarily with its history. Because of the nature of the industry and its importance, this book should be of particular interest to students of history, business, and economics.

This book is based on the premise that an increased understanding of the aircraft industry can be gained by discovering the forces and circumstances that have shaped it over time. It is with this primary purpose in mind that this book on the history of the aircraft industry has been prepared. A second purpose which the book fulfills is to make accessible a number of classic selections on the history of the aircraft industry, most of which are out of print and available only in limited copies.

Each selection in this book has been chosen on the basis of the quality of its discussion of the most significant developments affecting the aircraft industry during a particular period of history. Although the literature is limited, fortunately at least one representative study on each major period of the industry's history was available. Four of the selections were written by people in academic life, three by members of the aircraft industry, two by professional writers, and one by the inventor of the airplane, Orville Wright. The selections denote different points of view, perhaps reflecting the affiliations of the authors, which are indicated in the introductions to the individual essays. Each introduction briefly summarizes the outstanding features of the period under consideration. To ensure fuller coverage, in some cases an introduction also discusses relevant aspects of that period that are not covered or sufficiently emphasized in the selection. The readings are assembled chronologically to show continuity in the development of the industry's history.

The book divides the aircraft industry's history into five time periods. Each represents a distinct epoch in the sense that the industry's development then was largely influenced by factors peculiar to that period. The first period extends from 1903, when the airplane was invented, to 1930. The most outstanding feature of the era, after the invention of the airplane, was the impact that World War I had on the industry. Later in the period, legislation in 1925 and 1926, which was designed to sustain the industry in peacetime, had far-reaching effects on the industry's structure. By granting contracts for military aircraft, the government determined which few producers among the many could eventually survive. The structure of the aircraft industry today is a consequence of these early procurement policies of the government. Another characteristic of this period was the short-lived boom in demand for civil aircraft—the "Lindbergh Boom"—which took place between 1927 and 1930.

The second period extends from 1930 to 1940. The era had several unique characteristics. There was a sharp fall in demand for civil aircraft, coincident with the depression that forced out of the industry most producers who were not fortunate to have military aircraft contracts. Very important during this time was the growth of industrial concentration through merger movements and holding-company acquisitions that were expected by the participants to ensure survival and enhance competitive strength. Another distinctive feature of the period was the growth in aeronautical exports supplied by the surviving members of the industry as international relations deteriorioated.

The third period includes World War II. The achievement of immense expansion in the production of military aircraft, and the problems connected with it, were the main features of the period. It was during this tragic but dynamic era that the United States aircraft industry became the largest single industry in the world.

The next period extends from 1945, the end of World War II, to 1955, and includes the Korean War. The industrial consequences of the postwar contraction and the expansion caused by the Korean War were the two most important topics of that interval.

Finally, the decade since 1955 was marked by several dynamic forces. The development of commercial jet transports, the effect of the substitution of missiles for military aircraft, and the industrial opportunity that space programs were offering and will offer in the future all caused more revolutionary technological changes in the industry than had occurred during any previous period.

Developments in the aircraft industry have been more violent than in any other industry of its size. This is largely true because throughout its history it has been primarily a defense industry whose sales have been periodically large in wartime and, by comparison, small in peacetime.

Moreover, the crucial necessity for technologically superior weapons and their development has led to a high rate of obsolescence of products as well as techniques and facilities to produce them, thereby forcing frequent drastic industrial changes. Although the subject has been neglected and is unfamiliar to most people, the development of the aircraft industry is one of the most interesting topics in American history.

I am particularly indebted to the authors and publishers who have granted permission to reprint the selections contained herein. In several cases, they have graciously permitted me to edit their works to make them more suitable for the purposes of this book. I also wish to thank Professor John B. Rae of Harvey Mudd College for several helpful suggestions relevant to the manuscript.

G. R. SIMONSON
Long Beach, California
August 1967

Contents

Part I

Early Industrial Development, 1903–1930

1. Invention of the Airplane   3
   Orville Wright:
   "How We Invented the Airplane"

2. The Rise of the Aircraft Industry   23
   Howard Mingos:
   "Birth of an Industry"

Part II

The Aircraft Industry in the Depression Years, 1930–1940

3. Depression, Industrial Concentration, and the Growing Export Market   73
   Elsbeth E. Freudenthal:
   "The Aviation Business in the 1930's"

Part III

World War II, 1940–1945

4. Conversion to Wartime Production   119
   Tom Lilley et al.:
   "Conversion to Wartime Production Techniques"

5. Wartime Performance of the Industry   141
   Reginald M. Cleveland and Frederick P. Graham:
   "Aviation Manufacturing Today in America"

6. The Industry's War Record and Postwar Recommendations   161
   The Aircraft Industries Association of America:
   "Aircraft Manufacturing in the United States"

Part IV

Postwar Developments and the Korean War, 1945–1955

7. The Consequences of the Postwar Contraction 181

    William Glenn Cunningham:
    "Postwar Developments and the Location of the Aircraft Industry in 1950"

8. The Korean War Expansion 209

    John S. Day:
    "Accelerating Aircraft Production in the Korean War"

Part V

The Aircraft Industry in Transformation, 1956–1965

9. The Missiles Impact 227

    G. R. Simonson:
    "Missiles and Creative Destruction in the American Aircraft Industry, 1956–1961"

10. The Space Age Opportunity 243

    Leonard S. Silk:
    "Outer Space: The Impact on the American Economy"

Bibliography 261

Index 267

Part I
Early Industrial Development
1903–1930

1. The Invention of the Airplane

The invention of the airplane in 1903 by Wilbur and Orville Wright marked the beginning of the aircraft industry. This invention is generally regarded as one of the truly great technological achievements of all times. The impact that the airplane has had on civilization, both as a mode of transportation and a means of warfare, has been all encompassing. The monumental nature of the technological breakthrough that the Wrights achieved is suggested in this statement made by Donald Douglas upon being awarded the Collier Trophy for the development of the DC-2: "There is nothing revolutionary in the airplane business. It is just a matter of development. What we got today is the Wright brothers' airplane developed and refined. But the basic principles are just what they always were." The breakthrough had been achieved by the Wrights. Any subsequent advances in the development of aircraft with respect to speed and ability to transport would be as a result of improvements in the areas of airframe aerodynamic structural qualities and engine power to propel the aircraft.

    The following article by Orville Wright is a classic in aviation history; it explains how the Wright brothers overcame the problems connected with human flight, particularly that of instability, and thereby made way for the aircraft industry.

How We Invented the Airplane*
Orville Wright

Our first interest [in the problem of flight] began when we were children. Father brought home to us a small toy actuated by a rubber string which would lift itself into the air. We built a number of copies of this toy, which flew successfully.... But when we undertook to build a toy on a much larger scale it failed to work so well. The reason for this was not understood by us at the time, so we finally abandoned the experiments. In 1896 we read in the daily papers, or in some of the magazines, of the experiments of Otto Lilienthal, who was making some gliding flights from the top of a small hill in Germany. His death a few months later while making a glide off a hill increased our interest in the subject, and we began looking for books pertaining to flight. We found a work written by Professor Marey on animal mechanism which treated of the bird mechanism as applied to flight, but other than this, so far as I can remember, we found little.

In the spring of 1899 our interest in the subject was again aroused through the reading of a book on ornithology. We could not understand that there was anything about a bird that would enable it to fly that could not be built on a larger scale and used by man. At this time our thought pertained more particularly to gliding flight and soaring. If the bird's wings would sustain it in the air without the use of any muscular effort, we did not see why man could not be sustained by the same means. We knew that the Smithsonian Institution had been interested in some work on the problem of flight, and, accordingly, on the 30th of May 1899, my brother Wilbur wrote a letter to the Smithsonian inquiring about publications on the subject. Several days later we received a letter signed by R. Rathbun, assistant secretary.

Among the reprints of the Smithsonian sent to us and mentioned in the letter was the *Problem of Flying and Practical Experiments in Soaring,* by Otto Lilienthal; *Story of Experiments in Mechanical Fight,* by S. P. Langley; and, I think, a paper by Pettigrew, as well as a copy of Mouillard's *Empire of the Air.* We sent for copies of Chanute's *Progress in Flying Machines,* Langley's *Experiments in Aerodynamics,* and the Aeronautical Annuals of 1895, 1896, and 1897. On reading the different works on the subject we were much impressed with the great number of people who had given thought to it—among these some of the greatest minds the world has produced. But we found that the experi-

---

* Reprinted by permission of the publishers from Orville Wright: *How We Invented the Airplane,* ed. by Fred C. Kelly (New York: David McKay Co., Inc., 1953), pp. 18–57. The essay was dated January 13, 1920.

ments of one after another had failed. Among these who had worked on the problem I may mention Leonardo da Vinci, one of the greatest artists and engineers of all time; Sir George Cayley, who was among the first of the inventors of the internal-combustion engine; Sir Hiram Maxim, inventor of the Maxim rapid-fire gun; Parsons, the inventor of the turbine steam engine; Alexander Graham Bell, inventor of the telephone; Horatio Phillips, a well-known English engineer; Otto Lilienthal, the inventor of instruments used in navigation and a well-known engineer; Thomas A. Edison; and Dr. S. P. Langley, secretary and head of the Smithsonian Institution. Besides these there were a great number of other men of ability who had worked on the problem. But the subject had been brought into disrepute by a number of men of lesser ability who had hoped to solve the problem through devices of their own invention which had all of them failed, until finally the public was led to believe that flying was as impossible as perpetual motion. In fact scientists of the standing of Guy-Lussac, the great French scientist and engineer, and Professor Simon Newcomb, one of the greatest of the American scientists and mathematicians, had attempted to prove that it would be impossible to build a flying machine that would carry a man. Admiral Melville, chief engineer in the United States Navy, a little later, in 1901 or 1902, published an article in which he pointed out the difficulties of building a flying machine to carry a man, and stated that the first flying machine would be more expensive than the most costly battleship.

    After reading the pamphlets sent to us by the Smithsonian we became highly enthusiastic with the idea of gliding as a sport. We found that Lilienthal had been killed through his inability to properly balance his machine in the air. Pilcher, an English experimenter, had met with a like fate.

    We found that both of these experimenters had attempted to maintain balance merely by the shifting of weight of their bodies. Chanute, and I believe all the other experimenters before 1900, used this same method of maintaining the equilibrium in gliding flight. We at once set to work to devise a more efficient means of maintaining the equilibrium. . . .

    The first method that occurred to us for maintaining the lateral equilibrium was that of pivoting the wings on the right and left sides on shafts carrying gears at the center of the machine, which, being in mesh, would cause one wing to turn upward in front when the other wing was turned downward. By this method we thought it would be possible to get a greater lift on one side than on the other, so that the shifting of weight would not be necessary for the maintenance of balance. However, we did not see any method of building this device sufficiently strong and at the same time light enough to enable us to use it.

A short time afterward, one evening when I returned home with my sister and Miss Harriet Silliman, who was at that time a guest of my sister's in our home, Wilbur showed me a method of getting the same results as we had contemplated in our first idea without the structural defects of the original. He demonstrated the method by means of a small pasteboard box, which had . . . the opposite ends removed. By holding the top forward corner and the rear lower corner of one end of the box between his thumb and forefinger and the rear upper corner and the lower forward corner of the other end of the box in the like manner, and by pressing the corners together, the upper and lower surface of the box were given a helicoidal [*spiral*] twist, presenting the top and bottom surfaces of the box at different angles on the right and left sides.

From this it was apparent that the wings of a machine of the Chanute double-deck type, with the fore-and-aft trussing removed, could be warped so as to present their surfaces to the air at different angles of incidence and thus secure unequal lifts on the two sides.[1]

We began the construction of a model embodying the principle demonstrated with the paper box within a day or two. This model consisted of superposed planes each measuring five feet from tip to tip and about thirteen inches from front to rear. The model was built and, as I remember it, was tested in the latter part of July 1899 . . . . I was not myself present . . . .

[*Experiments with this five-foot apparatus, more a model glider than a kite, were confined to one day.*]

According to Wilbur's account of the tests, the model worked very successfully. It responded promptly to the warping of the surfaces, always lifting the wing that had the larger angle. Several times . . . when he shifted the upper surface backward by the manipulation of the sticks attached to flying cords, the nose of the machine turned downward as was intended, but in diving downward it created a slack in the flying cords, so that he was not able to control it further. The model made such

---

[1] Courts have held that the Wrights, as pioneers, had priority on *any* method for presenting the right and left wings at different angles. They had discovered the aileron principle.

a rapid dive to the ground that the small boys present fell on their faces to avoid being hit, not having time to run . . . .

We felt that the model had demonstrated the efficiency of our system of control. After a little time we decided to experiment with a man-carrying machine embodying the principle of lateral control used in the kite model already flown. From the tables of Lilienthal we calculated that a machine having an area of a little over 150 square feet would support a man when flown in a wind of sixteen miles an hour. We expected to fly the machine as a kite and in this way we thought we would be able to stay in the air for hours at a time, getting in this way a maximum of practice with a minimum of effort. In September of 1900 we went to Kitty Hawk,[2] North Carolina, and there assembled the machine, most of the parts of which we had made at Dayton.

From the United States Weather Bureau reports we had found that Kitty Hawk was one of the windiest places in the country, and that during the month of September it had an average wind in the neighborhood of 16 miles an hour. We wrote to the Weather Bureau man at the Kitty Hawk station, telling him of the nature of the experiments we wished to conduct and asking him in regard to the suitability of the ground in that neighborhood. We received a very favorable report from him, and also from the postmaster at Kitty Hawk, to whom he had shown our letter.

[The machine] had two superimposed surfaces measuring eighteen feet from tip to tip and about five feet from front to rear. The surfaces were spaced five feet apart and were connected at the extreme forward edge by six upright posts, and at about one foot from the rear edge by another row of uprights or struts. The struts were connected to the surfaces by means of flexible joints. The ribs were made of thin strips of ash, slightly bent near their forward extremities. These ribs were bound to the forward spar on the spar's upper side, so that the spar and curvature given to the ribs produced a [wing] curvature of about one-eighteenth to one-twentieth of the chord [the straight-line distance from front to rear edge of wing]. The spars were enclosed in a sheath formed

---

[2] Natives around Kitty Hawk showed only mild interest in the Wrights' hopes of flying, but they became much excited when they learned that the brothers had sent to Elizabeth City, fifty miles away, for a barrel of gasoline and intended to keep the highly explosive stuff right in their tent. Didn't these men know how dangerous it was? Mothers cautioned their children not to go near the tent. The Wrights wanted the gasoline not for a motor but for their cookstove. It was the first gasoline ever taken to the Kitty Hawk area.

Orville Wright 8

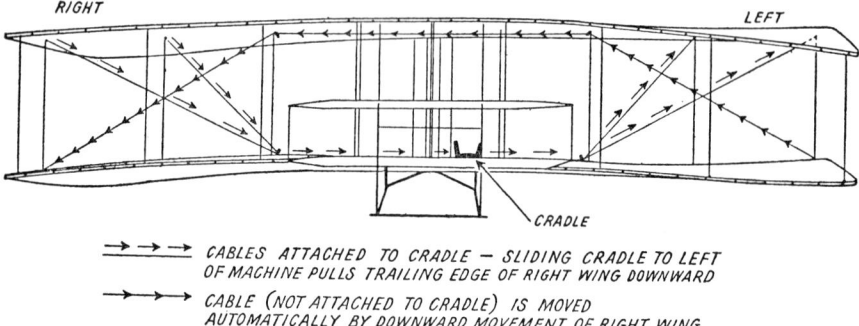

HOW THE WINGS WERE WARPED

→→→ CABLES ATTACHED TO CRADLE — SLIDING CRADLE TO LEFT
OF MACHINE PULLS TRAILING EDGE OF RIGHT WING DOWNWARD

→→→ CABLE (NOT ATTACHED TO CRADLE) IS MOVED
AUTOMATICALLY BY DOWNWARD MOVEMENT OF RIGHT WING

[*The accompanying picture of the Wrights' first powered machine (with motor and propellers removed) shows the method of twisting the rear of the wings. A movement of only an inch or two, to right or left, of the operator's hips resting on the little cradle was enough to give greater lift to whichever wing needed it, and to restore sidewise balance.*

And here is Wilbur Wright's own explanation, given as witness in the suit of The Wright Company against Glenn H. Curtiss and the Herring-Curtiss Company, of how the Wright system of control was used in making circular turns.]

In order to circle to the left, we moved the cradle slightly to the left, thus turning the tail slightly to the left and imparting an increased angle to the right wing and a smaller angle to the left wing. This caused the machine to tilt so that the left wing was lower than the right wing, which, of course, in turn, caused the machine to slide somewhat to the left. This side movement of the machine tended to cause the vertical rudder to strike the air at a greater angle than was necessary to compensate for the difference in resistance of the right and left wings.

This tendency caused the tail to lag behind in this lateral movement just as the feather of an arrow causes the feathered end to lag behind when the arrow is dropped sidewise. Thus the lateral movement of the main aeroplane sidewise, as the result of tipping, became combined with the rotary movement about its vertical axis, due to the vane-like action of the tail, and the machine proceeded on a circular course. But as the speed of the outside wing increased, and that of the inside wing decreased, by reason of the fact that the inner wing was traveling in a smaller circle than the outside wing, there was a tendency to tilt too much and this was corrected by gradually moving the cradle toward the high wing, thus increasing the angle on the low wing and decreasing the angle of the high wing and also setting the rudder over toward the high wing. This was done gradually, but only sufficiently to prevent the low wing from sinking lower and not enough to bring it back to the level. The machine then continued to circle to the left, with the vertical tail set over somewhat to the right, so that the machine turned in the opposite direction to that in which a ship would have turned with the ship's rudder set over to the right.

When it was desired to stop circling, a sudden movement of the cradle toward the high side gave the wings an increased warp and brought the machine up to the level. Then on setting the cradle back to its central position, thus restoring the wings and tail to their central positions, the machine proceeded in a straight line, with the wings level.

by sewing a strip of cloth over them, resulting in the elimination of all sharp angles or corners. The ribs were enclosed likewise.

Both the forward and the rear rows of uprights were trussed by wires much like the Chanute. The machine thus had two systems of rigid trusses laterally; but, unlike the Chanute machine, it was not rigidly trussed from front to rear. On the contrary, a flexible cable was connected to the upper surface at the extreme outer upright in the rear, passed diagonally downward through a pulley on the lower surface at the outermost forward upright, thence across to a pulley in a corresponding position on the lower plane on the opposite side of the machine, and then diagonally upward to a connection to the upper surface at the outermost rear upright. Another flexible cable was attached to the upper surface at its forward edge at the outermost upright on the one side, passed diagonally downward and backward and crossing the first-mentioned flexible cable to a pulley at the rear of the lower surface, then across to a pulley at the rear of the lower surface at the opposite side, and then up to the connection of the forward upright to the upper surface. A cradle in which the operator lay was connected to the cable running along the forward edge of the lower surface, so that when the cable was pushed to the right the upper rear corner of the machine was pulled downward and forward and the corresponding part on the opposite side of the machine was allowed to move upward and rearward. In this manner a helicoidal warp was imparted to the surfaces.

The horizontal rudder, or elevator, was attached to a framework about four feet forward of the lower main plane. This elevator was pivoted about one-third back from its front edge. To the forward edge of the elevator were attached two springs which extended horizontally forward to the framework which supported the elevator. The rear edge of the elevator could be raised or lowered by means of two arms extending from the operator and connecting to the rear edge of the elevator through links. Thus when the rear edge of the elevator was raised, the springs referred to prevented the front edge from moving downward to a like angle, and as a result a curvature was given to the elevator on its upper side. When the rear edge of the elevator was moved downward a curvature on the under side was produced . . . .[3]

We attempted to fly the machine as a kite with a man on board a

---

[3] The front elevator in the first power plane was operated differently.

number of times, but were successful in keeping it up only when the wind was about twenty-five miles or more an hour. It failed to perform in lifting as had been calculated from the Lilienthal tables of air pressure. However, when flown in the strong winds, it responded promptly to the warping of the wings, so that the side with the greater angle would rise

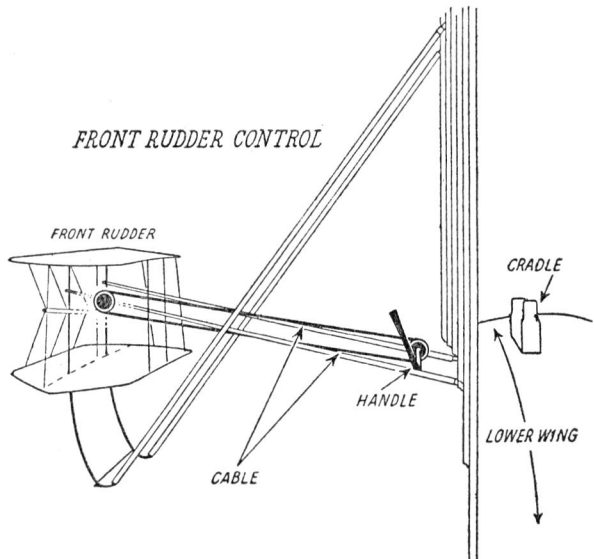

above the side with the lower angle and the machine would go sidling off toward the lower side, but the low side was brought up again by reversing the angles of the wing tips.

We also made a number of tests of it flown without an operator in which we attempted to measure the lift, the drift, and the center of pressure.

Before leaving camp for the year we carried it to the Kill Devil Hill, four miles from Kitty Hawk, and made about a dozen free flights, gliding down the side of the hill on the air . . . . The experiments were concluded near the end of October . . . .

Although we were highly pleased with the performance of the machine, in so far as lateral control was concerned, we were disappointed with its lifting ability. We did not know whether its failure to lift according to the calculations made previous to our going to Kitty

Hawk was due to the construction of our machine, or whether the tables of air pressure, at that time generally accepted, were incorrect. As a result we wrote to Mr. Chanute soon after our return from Kitty Hawk, giving him an account of the experiments just made, and asking his opinion as to the cause of the failure of the machine to lift, according to calculations. He suggested that it might have been due to the peculiar shape of wing curvature which we had used, and recommended that if we took up experiments again we use ribs having the curvature used by Lilienthal . . . .

In order to try to satisfy our own minds as to whether the failure of the 1900 machine to lift according to our calculations was due to the shape of the wings or to an error in the Lilienthal tables, we undertook a number of experiments to determine the comparative lifting qualities of planes as compared with curved surfaces and the relative value of curved surfaces having different depths of curvature. This was done by mounting the two surfaces to be compared at the extremities of the arms of an acute V-shaped structure made of wood. The V was pivoted on a vertical bearing at its point, the V lying in a horizontal plane. The surfaces were mounted vertically on the V, with their lifts opposed to each other. In this way we attempted to determine which had the greater lift by the amount one surface could push the other from the normal position. The surfaces while so mounted were exposed to the wind. The experiments were so crudely carried out that close measurements were not possible. But the results of these experiments confirmed us in the belief already formed that the accepted tables of air pressure were not to be altogether relied upon.

It was for this reason that we decided to increase the size of the machine of 1901, as well as to make the ribs and wings of a deeper curvature fore and aft. The 1901 machine was assembled at Kitty Hawk or, rather, near the Kill Devil Hill, in July 1901. The structure was very similar to that of the previous year. The method of imparting a helicoidal warp to the wings used in 1900 was used again in 1901. The area of the wings was increased from 165 square feet of the 1900 machine to 290 square feet, the wings having a spread of twenty-two feet, and a chord of seven feet. The depth of curvature of the wings was increased to one-twelfth of the chord, the deepest point being about 33 per cent back. . . .

This machine was tested a number of times in free gliding flight and also as a kite. In the gliding flights the fore-and-aft stability or control of the machine did not seem to be as good as that of the previous year. This we finally suspected was due to the difference in the curvature of the wings of the two machines. We also found that where the machine of 1900 continued to increase in speed as we glided down certain slopes of the hill, the 1901 machine did not do so. This seemed to indicate that the machine of 1900 was able to glide on slopes of less angle than the machine of 1901, and was therefore dynamically more efficient. The lateral control of the new machine appeared very effective. As a result of these experiments we soon decided to reduce the curvature of the wings, which we did by a system of posts and wires about midway between the front and rear spars.

These intermediate posts also served to prevent the ribs and wings from taking a deeper curvature due to the air pressure upon them. It had been found that the curvature of the wings was constantly changing during flight. The machine as thus modified was flown a number of times in gliding flights and as a kite with and without an operator on board. A number of measurements were made of the machine flown as a kite to determine the lift and the drift at various angles of incidence. The results obtained did not agree at all with the estimated values computed from Lilienthal and other accepted tables of air pressure . . . .

As we gained in proficiency in handling the machine in gliding flight, we began to encounter occasionally a phenomenon which we had not foreseen. Sometimes in warping the wings to recover lateral balance, it was found that the wing having the greater angle would at first tend to lift, but at the same time it would lose speed as compared with the opposite wing having a smaller angle of incidence.[4] As a result the machine

[4] In another lawsuit Wilbur Wright, in February, 1912, a little more than three months before his death, explained the angle of incidence as follows:
    The angle of incidence of an aeroplane is the angle at which the aeroplane surfaces and the air stream meet. It may or may not correspond with the angle of the aeroplane with the horizon. This angle, that is, the angle of incidence, is continually varying in flight in accordance with the speed of the machine. If the speed is low, a large angle of incidence is required to sustain the machine. If the speed is high, a small angle of incidence suffices to sustain the machine. When the machine is climbing to a greater height, the power of the motor is expended in lifting the weight. Consequently there is less power to drive the machine forward and the speed is less in this case, but the angle of incidence greater. Similar variations in the angle of incidence occur whenever the machine meets an air current of greater velocity or less velocity, or if the current has an upward or downward trend. If the load carried by the aeroplane is decreased, which normally happens by the consumption of oil and fuel, the angle of incidence decreases. If from any cause the power of the motor decreases, the angle of incidence increases. If an extra passenger is carried, the angle of incidence is greater than usual throughout the flight. If the air, from some cause, has a greater upward trend in one place than in another, the angle of incidence on one wing will be greater than the angle of incidence on the other wing. From these various causes

would begin turning a sharp circle, which generally resulted in a forced landing with the machine skidding outward on the ground. From this phenomenon we were led to the discovery that the relative velocities of the right and left wings of the machine bore a very important part in lateral equilibrium, a fact apparently never before considered by any investigators. I may state that in some of the flights just related, the wing having the larger angle and the lesser speed had a less lift than the other wing with the small angle and the greater speed.

The measurements of lift and drift, which were made in this year and the year before, I believe, were the first that were ever made upon a full-sized model; and I believe these were the first adequate tests that had ever been made, as to the accuracy of the accepted tables of air pressures.

We made a great number of measurements of the machine used as a glider. We accurately measured with a clinometer the angle of the machine's descent. With a Richard hand anemometer we measured the velocity of the wing at the height from the ground, when possible, at which the flight was made. The time during which the machine was in free flight was measured with a stop watch. The distance of the free flight over the ground was also measured. In many flights the speed of the machine relative to the air was measured by a man running beside the machine holding an anemometer in his hand. From the angle of descent as measured with the clinometer the ratio of the total lift of the machine to its total resistance can be easily and accurately computed.

We also made a number of measurements with the machine flying as a kite, sometimes empty and sometimes loaded with a bag of sand. These measurements were taken by measuring the pull on the flying cables at the two ends of the machine, when these cables were in a horizontal position so that the pull of the cables would neither add to nor detract

---

the actual angle of incidence is, under normal conditions, an angle sometimes above and sometimes below the average angle, which defendants refer to as the normal angle of incidence. It is very rarely that the machine flies, even for a short time, at the exact angle which they call the normal angle of incidence. More than 90 per cent of the time the machine is flying at some other angle. When the variations in the angle of incidence are produced by variations in load, variations in regard to ascent or descent, or by variations in the power of the motor, the variations in the angle of incidence continue for many minutes or even hours. In rapid climbing the angle of incidence of aeroplanes is usually ten degrees or more, that is, machines usually climb fastest when the forward speed is rather slow and the angle of incidence great, because then less power is expended in driving the machine forward and more is available for climbing. The angle of incidence which any particular machine normally utilizes in its work varies all the way from about 2½ degrees up to nearly 15 degrees.

from the load carried by the machine. As an example I will give a few measurements made on July 30, 1901. Wing velocity, 18 miles per hour; angle of incidence, 10°; lift, 100 pounds; drift, 18 pounds. Another set of measurements made on August 1, 1901, after the machine had been slightly modified, were as follows: Velocity, 17 miles per hour; angle of incidence, 6°; weight, 100 pounds; drift, 15 pounds. These measurements show a lift of about one-third of the estimates that had been made using the Lilienthal tables of air pressure.

Several hundred flights were made [in 1901]. I do not know the exact number. The flights ranged all the way from fifty feet to nearly four hundred feet in length. Quite a number were made of a distance of three hundred feet or more.

Changes in the arrangement of the spars were made several times during the series of experiments, the most important of which was produced by changing the length of the brace wires, so as to produce a curvature in the spars from wing to wing. The spars at the center of the machine were raised three or four inches above their extremities at the wing tips. The spars when the machine was first assembled were straight, the diagonal brace wires in each section being of equal lengths.

We had found in the free flights that when the wind entered the machine from one side or the other at an angle to the longitudinal axis of the machine, the wing on that side from which the wind was blowing received a greater lift, thus causing a disturbance in the lateral equilibrium of the machine. By giving the wings a curvature from side to side this disturbance was avoided, because the air entering from the side met the surface of the wing on that side at a smaller angle of incidence than it met the surface on the opposite wing. This, however, tends to produce a machine with unstable equilibrium laterally. While the equilibrium is disturbed less from side gusts, the machine tends to lose its own equilibrium when it slips sidewise on the air, but under the peculiar conditions existing on the Kill Devil Hill [partly the hill's convex surface] we found the advantages of the drooped wings more than overcame the disadvantages.

All the books and papers which my brother and I had read in which there was any reference to the travel of the center of pressure had taught that the center of pressure was approximately at the center of the surface when it was exposed at right angles to the wind; and that this center of pressure moved forward as the angle of incidence was decreased. We had built both the 1900 and the 1901 machines assuming this to be well verified. Our elevator was placed in front of the surfaces with the idea of producing inherent stability fore and aft, which it should have done had the travel of the center of pressure been forward as we had been led to believe. We found, however, that these machines were anything but inherently stable fore and aft. In our 1900 experiments we had even found inherent stability much improved when we tested the machine by gliding it down a hill loaded with a small sack of sand with the trailing edge of the main plane forward and the elevator trailing behind [*in short, when flying it backward*].

Doctor Spratt and Mr. Huffaker [then staying in the Wright camp] both suggested that there might be a rearward travel of the center of pressure on the curved surfaces at the small angles of incidence. We later demonstrated this fact by flying one of the surfaces alone as a kite. When the surface was exposed to the wind at large angles of incidence the pull on the flying cords was upward and when exposed at small angles of incidence the pull was downward. In the first case it was apparent that the center of pressure was in front of the center of gravity, and in the latter case behind the center of gravity. This clearly demonstrated that the center of pressure moved backward at small angles of incidence . . . .

Our experiments in 1901 were rather discouraging to us because we felt that they had demonstrated that some of the most firmly established laws, those regarding the travel of the center of pressure and pressures on airplane surfaces, were mostly, if not entirely, incorrect. At first we had taken up the problem merely as a matter of sport, but now it was apparent that if we were to make much progress it would be necessary to get better tables from which to make our calculations. In September we set up a small wind tunnel in which we made a number of measurements similar to those which we had attempted to make earlier in the year. The earlier measurements had been made in the open air, where it was difficult to determine the exact direction of the wind. The new measurements were made inside of the tunnel, through which a blast of air was forced. The new experiments were conducted with much more care than had been the first, but still they were not entirely satisfactory. We immediately set about designing and constructing another apparatus from which we hoped to secure much more accurate measurements. In this instrument the lift of the surface to be measured was balanced against a pressure created on a screen by the flow of the air through the tunnel. This enabled us to make very accurate comparative measurements of the lift.

We also designed and constructed another instrument for measuring the ratio of the lift to the drift. This utilized an idea which had been suggested by Dr. Spratt. During the following three or four months after October 1901 we made thousands of measurements of the lift, and the ratio of the lift to the drift with these two instruments. We measured the lift of square planes and rectangular planes of different aspect ratios, in order to determine the effect of the aspect ratio on the lifting qualities of the plane. We also made experiments of a number of similarly curved surfaces having different cambers to determine the effect of camber on the lift and also on the drift.

We also measured these curved surfaces to determine the effect of aspect ratio on their lifts and drifts. We measured a number of surfaces superposed with gaps ranging from one-fourth of the chord to one and one-eighth times the chord. We measured a series of surfaces having a regular camber like that of a sector of cylinder, [and] having different depths of curvature, as well as a great number of other surfaces having the greatest depth of curvature forward of the center, and some with the greatest depth back of the center. . . .

We decided to build another machine basing it upon calculations to be made from our own tables. We decided to attach a fixed vertical vane in the rear of the main plane, which we thought would maintain an equal velocity of the right and left wings when the wings were warped to different angles. Our tables made it apparent that we would secure a higher dynamic efficiency in the machine by using surfaces of smaller camber and of greater aspect ratio.

We went to Kitty Hawk in the last week of August 1902, and began the assembling of a machine embodying the changes which I have just mentioned. The wings of this machine measured 32 feet from tip to tip, and 5 feet from front to rear. The curvature of the wings measured from one twenty-fourth to one twenty-sixth of the chord of the surfaces. The front rudder, or elevator, contained 15 square feet of surface, and the rear vertical vanes had a total surface of $11\frac{2}{3}$ square feet. The area of the main planes totaled 305 square feet. These planes were spaced one 5 feet above the other. The wiring or trussing of the wings and uprights, as well as the arrangement of the cables for imparting the warp to the surfaces, was like that of the 1901 machine. The arrangement of the trussing and the method of producing the warp in the surfaces is clearly shown in Figure 1 of the Wright patent of May 22, 1906,

While this machine was being assembled, we made measurements of one of the surfaces flown as a kite, and found that the pull on the kite strings, in proportion to the load carried, was less than that of the surfaces of the 1901 machine. This was in accordance with the estimates which we had made from calculations based on our own tables. These measurements were taken when the kite strings stood in a horizontal position, so that only the drift of the surface was measured.

The assembling of the machine was completed about the 19th of September, when we began making glides with it. . . . In the first flight we found that the machine was able to glide with a much smaller angle of descent than either of our former machines. The first glides made with it, but which were not entirely free, led us to think that the lateral control had been improved by the addition of the fixed vertical vanes in the rear. In these first tests the wing with the larger angle would rise, while the opposite wing was depressed.

This machine was assembled with the spars straight from tip to tip, but as these first tests showed the same trouble that we had had with the 1901 machine when the wings were straight, on the 22nd of September we altered the truss wire so as to arch the surfaces from tip to tip, making the tips at least four inches lower than the center. We also made the angle of the surfaces at the tips greater than the angle at the center of the machine. We found that the trouble experienced before with a cross wind turning up the wing it first struck had been overcome, and the trials seemed to indicate that with an arch to the surfaces laterally the opposite effect was obtained.

Later, when we began to make free flights with the machine, we found that when the wings were warped, first with the larger angle on one side and then on the other, the machine descended the hill rolling from side to side. But later in some of the flights, when the machine was allowed to slide a little to one side or the other as the result of one wing being at an almost imperceptibly lower height than the other, we found that the fixed vertical vane, instead of maintaining an equal speed at the two opposite wing tips, as we had expected, as a matter of fact did just the reverse, and caused one wing to be checked and the other one to be speeded up. This was due to the fact that when the machine began sliding laterally a pressure was created on the fixed vanes on that side which was toward the lower side of the machine and the side toward which the machine was sliding. The increased speed of the high wing gave it a still greater lift, and the decreased speed of the lower wing produced a lesser lift upon it, with the result that the lower wing dropped and the higher wing went still higher. When the wings were warped in an attempt to recover balance, with the low wing having a greater angle of incidence than the upper wing, a still greater drag was produced upon the low wing, with a result that its speed was further decreased and the speed of the higher wing was increased. These flights ended usually with disaster to the machine in what is called today a "tail spin." . . .

Our first change in the machine, as the result of our experiences in these flights just mentioned, was to remove one of the vertical vanes in the rear of the machine. By doing this we hoped to remove at least a part of the disturbing effect of the vanes when the machine was sliding slightly sidewise. We found that this only slightly mitigated the evil influence of vanes. After a good deal of thought the idea occurred to us that by making the vane in the rear adjustable, so that it could be turned, . . . to entirely relieve the pressure on that side toward the low side of

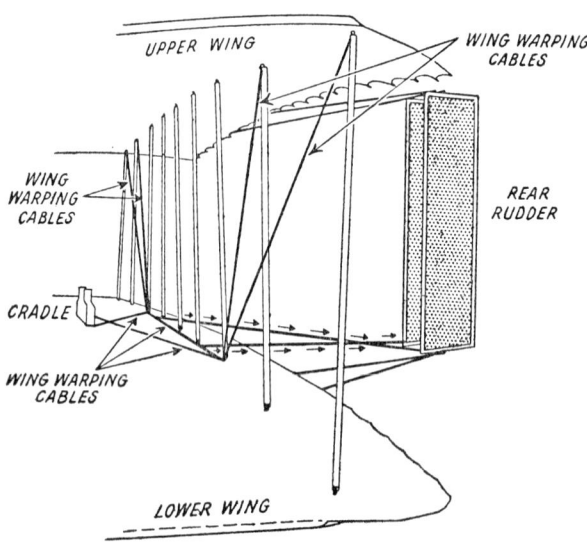

the machine, and to create a pressure on the side toward the high wing equal to or greater than the differences in the resistances of the high and low wings, due to their different angles of incidence, all of the good properties of a vane in the rear would be secured without any of its bad properties. But this was going to add one more burden to the operator. He would now not only have to think, and think quickly, in operating the front elevator for maintaining the longitudinal equilibrium, but he would also have to think so as to operate this rudder . . . to present its surface to the wind on that side which is toward the high wing, or the wing having the smaller angle of incidence.

While this change to make the vane adjustable was being made, the idea come to us of connecting the wires which operated the rudder to the cables which operated the wing warping, so that whenever the wings were warped the rudder was simultaneously adjusted, . . . to produce a pressure on that side of the rudder which was toward the wing having the smaller angle of incidence. [*Later the Wrights found it desirable, through the experimental stage, to operate the wings and rudder separately.*]

With the machine as now constituted we began a long series of gliding flights. The disastrous experiences which we had when the fixed vanes were used now seemed to be entirely avoidable. In fact, in the seven or eight hundred gliding flights that were made after the adjustable rudder was installed, not once did we encounter the difficulty we had experienced with the fixed vane . . . .

The fore-and-aft control of the 1902 machine had proved very effective, so that when at last we felt that the problem of lateral equilibrium had been entirely solved, we began to turn our thoughts to the construction of a machine to be driven with a motor. . . . To provide for the installation of a motor, propellers, etc., we thought a more rigid structure at the center of the machine would be useful. As a result we decided to rigidly truss the upper and lower planes of this 1902 machine in all excepting the outermost panel at each end. This was accomplished by putting in fore-and-aft stay wires, running diagonally from the upper end of the forward upright posts to the lower end of the corresponding rear posts, and from the upper end of the rear posts to the lower end of the corresponding front upright posts. In this manner we provided a rigid structure in the three center panels. Before this modification was made, in warping the wings, the upper and lower surfaces were drawn into diagonal positions with reference to each other. With the new form of trussing, the front edges of the upper and lower planes were maintained parallel to each other, so that only the rear edges of the outer panels at either end of the machine could be adjusted up and down for the purpose of securing different angles of incidence at the two opposite tips.

All of the later flights made with this machine in 1902, as well as the early flights made with it in 1903, were made with the wings trussed in the manner just described.

The flights of 1902 demonstrated the efficiency of our system of control for both longitudinal and lateral stability. They also demonstrated that our tables of air pressure which we made in our wind tunnel would enable us to calculate in advance the performance of a machine. Before leaving our camp at Kitty Hawk we began the designing of a new and larger machine to be driven by motor. The wings of the new machine had a spread of 40 feet 6 inches and a chord of 6 feet 6 inches, having a total area of a little over 500 square feet.

Immediately after our return from Kitty Hawk in 1902 we wrote to a number of the best-known automobile manufacturers in an endeavor to secure a motor for the new machine. Not receiving favorable answers from any of these, we proceeded to design a motor of our own, from which we hoped to secure about 8 horsepower. When the motor was tested it gave more power than we had anticipated. It developed a little over 12 horsepower and weighed about 160 pounds, without magneto, water, or oil.

We next proceeded with the construction of the parts to be used in this first power machine, and while we were doing this we began an investigation of screw propellers. At first we hoped to be able to procure a theory of the reactions on a screw propeller from works on marine engineering, but we soon found, after examining the few books we were able to secure in the Dayton Public Library pertaining to marine engineering, that water screw propellers at that time were not based upon theory but almost entirely upon empirical data. We had thought that we could adopt the theory from the marine engineers, and then by using our tables of air pressures, instead of the tables of water pressures used in their calculations, that we could estimate in advance the performance of the propellers we would use. When we found we could not do this, we began the study of the screw propeller from an entirely theoretical standpoint, since we saw that with the small capital we possessed we would not be able to develop an efficient air propeller on the "cut and try" plan. As a result of this study we developed a theory from which we designed the propellers which we used in this 1903 power machine.

These propellers had an efficiency of over 66 per cent, an efficiency, I believe, rarely exceeded by the marine engineers, and never approached by any of the aeronautical investigators up to that time. . . .

We went to Kitty Hawk the latter part of September 1903, and after a few days spent in establishing camp and in erecting a building in which to assemble and house our new machine, we began the work of assembling . . . . While in general the structure of these wings was similar to that of the previous gliding machines which we had built, yet a number of changes in design were made, among which I may mention that of the ribs and the covering of the surfaces with cloth. Instead of using thin strips of ash, bent to the desired curvature, as had been used in the earlier machines, for the new machine the ribs were made by [sawing] a piece of ash, with a cross section of about three-eighths by one-half inch, . . . from one end to within a few inches of the other, inserting blocks of wood between the two halves of the strip and gluing and nailing them in position. . . . Through this structure we secured at the same time great strength and lightness. Ribs of this type are used in practically all flying machines of today. The cloth was stretched over both the top and bottom sides of the spars and ribs.

These, I believe, were the first double-surfaced planes ever designed or built. . . . The control of this machine was the same as that of the 1902 machine. Like the 1902 machine in the later part of the season, the central portions remained fixed, while the outer portions of the wings were adjusted to different angles of incidence. . . .

The first attempt to fly this machine was made on the 14th of December, but through a mistake in handling it at the start the machine was broken slightly, so that repairs had to be made before another attempt could be undertaken. Five men from the Kill Devil Life Saving Station were present when this test was made. . . . The next trial was made on the 17th of December, in a wind blowing 20 miles, and four more flights were made. The first of these covered a distance of about 100 feet, measured from the end of the track, and had a duration of about 12 seconds. The second and third flights covered about 175 feet, and the fourth flight 852 feet. This last flight had a duration of 59 seconds.

These flights started from a point about 100 feet to the west of our camp. The ground was perfectly level for a mile or two in every direction excepting those toward the big and the smaller Kill Devil Hills. The ground was level in the directions toward these hills for a distance of a quarter of a mile.

The machine was launched from a monorail track. . . . This track was laid in a slight depression, which a few days before had been covered by water. We chose this spot because the action of the water had leveled it so nearly flat that little preparation of the ground was necessary in order to lay the track. The starting end of the track lay a few inches below the end from which the machine lifted into the air.

A small two-wheeled truck ran on the track. Across the truck extended a beam, upon the two opposite ends of which the skids of the machine rested. A bicycle hub was attached at the forward end of the skids, beneath the elevator. This supported the forward end of the machine and guided the machine on a rail.

The machine was launched entirely through the power of the motor and the thrust of the propellers.

In the last flight the rate of travel over the ground was approximately 10 miles per hour against a wind of approximately 20 miles per hour, making the real speed of the machine through the air about 30 miles an hour.

The first of these flights . . . was the first time in the history of the world that a machine carrying a man and driven by a motor had lifted itself from the ground in free flight.

Witnesses of this flight, besides my brother and myself, were John T. Daniels, W. S. Dough, A. D. Etheridge, from the Kill Devil Life Saving Station; W. C. Brinkley, of Manteo; and Johnny Moore, a boy from Nags Head, North Carolina.

2. The Rise of the Aircraft Industry

There was hardly any American aircraft industry to speak of before World War I. Even as late as 1914 records indicate that only 49 aircraft were produced that year. Except for the brief war period, since the invention of the airplane in 1903 to 1926 the aircraft industry had difficulty surviving. The combined civil and military demand for the industry's products was not sufficient to permit the industry to grow significantly. But in 1917 and 1918 the situation was very different. During World War I production expanded almost unbelievably to 14,020 aircraft in 1918 as domestic and foreign expenditures on the products of the American aircraft industry approximated $350,000,000. When the war was over and the demand for military aircraft was curtailed, the industry underwent a severe contraction.

Shortly before the Armistice was signed there was a shocking scandal in the aircraft industry. It was charged that excess profits were received, resulting from fraudulent misdealings on the part of government officials and members of the industry. The former Supreme Court Justice, Charles Evans Hughes, who was appointed to investigate these charges, confirmed that many of them were true. The Hughes findings and those of other investigations of the postwar period in effect censured the industry for certain acts of irresponsible behavior in its dealings with the government during the war. In the selection that follows, however, the author, Howard Mingos, notes that the Hughes investigation was not critical of the Manufacturers Aircraft Association or their cross-licensing agreement as such.

The depressed postwar state of the industry ultimately resulted in the appointment of the Morrow Board by President Coolidge to investigate United States air power needs. The findings of this board and other dramatic appeals led to the passage of several acts that helped to maintain a demand for aircraft. The Air Mail Act of 1925 was intended "... to encourage commercial aviation and to authorize the Postmaster General to contract for air mail service." The Air Commerce Act of 1926 gave the Secretary of Commerce the responsibility of fostering air commerce through the establishment of airports, civil airways, and navigational aids. It also authorized him to provide for registration of aircraft and certification of flying personnel to ensure safe operation of aircraft.

Two more acts, referred to as the "five-year programs," were formulated with the purpose of supporting the industry by enlarging the demand for military aircraft. Under the first act, the Navy was authorized to procure 1,614 aircraft between fiscal years 1927 and 1931. The second act authorized the Army Air Corps to equip itself with 1,800 airplanes during the same time period.

The industry was provided with an additional stimulus by 1927 as flying records set by Charles Lindbergh and others captured the imagination of the public. The increased demand for civil aircraft that resulted during this period was referred to as the "Lindbergh Boom." The value of aircraft sales rose from $21,162,000 in 1927 to $71,153,000 in 1929, largely as a result of the growth in demand for civil aircraft.

These were the outstanding developments during the era from World War I to 1930. Co-operation within the industry was significantly influenced by the Manufacturers Aircraft Association and, later, by the Aeronautical Chamber of Commerce.

The following selection by Howard Mingos, an official of the aircraft industry, is considered to be the best account of the United States aircraft industry's development prior to 1930. There are so few copies of this work accessible that the editor is extremely grateful for the privilege of reproducing this selection.

Birth of an Industry*
Howard Mingos

I

As everybody knows there was very little flying in the United States prior to the World War. Perhaps a half-dozen small shops were building airplanes, their products wholly experimental, their customers limited to a few exhibition pilots and sportsmen: with an occasional small order from the Army and Navy. Similar conditions existed throughout Europe.

When the war broke out the European aviators went up in their light, underpowered and rather treacherous planes. At first they flew over the front lines as scouts, observing the opposing forces, their numbers and troop movements. When they encountered an enemy machine they fought it out with shotguns.

It soon became apparent that the airplane might become a mighty auxiliary, not only as the eyes of an army or a fleet but as a combat weapon for harassing the surface forces on the front, destroying munitions behind the lines and raiding enemy territory.

At first Germany took the lead. She launched swarms of machines across the allied fronts, over their borders and into the heart of their war effort. Some of the German planes dropped explosives; others escorted them and warded off attacks, until the Allies realized that Germany was accomplishing every one of the several objectives which inspired the air raids.

Those objectives were written into the official records of the German High Command at that time. They are set forth here because they have guided the policy of all nations since the war. The main purpose was to interfere with manufacture and procurement of supplies and munitions. Next, to wreck points of military value—docks, railway yards, arsenals, munitions factories, warehouses and banks. Germany tried her best to blow up the Bank of England and throw Britain's monetary and financial system into hopeless confusion.

The third big reason was to compel the enemy to maintain at home huge forces which otherwise should be at the front. A half million men were kept in the United Kingdom to repel aerial invasion. About five hundred guns were used for anti-aircraft defense in the British Isles when they were needed on the continent.

Another objective was to destroy the morale. Millions of persons in the allied countries lived in a state of high nervous tension, even fear,

---

* Reprinted from Howard Mingos: *Birth of an Industry* (New York: W. B. Conkey Co., 1930), pp. 10–95. Photographs appearing in the original text have been omitted.

for days and weeks at a time. The false alarms of air raids were as effective as the actual attacks for they darkened whole districts, interrupted all work and caused the people to huddle under bomb-proof shelters while they awaited the explosions and fires.

The Allies admitted, that is, their military leaders agreed, that aircraft had become a powerful offensive weapon; and further, that the airplane is the best weapon with which to combat an enemy in the air. Under that stimulus the Allies commenced developing their own aerial strength. In 1915 they placed their first orders with some of the American companies.

Meanwhile our own military and naval observers had been sending back secret reports on the growing importance of aircraft in war. As official Washington knew that only a miracle could keep the United States out of the conflict the Army and Navy increased their orders for airplanes.

But the American industry was in bad shape. There were then about one hundred and thirty airplane patents, actually issued. Others were pending. Of those already issued some were basic and without which no real plane could be built. There were others, say half of the total number, which were of doubtful value. But each patent could cause a lawsuit. When a builder turned out a flying machine he invariably was threatened with court action for infringement on an airplane patent.

He might even pay royalties to one or two patent owners and still be confronted with claims from several others. Thus all the constructors, designers and experimenters were snarling and yipping at one another, some of them jealous of the prior claims advanced by competitors, others defiant and prepared to fight for what they believed to be their rights to use any patent. Had there been no war, those conditions might have continued and repeated the history of other industries.

Months before the United States assumed a stellar role in Europe's tragedy our War and Navy departments asked the National Advisory Committee for Aeronautics to bring into the industry some degree of peace so that it might produce airplanes. In January, 1917, Secretary of the Navy Josephus Daniels addressed to the Committee a letter in which he explained the situation in these words:

"Various combinations are threatening all other airplane and seaplane companies with suits for infringement of patents. The result is the demoralization of the entire trade. It is difficult to get orders filled because some companies will not expend any more money on their plants for fear that suits brought against them will force them out of business. To protect themselves, in case they are forced to pay large license fees, the companies have greatly increased the sale prices of their products. As the Army and Navy are the principal purchasers of aircraft in this country they are bearing the brunt of this levy. It is thought that the National Advisory Committee for Aeronautics might be able in some way to render assistance to the Navy by undertaking the study of this question and suggesting some line of action to be taken."

Secretary of War Newton D. Baker added this comment:

"It is believed that this is a subject of such importance as to warrant its immediate consideration by your Committee, to the end that a just and equitable solution to all concerned may be reached, which will apply not only to this department but to all other departments of the Government purchasing airplanes."

The National Advisory Committee for Aeronautics at once called a meeting of departmental heads and the leaders of the aircraft industry. There were many sessions. A few of the companies had been trying to form a trade organization to promote better understanding among themselves; but it was a difficult task for many of the leaders were not on speaking terms with one another.

They could not forget the old rivalry and jealousy, though the possibilities of a vast increase in business promised to place them in the same class with big business. The talk and the conferences in Washington were still in progress when in April, 1917, the United States entered the war.

The War Department at first planned to send abroad an army of one million. The strategists thought there should be one airplane for every thousand men, with possibly two in reserve—in all about 2,500 machines. The existing companies felt that they could produce that number at once, without further expansion, for they had, as a result of their foreign orders, about 5,000 employees trained in that work.

Then the English, French and Italian missions arrived, all hot and eager to tell us how we might contribute the most effectively to the allied aerial strength.

"Twenty-five hundred airplanes!" they exclaimed. "That's nothing at all! France, Italy and Belgium need planes badly. England is building her limit, but she is losing as many machines as she builds, month by month. Conditions are such, the importance of airplanes has become so great, that we shall need 25,000, perhaps more, from the United States."

That was a big order. It meant that all facilities must be expanded tenfold. Plants, raw materials, skilled labor and the proper executive and inspection staffs—all must be procured in a hurry. But the foreign experts insisted that there was no time to lose. They explained that the Allies were at the limit of their resources in manpower, factory output and raw materials.

Other committees were formed in Washington. Leading business men were summoned to the capital. Some of them were put into uniforms. Others were appointed civilian heads. The Bureau of Aircraft Production was organized. Civilians and Army officers set out to procure the 25,000 airplanes. Others were to train aviators and organize aerial squadrons for the Army. The Navy was to have its own program, buying the bulk of its planes and training its own aviators to operate with the surface forces.

Logically the important thing was first to put the aircraft industry into shape for this tenfold expansion. Many of the conferences in Washington lasted throughout a day and a night—between the military and naval experts, industrial and business leaders who had been called in, the National Advisory Committee for Aeronautics and the builders of airplanes.

A survey which had been made by the Council of National Defense had indicated that the motor car industry could handle a great deal of the aircraft work, particularly that of producing engines and metal parts. But the automobile people knew nothing about aircraft design, production methods and the tediously exact system of inspection which, by eliminating flaws and careless workmanship wherever possible, helps to protect the aviator.

And too, the motor car manufacturers did not like the patent situation. They knew that there were many lawsuits pending; and experience in their own patent controversies had taught them to avoid such situations. They hesitated to accept contracts which might involve them in costly litigation.

Thereupon the Government committee proposed to the aircraft companies that they draw up a patent licensing agreement whereby everybody making planes for the Government might use the patents. Because the War and Navy departments would have to pay the royalties which would be included in the price of the machines purchased, these two departments were directly interested. Under their leadership and with the impulse of the war spirit, that document, with all its terms and provisions, was drawn, submitted and approved within two weeks.

Similar to that under which the motor car industry had been working for years, yet providing for a lower royalty rate, the cross-license agreement was to be administered by a new organization of the aircraft industry. It was to be known as the Manufacturers Aircraft Association. Any builder of aircraft then or in future could become a member and have the use of all patents under the agreement. The Association was to collect a blanket royalty fee for each airplane and apportion it among the patent owners as stipulated. All disputes were to be settled by arbitration. Under a voting trust agreement the affairs of the Association were to be controlled by three trustees for five years.

Further, if any member received an order from the Government, he was to be supplied with designs of the machine specified, though they might be the original product of another member. That was the height of cooperation but it did not end there. The manufacturers skilled in airplane production undertook to teach the new trade to other concerns, especially those in the motor car industry, which might receive orders from the Government.

It was a pretty picture, painted in all the glowing colors of patriotism, for there is more than ample proof that one object dominated the making of the agreement and the first genuine organization of the aircraft industry. It was that the 25,000 or more airplanes might be turned out on schedule. And as such it was one of the most important undertakings in the American preparation for the war. For it meant that thus early in the game, July, 1917, the industry was equipped with the technical and legal machinery which would permit unlimited expansion without friction, without petty controversy or obstructionist methods.

Twelve companies joined the Association, and the aircraft builders returned to their plants, took off their coats and rolled up their shirt sleeves, now free to carry out their war contracts without patent lawsuits. For the Association was to handle all matters outside of those which dealt with the procurement or individual orders and contracts and the actual production of planes in the plants. Not only would it administer the cross-license agreement, it would be the spokesman for the industry, the medium through which would be solved a thousand and one questions arising from time to time. And to show how proud they were of their new organization, how important it was in the work of winning the war, all the members wore in their coat lapels the red, white and blue insignia of the Manufacturers Aircraft Association.

But one difficulty bobbed up to pester them at this time. The Association might accomplish all the various tasks awaiting it, but who could direct the Association? What executive? Surely not any individual picked from one of the member companies and who would have a partisan feeling or a material interest. He would have to be a neutral. And because every person familiar with aircraft then was either in the service or identified with an aviation concern it seemed almost impossible for the builders to find an efficient executive to guide the destinies of a new, expanding and vastly important war industry. Many persons were proposed but the manufacturers could not agree on any one of them.

II

August found the aircraft people still seeking an executive, when two men happened to meet in a dining car on a train rolling through Connecticut. One was Raymond V. Ingersoll, then Park Commissioner of Brooklyn. The other was Frank H. Russell, president of the new Manufacturers Aircraft Association. They fell to discussing the war.

"We are up against a hard proposition," said Russell. "We have an organization, but as yet we have not been able to find a man to head it, a general manager."

They talked about the qualifications necessary in a general manager. Then they parted. Russell went on to Marblehead, Mass., where he was managing the Burgess Company. Ingersoll, returning to New York, a few days later, wired Russell that he knew the very man whom the manufacturers were seeking. Russell replied that he would like to meet him.

The man whom Ingersoll had in mind was Samuel Stewart Bradley. He had managed a business of his own and retired from it because of an illness which had disabled him for more than three years. He and his wife had spent much of that period in France. The war was much more vivid to them than to the average American. They could feel it. Bradley, again in good health, was just aching to do his bit.

Ingersoll brought Russell and Bradley together. That meeting was followed by a number of interviews with other manufacturers. In Bradley they discovered a vigorous personality, possessing for all his gentle, modest demeanor, vast experience as a business executive. They also found him to have an original, inventive turn of mind which promised to be of value in the new organization where the work was largely without precedent.

He displayed a keen sense of humor, too. And throughout the interviews and meetings with the constructors he demonstrated that rare quality of patience which he was to need in his association with so many different minds and conflicting personalities. The manufacturers liked Bradley's patience and his good sense. They approved of this candidate.

They took him to Washington and showed him to the big officials and officers who were beginning to make things hum in a dozen or more bureaus concerned with the airplane program. Bradley met them all, from cabinet officers down to the chief clerks, and then he went back to New York as general manager of the Manufacturers Aircraft Association.

As this is written late in 1929 Bradley is still on the job. But he has made more than a job of it. He has established a position for himself among the pioneers of the industry.

Many of the pioneers were active during the war. Orville Wright was consulting engineer for the new Dayton Wright company. Glenn H. Curtiss was still with the company which he had founded. Glenn L. Martin was then with the Wright-Martin Company of California and soon to organize his own company. The Thomas brothers were with the Thomas-Morse company. Charles F. Willard was chief engineer for the Aeromarine company.

Others were making reputations for themselves and preparing to occupy places of prominence in the industry. William E. Boeing was in the naval reserve. R. H. Fleet was an Army pilot. Richard F. Hoyt was in the Army engineering division at McCook Field. C. M. Keys was treasurer and active in the management of the Curtiss company which he was soon to control as president. Charles L. Lawrence was doing engineering work for the Navy and developing the air-cooled engine. Grover Loening was designing military planes for the Army. Albert Loening was an officer in the Air Service. Frederick B. Rentschler was handling aircraft production for the Army in the New York district. William B. Stout was doing experimental work for the Government. Chance Vought was designing airplanes for the Army.

But many of the men who labored to organize the industry during those early days of the war are no longer in aviation. They dropped out of the picture before the recent expansion. Few have received the credit due them for what they accomplished during the war, and in some instances their names are never heard in connection with aeronautics. So it seems fitting that they should be mentioned here along with those who have remained with the industry from the beginning.

Frank H. Russell, who introduced Bradley into aviation, had been the first manager of the old Wright company, leaving that to become an executive with the Curtiss group and president of a subsidiary, the Burgess Company. Russell is now vice-president of the Curtiss Company. There was George H. Houston, a partner of General George W. Goethals and president of the Wright-Martin Aircraft Corporation. Russell and Houston represented their companies as the two principal patent owners in the new organization.

The other members of the Association were equally well-represented. They had Albert H. Flint, the vice-president, and their choice as one of the three trustees. Flint had been a railroad executive before he became president of the L. W. F. Engineering Corporation and a builder of airplanes. They had as secretary, Benjamin S. Foss, president of the Sturtevant Aeroplane Company; their treasurer, Harry Bowers Mingle, president of the Standard Aircraft Corporation.

The directors included Inglis M. Uppercu, president of the Aeromarine Plane & Motor Company; Harold E. Talbot, Jr., president of the Dayton Wright Airplane Company; Frank L. Morse, president of the Thomas-Morse Aircraft Corporation; and John P. Tarbox.

And still others. We have mentioned Flint as one of the three trustees. The Wright-Martin and Curtiss groups, owners of the basic patents, appointed as their trustee, W. Benton Crisp. He was a former judge and a patent lawyer who had distinguished himself when he represented Henry Ford in the Selden automobile patent case and the Hudson interests in the Hudson crankshaft case. With them as the third trustee and a neutral was Dr. Joseph S. Ames, then Professor of Physics and now president of Johns Hopkins University and chairman of the National Advisory Committee for Aeronautics.

All those men, while directly concerned with the reorganization of the industry, had other interests. They were experienced business men or scientists. While we are amazed at the rapid strides made in aviation, while we often wonder at the manner in which the industry has progressed for more than twelve years without panic and failure, we must hand a large share of the credit to the principles and policies which they established at such an early stage.

And many others helped, either directly or by giving sage advice to the manufacturers, in the innumerable conferences held in Washington during the war.

There was Howard E. Coffin, member of the Council of National Defense and chairman of the Aircraft Production Board, who has continued his energetic and constructive work in behalf of American aviation. He was the principal founder of the National Aeronautic Association and its first president.

Dr. William F. Durand, of Leland Stanford University, and Dr. Charles D. Walcott, then secretary of the Smithsonian Institution, were two members of the National Advisory Committee for Aeronautics who helped to guide the industry through the difficult period.

Several men abandoned their own business affairs that they might assist in building the industrial foundation for the American strength in the air. Among them was Colonel Edward A. Deeds, of Dayton, Ohio, who became the officer in active charge of aircraft production. He now is chairman of the executive committee of the United Aircraft and Transport Corporation. Others were Sidney D. Waldon and Harold H. Emmons, of Detroit, and Robert L. Montgomery, of Philadelphia.

There were many other civilians whose aeronautical activities have been submerged by the sheer brilliancy of their achievements in other fields—among them John D. Ryan who succeeded Coffin as chairman of the Aircraft Board. Associated with Ryan and Coffin were William C. Potter, president of the Guaranty Trust Company, of New York; H. B. Thayer, formerly chairman of the board of the American Telephone & Telegraph Company; R. G. Howe, of the International Harvester Company; Archer A. Landon, formerly president of the American Radiator Company; and C. W. Nash, president of Nash Motors.

A word about the officers who served in the aircraft bureaus. The industry was aided repeatedly through their sympathetic advice and assistance. Major General George O. Squier, Chief of the Signal Corps, Rear Admiral D. W. Taylor, Chief of the Bureau of Construction and Repair of the Navy, and a number of subordinate officers served on the aircraft boards and coordinated with work of the aviation program.

We have devoted space to the men mentioned above because their efforts in many and various ways were responsible for the achievements of the new industry. They, like our war aviators, won places in the history of flying.

III

Having finally discovered a general manager for their aircraft association the manufacturers and Government officials gave Bradley some insight as to the duties of the job. He was to be the spokesman for the entire industry, its liaison in welding all the various units which had been opposed to one another, bring about a mutual understanding between them and the Government, and briefly, reduce friction in the machinery which was to produce the thousands of war airplanes. He set to work early in August, 1917.

One week later the newspapers carried a scarehead story about the "aircraft trust."

Now when it is used as a catch phrase in a sensational manner "trust" implies a combination in restraint of trade, a selfish, grasping group of "highbinders" who contrive to so dominate a business that all healthy competition shall be stifled. And where that business deals with Government purchases it connotes graft. The word "trust" in that sense is anathema to Americans.

Here was the first breath of wartime scandal to be wafted into the sensitive nostrils of an excited public. The charge had emanated from the Aeronautical Society of America, which sounded big and official and seemed to give it a tone of authority; though actually that organization of engineers and inventors had not been conspicuous for constructive effort. But people generally knew nothing about aircraft. They could be told and were prepared to believe anything.

That first story was followed by other blasts, special articles and pamphlets—a virtual hymn of hate against the new organization of aircraft builders who at first paid no attention to it. They were setting up new jigs, scrambling for raw materials and hiring new hands to carry out their promise to the Government. They had their own individual problems and they either did not hear or they ignored the cry of "trust." They left to their new Association all such general matters.

At first Bradley did not know what it was all about. The thought that he might have become the bell cow in a herd of grafters had never occurred to him. His conversations with the Government heads and others had led him to think otherwise, that his organization was a very constructive expedient and calculated to help win the war, which was the main thing.

He went to Washington. There he found that the criticism and the publicity accorded it had wrought a mischievous influence in high places. At a time when the officers and other officials were feverishly at work on their war plans, getting out specifications for planes, passing on designs and awarding contracts the production end of the whole program was under grave charges of conspiracy. That was what the hue and cry amounted to when the most important companies were accused of forming a "trust."

Secretary of the Navy Daniels had begun to worry as to whether the organization was legally right or wrong. Secretary of War Baker, being a lawyer, had his own ideas which had led him to encourage the organization from the beginning. Still he did not want to be party to something which later on might be denounced in court. Those two Cabinet officers asked an opinion from Attorney General Gregory. And pending his opinion the subordinate officers in various bureaus would not proceed with certain phases of the production program.

They were justified in thus protecting themselves from possible scandal and no blame could be attached to them. Nevertheless, nothing that the enemy could have done would have put more of a crimp in the aircraft production program at that time. It caused a delay of about six weeks, when the Attorney General rendered his opinion, in October, 1917, giving the manufacturers' association a clean bill of moral health and the cross-licensing agreement his unqualified approval.

Having been assured of the legality of the agreement the Bureau of Aircraft Production then drafted three leading patent lawyers to survey the situation and advise the bureau as to whether the amount and rates of royalties and other phases of the manufacturers' agreement were reasonable and proper. They gave their opinion in January, 1918, stating that the royalties were reasonable and, referring to two single patents, added that the royalties for either were "in all probability less than the basis of recovery a court would allow in a suit against a private individual or concern."

That settled the question, for the time being.

Meanwhile, American factories were turning out airplanes and aircraft engines, not without some confusion occasioned by the foreign aviation missions, the British, French and Italian experts. Their task, as they saw it, was to facilitate the procurement of supplies for their own forces. Each mission was ambitious to have duplicated here copies of machines, engines and spare parts which had been designed in its own country.

They said in effect:

"Our problem abroad is to get airplanes to the front. The service of supply is the weak link in the chain. Our designers are competent, our plants capable of assembling aircraft; but we haven't the resources in labor and raw materials with which to produce the parts. Let the United States make the parts. We shall do the assembling."

That did not sound very agreeable to Americans. It was especially obnoxious when the foreigners insisted that the American plants should reproduce the foreign designs. The question was complicated, because many of the older companies had spent large sums on experimental machines of their own design. They felt, reasonably enough, that they should be permitted to develop them. Unfortunately, no fast fighting or combat planes had been completely developed and tested in the United States. Only the belligerents had accomplished anything in that direction.

The French had their Spads, the British their Bristols and De-Havillands. The Government had to yield the foreign missions a point there, and it agreed that the American factories should produce some of those types. But which ones? Another argument developed, this time between the British and the French; and it caused further delay in the production of airplanes fit to be flown over the front lines.

By that time the program had expanded. It demanded 20,000 combat planes and 9,000 training machines. The training planes were coming out of the factories on schedule, the greater number of them the famous Curtiss J.N.4 with the original Curtiss OX engine. Nearly 10,000 American aviators were trained in those planes. The Navy, too, was receiving its planes on schedule, seaplanes and flying boats designed here and built in American plants.

The production of combat planes awaited the decision in Washington as to which type should be adopted. Finally the British won; and a number of American plants were turned over to a full production schedule. Then it was learned that the working drawings of the De-Havilland plane had not arrived in this country; and there was another delay until the plans could be procured from England. Again, it was decided to modernize the old DeHavilland type and alter the design accordingly. But eventually the plants got under way with orders for production of battle planes, late in the autumn of 1917.

Still the foreign missions were not satisfied. They continued urging that the United States send abroad only parts, engines and machines which had not been assembled. And because they would occupy less space in the ships, quantities of airplanes were sent to Europe as parts, to be assembled in the foreign plants.

In time it became apparent to the manufacturers on this side that the British, French and Italians had adopted a policy of nationalism in safeguarding the future interests of their aircraft industries. Their governments had decided that no demand should be made upon the United States which would develop the American industry and leave it as a competitor after the war. That the French manufacturers and Government officials had hopes of entering the American market after the war was recorded in a report dated in April, 1917. But the Americans did not know it at the time.

They had their hands full taking care of their individual orders. All other matters were routed through the office of the Manufacturers Aircraft Association. It became a common meeting ground where the members could get together and thresh out their mutual problems.

But for the most part they were not accustomed to conferring with one another. They did not like to betray weakness before a competitor. Some of the old distrust and professional jealousy still lingered. But they could take their troubles to Bradley, the general manager and their mutual confidant and spokesman.

One of the most serious problems concerned labor. Thousands of artisans had volunteered for military service and the draft threatened to deplete their ranks still further. The other industries had been able to claim exemption for their employees and were raising wages in order to hold them. The aircraft people knew not where to turn. They had to expand their working forces. The new employees must be intelligent enough to be trained in piecework, the accuracy of which involved the lives of aviators. Training would require time. The best employees would be those who were experienced in trades somewhat similar to the fifty or more different occupations which figured in the construction of planes and engines.

Bradley took this problem to the officials in charge of the draft and with them developed a plan whereby certain classes of workmen were either assigned to the industry or held in reserve. There was no telling at the time just how many of them would be needed. It was the belief in military circles that the war might last five years. The industry had been advised to provide a capital structure and a reservoir of trained men for that period. This really meant raising a small army, and it was accomplished. The number of employees mounted rapidly from the original 5,000, until at the time of the armistice 175,000 men and women were working on aircraft production.

The question of obtaining raw materials kept bobbing up. One company would be able to procure the woods and metals required for an order and another would find shipments delayed or held up altogether. These matters had to be taken up in Washington, and the materials given priority.

The expansion of some of the companies was not accomplished without difficulty. Capital was available but the bankers and others who controlled it often doubted the good faith of the Government in handing out such large orders for planes. They had to have some assurance, and they were not always satisfied with the crisp replies received when they queried officers of the Government. So they went to the offices of the Association.

Very often there was no other place in which to find information. There was red tape in Washington, most of it spun out by the rigid censorship. Each officer had his own job and he was not supposed to discuss even that. It developed that Bradley, who possessed much data, had to employ a delicate sense of discretion in public relations. And that was no small task.

There was the matter of plant protection. A system of safeguards to prevent espionage was worked out through the Association. Freight rates, classification of materials and the eternal struggle to procure deliveries were items of continuous importance; for without priority orders no shipping was permitted.

The general manager of the Association was called upon to supervise on behalf of the industry the organization of vocational schools which soon were sending to the aircraft plants men and women who normally were not artisans but who had volunteered for such labor for the period of the war. This was an important contribution to the personnel; and had the war continued another year or so, it would have been essential to the expanding production program.

Insurance in all its various forms at first threatened to become a serious problem, for there was no precedent by which the underwriters could establish premium rates in a new industry working day and night on war contracts. The information and the views of the aircraft builders were assembled by the Association and its general manager conducted the negotiations with the insurance people. Likewise in the bonding of the companies which, without a central organization to give them other than a local standing, might have paid exorbitant rates for their surety.

There were family troubles too; some of the plants at first betrayed a tendency to steal one another's prize men; and that wrinkle was ironed out in the headquarters of the Association; until there developed quite a friendly spirit of cooperation which took tangible form in the interchange of information concerning improved methods of administration and manufacture. When one company discovered a better method of doing a thing it was passed on to the others.

Then the inventors came in, some who were and many more who distinctly were not. They had their own ideas for revolutionizing the industry. They had models of machines and tools and instruments, fantastic designs for flying craft and thousands of half-baked ideas for bringing destruction to the enemy by way of the air. If they went to Washington, they received scant attention from the Government. If they went to an individual company, they received even less. There was a war in progress. It was no time for doubtful and expensive experiments. To rid themselves of this bother they sent the inventors to the Association. It had its patent committee, but first all those people had to see Bradley.

There were others, many of them men noted in science, industry or business. Some of them wanted important jobs; others had grievances. They had tried to sell the Government a new kind of flying machine which existed only in their own minds. Or they had tried to organize an airplane company or develop an utterly new type of motor. Failing in their purpose they were usually as mad as hornets.

Others were mere gossips, scandal-mongers, time-wasters, fakers or just plain ordinary crooks. Occasionally there would be one who had sworn vengeance against some of the officials in Washington. It seems impossible, but there were thousands of useless persons in this country who during the war endeavored to exploit aviation for their own selfish purposes. And Bradley's office was their wailing wall. But more than that it was also the source of inspiration and courage for the industry.

It was not long before the Association possessed complete knowledge of the ins and outs, the real people and the fakers. Then the manufacturers and the Government officials commenced calling upon Bradley for advice and information.

Most important were his contacts with the newcomers in the industry. While the older plants were sending whole fleets of training planes to the flying fields, seaplanes to the naval stations and an ever-increasing number of combat planes on the way overseas, new manufacturers were entering the field. They wanted to know all about this organization which at first glance appeared to be a rather small family group desiring no additional members. These people had to be sold the new idea of cooperation; but one after another they saw the many advantages and decided to join. This involved a difficult task; for despite the opinion of the Attorney General and the three disinterested patent lawyers, criticism of the industry was again revived late in 1917, and a number of the aircraft bureaus in Washington were brought under fire.

The attacks came from different quarters, from personal enemies of the officials, from self-seekers who thought they had been unjustly rebuffed when they tendered their services, from disgruntled persons who had been clinging to the skirts of aviation in an amateur way and from others who undoubtedly were in the pay of persons or organizations desiring to throw the airplane program into confusion.

Agents from the Department of Justice, the Post Office Department and the Intelligence bureaus of the Army and Navy investigated the activities of different groups of accusers. There are on file in the various departments today voluminous reports indicating that the criticism and the continued efforts to create an aircraft scandal sprang from an enemy source.

All of the attacks were aimed at the "aircraft trust." The manufacturers were paying to their Association, for distribution among the patent owners, a royalty of $200 for each plane; and that in turn was included in the prices paid them by the Army and Navy. Successive newspaper articles, which had been inspired by persons working in the dark or shielded behind the names of so-called patriotic organizations, finally had their effect. They developed public hysteria.

People began to believe that most of the manufacturers were mulcting the Government of huge sums. They overlooked the fact that the cost of developing and acquiring the airplane patents had amounted to huge sums, and that the stockholders in the companies owning the patents, having surrendered their patent monopoly, naturally expected to recover at least their remaining equity.

Finally the War and Navy secretaries called upon the manufacturers to do something which might prevent that kind of criticism. The manufacturers sent Bradley as their spokesman.

Some of the officials had about concluded that possibly the idea of the Government paying royalties was wrong. At first they took the stand that the Government had granted the patents in the first instance; and that which the Government granted it should have the right to take back. It was not sound business logic but it would have been a popular move at the time. And Bradley had the disagreeable task of showing those officials that what they proposed doing was nothing short of confiscation of private property based on a principle which, once established, would discourage invention and destroy vast sums of capital in many different industries throughout the country.

Secretary Baker, as a lawyer, agreed with the manufacturers; but felt that a satisfactory compromise should be effected. The manufacturers agreed to that. They took the stand that the important thing was to get out airplanes and all else was of little account. A supplement to the cross-license agreement was worked out, providing that the royalties during the period of the war should be cut in half.

IV

But still the veiled attacks persisted, and this time they were directed chiefly at the vast expenditures and the management of the aircraft bureaus. Volunteer investigators commenced handing to the newspapers sensational accounts of a promised scandal. They stated that Congress had appropriated a "billion dollars for aircraft" and was getting little or nothing for its money.

The publication of these sensational stories in the spring of 1918 knocked official Washington into a cocked hat. Officers who had been plugging along working day and night at their job of building up our aerial strength immediately froze up, suspected their colleagues of possible chicanery and were half convinced that everybody concerned with aviation was a crook except themselves.

Some commenced playing safe. They declined to put their signatures to any paper. They refused to discuss anything. They wouldn't tell a stranger the day of the week. And thus the "great aircraft scandal" burst wide open and flowered on the floors of Congress. Every act of the officials became subjected to the closest scrutiny. Mistakes and errors of judgment were magnified into grievous faults, even crimes. And before long some of the more important executives, both the civilians and high ranking Army officers, were being transferred to isolated posts or permitted to retire.

President Wilson appointed Snowden H. Marshall to head an investigating committee which would get at the facts. Marshall was one of the most prominent lawyers in New York. Associated with him was Gavin McNab, a leader among the attorneys on the Pacific Coast. Their investigation drew from Marshall this comment, made in the course of a speech after the war:

"I think I will be violating no confidence at all if I say that every member of our committee, after going up and down and all over the country, and looking at all of the people and discussing things with the manufacturers, and with the Signal Corps, and with everybody concerned, unanimously formed the opinion that there was no truth whatever in the false and libelous charges that had been made against the body of the people who were working on this; but that we had been in contact with an able, a patriotic, and an honest body of men who were striving under great handicaps to accomplish a great good for their country."

Still the attacks were continued after the Marshall investigation; and President Wilson, in order to prevent the question of aircraft production from becoming involved in a political controversy, enlisted the services of his former political opponent, Charles Evans Hughes, and authorized the former Justice of the Supreme Court to conduct an investigation covering all charges.

At the same time a sub-committee of the Senate Military Affairs was appointed to hold an investigation. After a lapse of several weeks the secretary of that committee was asked about the investigation; and he replied that the whole thing was a hoax, there was nothing to investigate. Justice Hughes finished his investigation and made a thorough report about two weeks before the armistice. He found nothing to criticize about the manufacturers' association or their cross-license agreement.

One would have thought that the great aircraft hoax should cease then and there. But it did not. The reports persisted and some newspapers continued to print editorials concerning the failure of the aircraft industry and the Government's production program.

Many months were to elapse before the statisticians were able to unscramble the facts and determine the truth, but they managed it finally; and their reports embodied in a score or more of public documents, which are on file in Washington and readily available, throw much light on that matter of "a billion dollars spent for aircraft."

As a matter of fact the United States did not spend a billion dollars on aeronautical activities during the war. The Government's aircraft production program was not a failure. The aviation industry did not fail.

Congress, it is true, appropriated more than sixteen hundred million dollars for the Army air service during the twenty-one months of the American participation in the war. But nearly half of that amount remained in the United States Treasury. It was never incumbered, much less spent. The balance of the appropriations available covered everything spent on military aviation here and abroad in one of the most stupendous undertakings in history. And after the war a large sum was recovered through liquidation and sales of supplies. The net cost of the wartime aviation program was less than four hundred millions.

More than ten thousand aviators were trained and equipped along with a hundred thousand enlisted men in the air service. In the United States thirty-five flying schools and fields were built and operated. There also were radio, aerial gunnery and aerial photographic schools, balloon division and other stations. The construction of air service stations in this country alone cost about seventy millions. And there were purchased in this country supplies such as gasoline, oil, one hundred thousand machine guns, thrice that many bombs, an equal number of instruments, forty thousand propellers, and a limitless variety of tools, lumber, metals, transportation facilities and other auxiliaries to the air force, all of which cost about fifty millions more. The Army's share of the helium gas development during the war was more than a half million dollars, to mention one among 150,000 separate items.

And further, the Army's air service expenditures abroad, in England, France and Italy, were allotted to so many different projects that two years were required to effect settlements with the foreign governments and companies. More than eight millions were spent abroad for hangars, tents and similar equipment. The air service had abroad about thirty flying fields, balloon schools, depots, warehouses and other stations, the construction of which cost more than sixteen millions. Supplies, transportation and equipment purchased abroad cost more than fifty millions.

Besides that the Army purchased from England, France and Italy 5,229 airplanes and 7,059 aircraft engines which with spare parts and all the other supplies mentioned above brought the total foreign expenditures to more than one hundred and thirty-nine million dollars.

In this country about three hundred and fifty million dollars was devoted to airplanes, engines and spare parts. Approximately two-thirds of that was spent for the engines. Let us see what the Government got for its money.

Remember, it started with nothing. The lack of preparedness in the air necessitated a sudden expansion in an emergency. And the cost of that sudden expansion had to be borne by the Government. As we have said the Government did not depend upon the old aircraft companies alone. It went to the motor car industry and to others willing to abandon the manufacture of peacetime products and turn their plants into airplane and engine factories.

During the twenty-one months of war effort the Army received from American manufacturers a total of 13,894 airplanes and 41,953 aircraft engines, including spare parts for both planes and motors. From those companies which could be classified as belonging to the aircraft industry the Army received 9,742 airplanes and 14,765 engines.

That was not all. The Allies kept insisting that the American plants confine their production to spare parts and other equipment which could be shipped to Europe and assembled there. The manufacturers devoted much of their production to that kind of effort.

Further, they built for the Navy airplanes, seaplanes and flying boats. These American machines and engines were being used by the Army and Navy not only in training thousands of aviators but in patrol work with the fleet and from shore stations on this side of the Atlantic, with the American squadrons in foreign waters and with the American armies on all fronts.

Of the forty-five American Army squadrons at the front when the armistice was signed thirty-three of them were equipped with foreign-built machines. The remaining twelve squadrons were using American-built airplanes. Actually 2,091 American-built airplanes had been shipped in France at the time of the armistice, and 1,040 others were on the docks awaiting transportation. Those figures do not seem so small when we learn that the Central Powers had only 3,309 airplanes on the front at the time of the armistice.

Still, the American contribution was nothing when compared to what it would have become within a few months. For the Government had based its plans on several years of war. Its program then called for a constantly increasing number of airplanes, an unlimited number, to be sent to Europe. At the time of the armistice the American factories were geared up to an output of 21,000 airplanes a year. They were actually producing more than all the Allies combined; and thousands of Americans were being trained to fly them. The next few months would have found American machines virtually swarming over the enemy lines by the thousands. It was this rapidly growing air power of the United States, and Germany's knowledge of it, which helped to force the war to an early conclusion.

V

The part played by the aircraft industry in developing the American aerial strength until at the time of the armistice it surpassed the combined efforts of the Allies, was nothing if not a miracle of modern business. Impartial observers have made exhaustive studies of the reorganization which took place in the industry during the twenty-one months of war. They have examined closely the production of planes and engines and the progress made on new training and combat types. And they have been amazed at the accomplishment.

But the armistice threw the industry into utter chaos. There were, all told, twenty-four aircraft companies, some of them large, others small and experimental, but all of them getting under way. They represented a total capital investment of about twenty-three million dollars.

Within three days after the armistice more than a hundred million dollars worth of contracts were cancelled. The Army and Navy had more airplanes and engines than they could use—all war machines of doubtful value in commercial flying. The American industry was left flat, over-capitalized, over-stocked with raw materials, over-organized in all executive and inspection departments and over-manned by expert personnel and skilled labor.

Many of the companies promptly went out of business, liquidating their assets and retiring permanently from aeronautics. Some of the others, which had entered aviation solely as a war expedient to bridge the gap in the market for their peacetime products, returned to their prewar business. But the pioneer companies held on, clinging to the hope that aviation might be popularized.

Here they were up against an unknown proposition. No precedent had been established prior to the war; for people had paid little attention to flying and the number who had been interested in using aircraft was remarkably small. The war had not enhanced its popularity. The flying machine had been developed solely as a military weapon. Whatever favorable notice it received had related to thrilling aerial battles over the front lines, the more casualties the greater the thrill and resulting publicity. Most persons looked upon flying as a military operation and nothing else.

Three months after the armistice the aircraft industry was being liquidated to a degree within ten per cent of its war strength. The remaining companies, having in mind the spirit of cooperation with which they had been working through their trade organization, the Manufacturers Aircraft Association, undertook to utilize it as the principal agency in the development of commercial aviation. They persuaded their general manager to continue on the job, and Bradley, who had expected his work to cease with the armistice, now found himself the spokesman for a struggling, peacetime industry.

The principal work then involved a campaign of public education as to the commercial possibilities of aircraft. It appeared rather simple, at first. One told the people all about it, and they, of course, would believe it; in other words, they would use airplanes.

The Manufacturers Aircraft Association early in 1919 published the first Aircraft Year Book, and from then on, annually for ten years, Bradley, in the course of the day's work edited, compiled and guided the policies of this official and valuable compendium of American aeronautics. He not only saw to it that the facts were set forth honestly and properly, but he interpreted those facts, their relative importance and their influence upon the slow but steady progress of commercial aviation.

From the beginning the Aircraft Year Book became the standard authority in libraries, schools and colleges, banking and business houses, in the newspaper offices, and in the various Government bureaus having anything at all to do with aviation. That was proper, for the Association, eager to continue the method originally a war expedient of having the Government working heart and soul with the industry, now called upon the Government officials for help in promoting the popularity of flying.

The wisdom of this course was apparent; for if the industry then was dependent upon the Federal agencies, the future safety of the country was no less dependent upon the growth of the aircraft industry. If one doubted that, a trip to Europe in the summer of 1919 would have caused him to change his mind.

The Government at that time appointed an aviation mission to visit the European countries and make a thorough study of aeronautics, both military and commercial, with a view to preserving for the United States some benefit from its aeronautical expenditures during the war.

The members of the American Aviation Mission included Assistant Secretary of War Benedict Crowell; Howard E. Coffin, representing the Council of National Defense; Captain Henry C. Mustin, U.S. Navy; Colonel Halsey Dunwoody, Army Air Service; Colonel James A. Blair, Jr., of the Army General Staff; C. M. Keys, president of the Curtiss

Aeroplane & Motor Corporation; George H. Houston, president of the Wright Aeronautical Corporation, and Samuel Stewart Bradley as general manager of the Manufacturers Aircraft Association. Bradley was elected secretary of the Mission, and he compiled its report.

These men had not been in Europe many days before they discovered that conditions there were similar to those existing in the United States. Europe had thousands of military aircraft and an industry limping about trying to keep itself alive on hope for the commercial future. The various governments, recognizing that they must have an industry if they were to maintain air forces, were even then projecting air transport routes to be financed largely by subsidies.

But more than that was embodied in the report of the American Aviation Mission. Its recommendations formed the first constructive program for placing commercial aviation on the road toward its present progress. It may be of interest to quote a paragraph or two.

"Any future war will inevitably open with great aerial activity far in advance of contact either upon land or sea, and victory cannot but incline to that belligerent able to first achieve and later maintain its supremacy in the air.

"For economic reasons, no nation can hope in time of peace to maintain air forces adequate to its defensive need except through the creation of a great reserve in personnel, matériel and producing industry, through the encouragement of civil aeronautics. Commercial aviation and transportation development must be made to carry the financial load.

"No sudden creation of aerial equipment to meet a national emergency already at hand is possible. It has been proven within the experience of every nation engaged in the war that two years or more of high pressure effort have been needed to achieve the quantity production of aircraft, aircraft engines and accessory equipment. The training of personnel including engineering, production, inspection, maintenance and operating forces—covering some fifty distinct trades and some seventy-five industries—has proved itself a stupendous task when undertaken upon the basis of the war emergency alone.

"Past experience and every economic consideration point to the vital need for the formulation by the United States, of a definite, comprehensive and continuing policy for the development of every phase of the aircraft art. Our Government is now faced with the task of nursing and actively encouraging a new transportation industry, whose healthy growth is vital to the future progress and defense of the nation."

Thereupon the report recommended a national air law, Federal control of all flying operations and a continuing program for fostering commercial aviation.

The Government was asked to pay private enterprises for flying the mails, or at first to operate mail lines until they should be proven commercially successful. That was calculated to provide at least a small market for the manufacturers until they could sell commercial planes. The members of the Mission also recommended that the aircraft factories should be conserved by a well-defined and continuing program of production for military and naval purposes, over a period of years—long enough for commercial aviation to get a fair start.

All that and more the American Aviation Mission conceived for the benefit of American aeronautics. It went into the smallest details concerning aerial regulations, the licensing of planes and pilots, aircraft insurance, the kind of organization the Government should have in order to exercise the proper supervision and the manner in which it should deal with the industry at large.

And in one form or another everything recommended by those men who studied the question in 1919 has become an actuality today. A newcomer in aviation might read their report and believe that what they then urged was adopted immediately. But that was not the case. Years were to pass before any of the important recommendations, save one, was put into effect.

That one exception was the air mail. The air mail had been first proposed in 1912 but popular indifference had led Congress to refuse an appropriation of $50,000 requested by the Post Office Department.

The War Department had opened up the first air mail route between New York and Washington in May, 1918. The enthusiastic cooperation of Otto Praeger, then Second Assistant Postmaster General, combined with the efficiency with which the military aviators carried on the work, quickly won public approval, and plans for extending the service were developed even during the war.

On the day of the false armistice Praeger and Bradley were at Harrisburg in conference with the Pennsylvania Forestry Commission on a plan for providing emergency fields along the proposed air route over the Alleghenies. Shortly after the war the actual flying of the mails was taken over by the Post Office Department and the service was expanded from then on until it had spanned the continent.

VI

The operation of the air mail was the first concrete demonstration of practical commercial aviation; and accordingly, it attracted the attention of municipalities, chambers of commerce and other civic bodies throughout the United States. These people, desiring to gain whatever advantage might be procured by having the mail enter their towns, sought the help of the Manufacturers Aircraft Association.

Bradley's efforts in fostering goodwill in the industry had borne fruit outside of it. His advice and cooperation were sought by every reputable concern interested in aeronautics, and they in turn referred inquiries to him.

This required the expansion of an information department which was soon supplying all kinds of data—to the newspapers and magazines, the civic and trade bodies, the Federal and State authorities and to all the allied industries. Within a year every intelligent person had an opportunity to know that aircraft could be made commercially practicable.

Encouraged by the apparent public interest a few of the manufacturers boldly entered the commercial field; some of them producing newly designed mail and passenger planes. Others organized air transport lines. But the public did not respond.

It wasn't lethargy and lack of interest which caused the failure of those early postwar attempts to establish commercial aviation. It was a combination of circumstances, chief among them being the lack of proper landing facilities.

Outside of the few military airdromes and fields established by the Post Office Department as it extended the transcontinental route there were no airports. There was no air law to safeguard the passengers and assure them that they were riding in an air-worthy machine. They could not buy insurance at any premium. And knowing all that, the majority of persons in control of capital—bankers and financiers—repeatedly declined to support aeronautical ventures.

For three years after the war practically all the commercial flying was accomplished by one or two services, which were supported by manufacturing companies, and a hundred or more aviators, war veterans who had purchased planes from the surplus stores of the Army and were barnstorming about the country, stunt-flying, carrying passengers on short hops—and cracking up all over the lot. Lacking facilities for repair and maintenance they usually overlooked such details. Without landing fields they made emergency landings in hay fields and pastures. They repaired their machines with whatever materials they found convenient. There were accidents galore. It was a question as to whether the gipsy fliers were retarding commercial flying or promoting it. At their best the gipsies in those days could not afford to buy new commercial planes.

The industry, the entire field of aviation, became involved in a vicious circle. It could not sell machines; and without sales it could not finance research and improvements in its products. And until it could produce better airplanes, machines which could be operated at a profit, there was small chance of procuring the financial support necessary for commercial expansion and technical development. The Army and Navy were the only customers.

At about this time—during the Spring of 1920—agitation against the "aircraft trust" was again revived. At first the manufacturers and officials of the Government were at a loss as to the reason. There seemed little to be gained by anyone in criticizing an industry which was almost down and out.

One day a young man walked into Bradley's office. He stated blandly that he had a commission to draft an airplane sales campaign on a nation-wide scale. Bradley listened attentively, gave the visitor the information requested but immediately after his departure, set out on a private investigation of his own. He learned that the representative of a foreign manufacturer had been recruiting all the malcontents and erst-while critics of the "aircraft trust" in a scheme to market here in the United States the surplus war stocks of foreign plants.

The plan was simple; it was to so discredit the American manufacturers that they would have no influence with the public or the Government officials; and therefore would be unable to oppose the importation of the junk from Europe. Once having sold the foreign machines and, as they contemplated, having put the American manufacturers out of business, the European constructors might build up a permanent market here in the United States.

That was at a time when the manufacturers were protesting, feebly enough, against the sale of the American surplus war machines because they were not adaptable to commercial flying and could accomplish no constructive purpose.

In fact, a committee of Congress had scheduled hearings on an aircraft anti-dumping bill. There was no opposition to the measure.

Everybody appeared to be in favor of it, when the agents of the foreign combine commenced sending to the committee telegrams of appeal "on behalf of America's ten thousand aviators now in need of airplanes which the 'aircraft trust' will not let them have."

The senders of the telegrams professed to represent various organizations with patriotic motives. And they achieved their purpose. They delayed the committee's consideration of the bill until they could appear at the hearings and make their statements. But as quickly as the committee found that their claims were not supported by the facts it ignored them and reported the bill favorably. It was passed by the House of Representatives and was on its way through the Senate when Congress adjourned. The foreigners seemingly had won; they had succeeded in delaying the proceedings until it was too late for Congress to pass the desired legislation. They commenced shipping their old war machines into the United States.

The patent owners then decided to go into court and demand injunctions against the importers on the ground that they were infringing on American patents. While machines could be built abroad under the terms by which patent rights had been granted, they could not be imported here without payment of royalty fees.

That step whereby the patent owners were to sue for injunctions required a reversal of policy. The manufacturers owning the basic patents had not brought a lawsuit for infringement since the beginning of the war and the organization of the Association.

Several companies had been operating in this country without licenses or paying royalties direct to the patent owners. But the manufacturers had agreed that it would be better for commercial aviation in the long run to permit all possible experimentation and demonstration of flying craft. They believed that if airplane production should become a paying proposition, they would have little trouble with the new members of the industry. And as events proved, they were correct in that assumption.

But here was something vastly different; it amounted to a foreign invasion of a key industry. It meant life or death to the aircraft industry, and to a certain degree it meant just that to the potential buyers of the foreign planes.

We had no laws to regulate the construction or design of aircraft. Here our manufacturers were building machines which conformed to the rigid safety requirements established by the Army and Navy. They could be depended upon; but the foreigners could send over what they pleased, in any condition; and the gullible purchasers would never know, until they crashed, just what was wrong with the imported machines. Some of the planes brought in from Europe at that time were selling for prices as low as $300. They were not worth that.

So the manufacturers decided to take their case to court. They won out. Injunctions were granted. They made it impossible for the foreign builders to sell airplanes in the United States at bargain counter prices. Thereupon the manufacturers adopted another policy. They said that if Europe had airplanes which were better than those built here in the United States, then let the Europeans establish their own plants over here and build those machines with the help of American labor and American materials. In that case they would welcome the machines designed abroad.

The adoption of that policy convinced the European airplane builders that if they hoped to sell machines in the United States, then or in future, they must establish branch factories here or license other American companies to manufacture their types, both planes and engines. Today some of the most important units in the aircraft industry have grown out of the plants put up for the exclusive production of airplanes and engines originally designed abroad.

But the improvement of those machines may be attributed largely to the fact that they were built here, their builders having received sufficient financial support and cooperation from the rest of the industry to permit a development of engineering and design. And further, the fact that the planes were put into commercial operation here, in other words, run through the practical laboratory tests which flying alone can provide, pointed the way toward continuous improvement.

Meanwhile there had developed another situation which for perhaps three years threatened to ruin American aviation. A controversy arose as to the superiority of aircraft against the battleship and other surface armament. The high ranking officers of the Army and Navy who had served with the air forces during the war were enthusiastic in their claims that the day of the battleship, surface artillery and other arms of the defensive establishment was on the wane. Officers who had devoted their careers to battleship strategy and other surface auxiliaries were equally insistent that while extremely useful and potentially dangerous to anything on the surface, aircraft had not proven any overwhelming superiority.

Both sides commenced advancing their claims, in lectures, newspaper interviews and official reports. The question of superiority between the airplane and the battleship turned rapidly from an academic discussion into an argument, from an argument into a bitter contest in which several personalities figured. From the Army and Navy it passed into Congress and reached the committees which had before them all kinds of proposed measures designed to help commercial aviation.

There were bills providing for a national air law, extension of the air mail, and liberal appropriations which would enable the Army and Navy to acquire new and modern aircraft and engines. But the airplane-battleship controversy overshadowed all other questions and members of Congress took sides, became proponents of one or the other. The whole aviation program became scrambled in hopeless confusion. There followed the usual result of such controversies. Nothing at all was accomplished.

A minimum of money was appropriated for new aircraft; but there was little or nothing provided for the development of modern machines, improved designs and types. A half dozen manufacturers were able to procure small orders at irregular intervals; but these orders did not amount to much, and in fact, too little money was made available for experiment and research.

A manufacturer would receive an order for twenty or thirty airplanes. As quickly as he completed that order he was finished for the time being. He had to turn his factory over to other things—motor car bodies, steering wheels, boats, phonograph cabinets and the like. Many plants were shut down during this period. The management of the surviving companies happened to have access to private resources; or they were in the hands of a few financiers and capitalists whose vision of the future remained unchanged during this period.

In the East there were the Wright and Curtiss Companies, Loening, Vought, Thomas-Morse and possibly one or two others which were small, experimental firms. In the Middle West were the Glenn L. Martin Company, of Cleveland; Dayton-Wright, at Dayton; and a few new plants organized by veteran pilots. In the West there were the Boeing Airplane Company of Seattle, Douglas in Los Angeles and two or three very small concerns locally financed and struggling to get under way.

It wasn't much of an industry, all things considered. Both the Army and Navy in the confusion resulting from the airplane-battleship controversy and the personalities exchanged between the officers and officials in Washington had no real policy for the development of aircraft.

The engineering and new design which seemed imperative was undertaken in the aircraft factories maintained by the services and which were essentially experimental and intended originally for research and repair depots. When they commenced building their own service craft it added the finishing touch. The industry was about to become non-existent.

Even those companies which were not on the verge of bankruptcy had about decided to retire. But there remained that vision of what might be accomplished; and there were many executives who had either taken part or witnessed the amazing cooperation between the Government and the industry during the war. They also knew the thoroughness with which Bradley and his staff had been conducting the campaign of popular education; and they felt that something might still be accomplished.

First, the manufacturers, through their organization, appealed to the National Advisory Committee for Aeronautics and the War and Navy departments. Official Washington appeared willing to listen, and it finally agreed that the airplane industry must be saved. But how? That was the question.

The manufacturers met them more than halfway with a proposal. Said they, "If the Government will spend its money with the airplane builders, we in turn will devote all our profits toward designing and improving equipment until the United States Army and Navy have the best flying machines in the world."

Their proposition was accepted. The constructors went back to their plants and commenced the profitless task of developing modern planes and motors, at first experimental planes with clipped wings and superfine streamline fit for racing and speed trials. Races were held. The Army and Navy pilots began taking world's records away from their European rivals. The American public took to congratulating itself that it had such able engineering talent in this country, but the pilots received most of the acclaim.

Bradley, however, continued to point out the urgent need of commercializing the industry. He was drafting memorandums, visiting important groups of business executives and conferring with official committees which had called upon him for information.

His plea was this: "If we are to continue looking upon aircraft as military weapons, we should abandon all attempts to commercialize flying. We shall never have an industry if we remain solely munitions makers. We do not require a big industry if we are to be simply purveyors of the Government. But if we are to develop the airplane as a vehicle of transportation, then we must procure capital and other forms of public support such as air law and regulations, landing fields and charted aerial highways."

In May 1921, Bradley conceived the idea for one great central trade organization which would include not only the manufacturers but all others interested in aviation. This idea was presented to a special committee of the Association which was then considering the advisability of either carrying on the promotion work or abandoning it altogether.

His memorandum addressed to the committee showed the deplorable state of mind into which the entire industry had fallen at that time; and it pointed to the creation of one all-embracing organization of aircraft interests as the best means of promoting commercial aviation.

After reviewing the work which had been accomplished he stated:

"Having fully developed a consciousness of the need for military aircraft, it now remains to force home the facts: (a) There can be, in reality, no military aviation in this or any other country, unless there also be developed commercial aviation. (b) Commercial aviation must be developed in this country in order to sustain our economic and commercial independence.

"From the above brief summary it appears that the national interests and the individual interests of the aircraft manufacturers are identical. We must secure complete recognition of these facts.

"Our duty and responsibility is clear and inescapable. If this work is not done, the entire country may suffer. The importance of the work is so great that it should command the best effort and ability. The manufacturers of aircraft, having in addition to their investment of capital the same interest as every other patriotic citizen, must either individually or collectively accept this responsibility and fulfill this duty. Their greater and more complete understanding of the need imposes the necessity of their continuing this work whether current orders and financial returns cover the expense or not."

And further on the report added:

"As above indicated, during this period we should prepare and develop a complete plan for a broader organization, including under various classes of membership the balloon and dirigible interests, accessory manufacturers, the operators of commercial aircraft, dealers and distributors. If we continue to do our work conscientiously and well, we will attract to the new organization all of these different interests as soon as any one or all of them have developed sufficient substance to have belief in themselves and the future of this business."

Bradley's conception of a worthwhile trade organization was to have in it all the elements which might be interested in aeronautics. But this was not such a simple matter as it appears. The leaders among the manufacturers, a few of the more important operators and a small number of the accessory people agreed that it was a good idea. Others frowned upon it at first. The different groups still had a tendency to hang apart. Aside from the airplane manufacturers they never had been united into any kind of cooperative effort. The industry was full of individualists who liked to run their own show without help from others. It turned out to be quite a struggle before a fairly representative cross section of the industry was finally committed to the idea. The Aeronautical Chamber of Commerce of America was organized on January 1st, 1922.

VII

The membership of the Aeronautical Chamber of Commerce soon included twenty-six manufacturing and engineering companies in both heavier and lighter-than-air, thirty-one operators and distributors—the majority of them doing a pitifully small volume of business—twenty-nine manufacturers of accessories and supplies, eight trade publications, one insurance underwriters association and possibly a hundred individuals—executives, engineers and designers.

The first president was Grover Loening; the vice-president, Charles F. Redden; general manager of the Aeromarine Airways then operating a mail and passenger service between Miami, Key West and Havana. Among the governors were Bradley; Charles H. Colvin, head of the Pioneer Instrument Company; Sherman M. Fairchild, then developing his aerial camera and the Fairchild Aerial Surveys; Frederick B. Rentschler, who had become president of the Wright Aeronautical Corporation; Frank H. Russell, vice-president of the Curtiss Company; Lawrence Sperry, who had his own experimental company; and Charles C. Witmer, president of Airships, Incorporated. They represented all the different groups in the industry.

They asked Bradley to manage the Aeronautical Chamber of Commerce, chiefly because he had inspired its organization and more than any other understood the nature of the work which it must do in developing commercial aviation along the broad national course it since has taken. There was no money to pay Bradley for that work, and he assumed the responsibilities of the position without receiving a salary for it. At the same time he performed his duties as general manager of the Manufacturers Aircraft Association.

With his broad gauge view of the industry as a whole he had suggested that the old wartime cross-licensing agreement should be revised; and a committee of the manufacturers—Charles L. Lawrance, Frank H. Russell and Chance Vought—had reported favorably on the idea. The work of revision and negotiations between the Government and the manufacturers fell to Bradley.

For eight and a half years the two organizations occupied the same offices in New York. During the first nine months all expenses of the Aeronautical Chamber of Commerce were paid by the Manufacturers Aircraft Association. And for years, until the growth of the industry put real money into the treasury of the Chamber, it had the use of the Association's library, information files, office furniture and other facilities. In other words the Chamber had better offices and facilities than it could have paid for at that time. And this circumstance bore immediate results.

Banks, oil companies, tire manufacturers, the great corporations in the electric, lumber, metal and other industries allied to aviation sent their representatives to the offices of the Chamber. The visitors found them well-located in the Grand Central zone in New York, well-equipped and ably managed. They reported the facts. The big corporations and banking houses concluded that the aeronautical industry believed in its own destiny and that it was chock full of promise. They joined the new trade organization. In a short time the Aeronautical Chamber of Commerce represented some fifty allied industries and a rapidly growing number of business and commercial institutions determined to help promote aviation because of the speedy transportation which aircraft might provide.

The source of inspiration in this early work of popular education was the headquarters of the Aeronautical Chamber of Commerce. Bradley and his staff of assistants carried on extensive research in all phases of aviation. For years they were the principal distributors of information—to the newspapers and periodicals, schools and colleges, trade organizations, legislative bodies, lecturers, motion picture companies and others.

They initiated a public landing field campaign and interested municipalities throughout the country in providing airports and other facilities. They appeared before advertising clubs, engineering societies and various civic organizations, managed flying meets, air races and aircraft shows. Wherever expert knowledge of aeronautics was required there a representative of the Chamber would appear.

The Aircraft Year Book, started by the Manufacturers Aircraft Association in 1919, and taken over by the Chamber, became the standard reference work on American aviation. The entire industry was kept fully informed—through bulletins and reports—of every development, technical, commercial and legislative.

The extension of the air mail service through from New York to San Francisco was accomplished with the aid of the Chamber, which went into the larger business houses and sold them the idea of patronizing the flying mails.

The air mail operations under the direct management of the Post Office Department soon created a demand for service which the Government could not give without entering the transportation business on a nation-wide scale. And that was contrary to Federal policy. The Post Office Department was operating mail planes and routes only until such time as the experiment should prove that air mail and other air transport were commercially practicable.

Local trade bodies in hundreds of cities and towns throughout the country commenced agitating for the development of air transport, inviting commercial lines to come in and do business. But there were no air transport companies. The Aeronautical Chamber of Commerce had sold the public on commercial aviation, but there was no organization to carry on operations.

"Why not?" People wanted to know.

"Because there are no adequate airports, no air laws, no weather facilities. There has been no demand for airplanes, and therefore we have no airplanes fit to operate commercially." The answer came from many groups which had been surveying the possibilities of organizing operating companies.

One might have continued:

"And without air law, airports and other surface facilities there never will be commercial airplanes worthy of the name."

It was all rather sad, this picture of a big nation ready to adopt flying as an everyday means of transport, yet lacking all the facilities. But it was the kind of a picture which the leaders of the aircraft industry desired to have presented.

Those leaders deserve mention here; for more than any of the others they paved the way for the real development which was soon to come. They included William E. Boeing, Sherman M. Fairchild, Harris M. Hanshue, Paul Henderson, Richard F. Hoyt, C. M. Keys, Charles L. Lawrance, Harold F. Pitcairn, Frederick B. Rentschler, Frank H. Russell and a score or more of other important figures in either the manufacturing or operating branches of aviation. They had maintained their interest in aviation throughout the long uncertain period. Each one had the support of other big business men, banks and financial houses. If and when they were ready to move, they could command all the capital necessary to finance air transport. Yet that very fact precluded all possibility of such a move on their part until they were assured that the time was ripe, that the proper facilities should be made available. But they continued to promote aviation, working with Bradley and his staff in the Aeronautical Chamber of Commerce.

Still the six requisites for safe flying were lacking—the inspection and certification of airplanes, engines and pilots, the establishment of airports, charted and lighted airways and a nation-wide meteorological service. There were several others, including better planes and engines, the development of navigational instruments, and adequate capital and properly trained management. But all these related to the industry, the manufacturers and the operators, and they could be depended upon to provide them when the six other essential factors should be supplied.

These factors awaited the adoption of a comprehensive national air policy, one in which the Government agencies would provide aerial safeguards and navigational aids as they were supplying lighthouses, harbors and other facilities for surface ships. The Post Office Department, the Army Air Service and the Navy Bureau of Aeronautics were doing much that was constructive.

The Army Air Service, with moderate funds and inadequate personnel had been laying out and charting a number of air routes. The Post Office Department had completed its main transcontinental system between New York and San Francisco, and was preparing to light the route for night flying.

But all those efforts were relatively slight when compared to the actual possibilities, the needs of the nation, if all sections were to have commercial aviation.

It was not until 1924 that a change occurred in national sentiment. At that time the efforts of the Aeronautical Chamber of Commerce commenced showing some tangible results. The work of the manufacturers in devoting all available funds to the improvement of planes, engines and accessories commenced bearing fruit.

Army aviators flew around the earth. The Navy sent its two airships, the Shenandoah and the Los Angeles, on long overland trips, carried scores of prominent persons and demonstrated to the public the practicability of airships. An Army pilot flew across the continent between dawn and dusk.

In that year American aviators captured thirty-two of fifty-nine world's records. It was on the whole a period of greater achievement and less disappointment than any since the armistice. But it was not what it should have been. Three of the most important world's records—speed, altitude and endurance—all held by Americans in 1923, had passed to French aviators in French machines.

The industry, through its trade organization, kept repeating what it had been saying for years, that American aviation could not be given a fair start without a comprehensive and detailed national policy. Bradley and the manufacturers, who since the war had retained the confidence of all the Government bureaus and committees, were called upon for definite information as to the exact conditions prevailing throughout civilian aviation and the steps necessary for correction.

As Bradley explained in one of his reports:

"I feel certain that if our work had not at all times been inspired by a sincere desire to help cooperate and build up all aviation, without bias or prejudice for any of its established, recognized, reputable elements, that our organization would have ceased to exist and that today there would not be in existence any comparable organization representing the common interests of the industry.

"I feel that it is equally true that had our activities even the appearance of organized effort to direct aeronautical legislation or appropriations, by maintaining direct contact with Congress and other representatives of the Government, through the maintenance of a lobby, or other means similar in character, our organization would not have survived.

"By avoiding the above and by studiously refraining from any activities of this character, and confining ourselves to the dissemination of correct information, by cooperating with and assisting all individuals and groups who have been sincerely endeavoring to advance aviation we have exercised a stabilizing, encouraging and wholesome influence on all such activities and have established for our organization a reputation generally recognized as a permanent, continuing and sane, affirmative influence which constantly manifests itself and whose support is sought and urgently demanded whenever any project for the development of aviation is under consideration."

VIII

In 1924 during the excitement occasioned by the controversy over the relative value of big guns and airplanes the "aircraft trust" hoax was revived. At the time a Congressional committee was just starting out to investigate the needs of the air services. This committee immediately turned its attention to the "aircraft trust."

Under the chairmanship of Congressman Lampert and with the examinations led by Congressman Perkins the committee conducted an exhaustive investigation. But instead of finding a "trust" it found that the airplane people were absolutely correct in their statements. Instead of aviation suffering from a "trust" it was being slowly stifled by the lack of a definite Government policy and legislation required to permit its growth. The report of the Lampert Committee made many recommendations which later were embodied in much constructive legislation of benefit to the industry.

Meanwhile, Major Lester D. Gerdner, then publisher of *Aviation* and a former Air Service officer with wide understanding of the problems of the services and the industry, invited the aircraft and engine constructors to a luncheon in New York. He suggested that a special committee of the industry be organized to look into its own responsibilities and study the means by which they might be more fully met and realized. The manufacturers appointed their committee. It included Charles L. Lawrance, chairman; Samuel Stewart Bradley, secretary; Frank H. Russell, Chance Vought, Albert P. Loening, Carl B. Fritsche, and Glenn L. Martin.

They held conferences with the Secretaries of War and Navy, and in response to an invitation from President Coolidge went to the White House and reported to him. They then went into conference with Herbert Hoover, who as Secretary of Commerce was later designated by Congress to administer our first national air law and to foster aviation by regulating all civil flying and developing the airways. President Coolidge in his message to Congress asked that something be done to encourage aviation. The National Advisory Committee for Aeronautics in its annual report stated:

"The present American aircraft industry is but a shadow of that which existed at the time of the armistice. Civil aviation has not developed as it was hoped it would, and this makes the situation more difficult. The aircraft manufacturers have had to rely for orders upon Government agencies, and the limited amount of Governmental purchases has forced a number of manufacturers to go out of the aircraft business. It is a matter of grave concern lest the productive capacity of the industry may be so far diminished that there may not remain a satisfactory nucleus. By a 'satisfactory nucleus' is meant a number of aircraft manufacturers distributed over the country, operating on a sound financial basis and capable of rapid expansion to meet the Government's needs in an emergency."

By New Year's day in 1925 everybody understood the general terms of a national policy, providing that it could be adopted. There were other highlights over the horizon, enough to promise the dawn of a brighter day for aviation. The Ford Motor Company started to build airplanes. A number of large corporations purchased machines which were flown about the country. People thought that they were growing "air-minded." The air-cooled engine was developed to a practical stage. American pilots broke more air records, notably those for speed over both land and water.

Then the service controversy broke out again in Washington. The flying officers as a class accused the other branches of trying to cripple the aerial arm. They were finding fault with the promotion system, the administration of the air services under the control of non-flying officers and the policy of maintaining aviation as a subordinate branch of the defensive establishment.

Their champion was the Assistant Chief of Air Service, Brigadier-General William Mitchell, an officer with a distinguished record dating from the Spanish-American War. Mitchell was a pilot. He was the first officer of the American forces to fly over the enemy lines after our entry into the war.

He took his arguments to the public in a series of magazine articles and later, after disciplinary measures had been taken against him, openly accused the military boards of discriminating against aeronautics.

This resulted in his resignation from the service, but it aroused the nation. The public demanded a thorough airing of Mitchell's charges and his contention that aviation was being neglected. Of course others had said the same thing many times. But Mitchell's methods were spectacular, therefore effective.

President Coolidge appointed an aircraft board under the chairmanship of Dwight W. Morrow. This board held hearings and rendered an exhaustive report. It clarified the situation, informed the nation as to exact conditions and pointed the way for Congress to act. There were manifold results.

The national air law was passed in 1926, placing in the Department of Commerce control of commercial aviation. Five-year procurement programs were adopted for the Army and Navy, providing for an increasing number of aircraft each year until 1932. The Army flying service under the leadership of Major General Mason M. Patrick and later, Major General James E. Fechet, and the Bureau of Aeronautics of the Navy, administered by Rear Admiral William A. Moffett, have maintained their progressive standing each year since the adoption of the five-year programs.

While passing that important legislation providing for the development of both civil and military aviation, Congress at the same time gave aeronautics a belated but none the less welcome representation in the administrative branch of the Government. It provided for three under-secretaries for air in the President's Cabinet.

William P. MacCracken, Jr., was appointed Assistant Secretary of Commerce to administer the national air law and the Bureau of Aeronautics in the Commerce Department. F. Trubee Davison became Assistant Secretary of War in charge of the aeronautical activities of the Army; and Edward P. Warner was named Assistant Secretary of the Navy for Aeronautics. Under those three secretaries the nation was provided with able management of all Governmental aviation activities and members of the industry once more were encouraged to plan for the future.

With a definite national aviation policy assured, the men who had been struggling for years to secure such a policy now undertook to organize air transport lines. An act of Congress enabled the Post Office Department to retire from the operating business, leaving the air mail to private contractors. In 1926 a number of lines were in operation and others were getting under way, ordering machines from the manufacturers and in some instances preparing to carry passengers and express besides the mails. That was the end of the twilight period in aviation.

The year 1927 was one of epic flights. Lindbergh flew from New York to Paris and public enthusiasm exploded. Aviation became popular overnight, popular at least to the extent that every man, woman and child commenced talking about it. Lindbergh was followed across the Atlantic by Chamberlin and Byrd. Maitland and Hegenberger flew from Oakland to Honolulu, followed soon by Smith and Bronte, Goebel and Davis, Jensen and Schulter. Brock and Schlee flew the Atlantic and on across Europe and Asia to Tokio.

All the long flights, however, were but the culmination of years of effort within the aircraft industry. Bradley writing the introductory chapter in the Aircraft Year Book for 1928 summarized that history in the following manner:

"As far back as 1919, three trans-Atlantic flights were successfully accomplished. Subsequently, American aircraft had won laurels through a wonderful series of exploits such as the flight around-the-rim of the United States, the flight of the fleet of planes from New York to Alaska and return, the transcontinental non-stop flight, the round-the-world flight of three Army planes in 1924, the dawn to dusk flight from New York to San Francisco, the North Pole flights, the good-will flight around South America and other similar events of outstanding importance.

"In addition, equally noteworthy results have been attained in high speed, endurance and altitude records. In the practical application of aircraft to more speedy transportation we had recorded the truly impressive performances of our air mail lines. Flying by night as well as by day in all kinds of weather, schedules had been maintained for more than 7,000 miles each twenty-four hours over most difficult terrain, crossing mountains, deserts, lakes and forests.

"These accomplishments had not gone unheralded. They had been duly appreciated by the press and the public and utilized as stepping stones for continued advancement. They marked the steady march of progress and paved the way for securing the long deferred but vital Governmental recognition which came in 1926. During that year aeronautics in the United States became permanently established upon a sound program of constructive legislation. Thus as the year 1927 was ushered in the stage was set for the next great step in our progress.

"With the passage of the Air Commerce Act and the five-year

programs for the Army and Navy we were in a measure prepared for the events which followed. We had, in addition to pilots and aircraft, the engineers, designers and manufacturers to carry on and secure the progressive development of all kinds of equipment. We had aerial transportation companies and aerial service operators in the field looking for business. We had the basic law giving legal authority for carrying on their work and for the assistance of the Government, through the Department of Commerce, in maintaining airways and aids to navigation. In fact we had about everything that could be desired except complete public recognition of flying as a practical means of transportation. The year 1927 changed all this. The flying events of that year supplemented the work which had gone before in such an admirable way that in the twinkling of an eye, Lindbergh flying alone from New York to Paris, gripped the consciousness of the entire civilized world. Public recognition and confidence seemed to come in an instant."

IX

The Aeronautical Chamber of Commerce played a most important part in the developments which followed during the next eighteen months. There was phenomenal expansion in every phase of aviation. New interests were plunging into the business with money and energy, and frequently with little or no practical experience in aeronautics. They required guidance, asked for it and got it. There was so much enthusiasm that certain undesirable promoters found the public gullible and steps had to be taken to protect the innocent. There was as much danger from over-inflation as from depression; and the Aeronautical Chamber again exercised a wholesome, stabilizing influence during this period of rapid expansion.

The organization had to develop facilities for assisting every branch of the industry. Late in 1927 Bradley had suggested a plan looking toward the decentralization of the Chamber. This provided for regional divisions and trade sections, the latter to include special groups made up of commercial airplane builders, motor manufacturers, transport operators, constructors of airships, airports, flying schools, purveyors of materials, equipment and supplies, jobbers and dealers, fuels and lubricants, publishers, aerial service operators, aerial photography and survey.

In August, 1928, the country was divided into seven geographical divisions, each one represented by a divisional vice-president in charge of a committee which would work through the parent organization. In addition general committees were appointed to handle shows, insurance, arbitration matters, technical standards, aeronautical education and Government relations.

The twenty-fifth anniversary of the airplane found flying well to the forefront among other means of transportation, and aviation was rapidly assuming the proportions of a major industry. The air transport lines in 1928 had flown twice the mileage of the preceding year, carrying three times the mail and four times the number of passengers. Traffic was increasing month by month. Local aerial service companies were being merged into state-wide and sometimes nation-wide organizations. The number of privately owned airplanes increased from hundreds to thousands. Airports were being established in the majority of cities and towns. And the airplane factories were producing more commercial planes than military, for the first time in history. They were employing more workers than during the war. Aviation was beginning to fulfill its promise, to justify the vision of those who entered the commercial industry after the war and remained steadfast. Through the efforts of those men, and because of the work which they accomplished through their central organizations aviation had reached an enviable position among the older industries.

Meanwhile the membership of the Chamber doubled within six months in 1928. It included sixty-seven aircraft manufacturers, eighteen engine companies, a score of trunkline air transport operators and hundreds of industrial enterprises in affiliated branches of the industry. This membership was distributed in all the states. Moreover the industry was undergoing a rapid transformation.

It was doing more business and it was developing into a number of big corporations, holding companies, investment trusts, consolidated manufacturing companies and transport lines merged into nation-wide systems. In many ways these concerns required help and cooperation from their trade organization. In several instances there were executives whose experience had been limited to one or two years. They required coaching, and most important, instruction in the code of ethics which had developed in the industry during the days of the war.

The Aeronautical Chamber of Commerce was soon functioning under its numerous committees. More personnel was added to the executive staff; and those men were trained by Bradley. An expositions company was organized to handle aircraft shows and flying meets. Then, early in April, 1929, the Manufacturers Aircraft Association claimed the undivided services of its general manager.

There was an amended cross-license agreement to administer. Scores of new companies were beginning to produce airplanes. The Manufacturers Aircraft Association promised such rapid growth that it would require all of Bradley's attention. He resigned from the Chamber in April, 1929. The Board of Governors in accepting his resignation paid him tribute in this resolution:

"There was a time when this body, which today embraces within its membership hundreds of corporations from all parts of the United States, existed only as an idea, and that idea was first expressed, nurtured and developed by Samuel Stewart Bradley.

"Since its inception in 1921, the Aeronautical Chamber of Commerce has been under the management of Mr. Bradley. That it was able to survive during its first difficult years was due to his untiring watchfulness. That it was able to meet the long-expected opportunity to serve the industry, when our commercial expansion began three years ago, was due to Mr. Bradley more than to any other man.

"In these seven years, Mr. Bradley has served the Chamber without compensation. He leaves this work with the realization that what was once an idea is now a tangible, powerful reality. The impartial spirit which has characterized his actions has, through his personal example, inspired in all the operations of the Chamber a spirit of mutual cooperation and good will. We are indebted to him. We are grateful to him. In accepting his resignation which he has several times offered, we are unwilling to admit that he shall completely separate himself from the work to which he devoted himself for so many years. While releasing him from labor now grown impossible because of other exacting duties, we shall still look to an unbroken continuance of his friendly association and mature counsel."

With Bradley's resignation from the Aeronautical Chamber of Commerce that body and the Manufacturers Aircraft Association became separate organizations in fact as well as in name. The Chamber moved its headquarters to another building at 10 East Fortieth Street, while the Manufacturers Aircraft Association retained its old address at 300 Madison Avenue, New York. Thus there were two trade bodies to work for the advancement of American aviation.

The Manufacturers Aircraft Association as a matter of course has limited its activities to the administration of the cross-license agreement. That agreement is vastly more important than it may at first appear. The amended agreement which Bradley had been negotiating for seven years covers the two basic airplane patents and more than three hundred other patents owned by members of the Association. Under its terms the members and subscribers to the agreement pay a modest royalty fee based on a sliding scale determined by the number of planes and the selling prices of the machines sold. Members are free to use one another's patents and are in a position to meet all patent problems intelligently and constructively.

The importance of that agreement is evidenced by a letter addressed to Bradley on December 20th, 1928, and signed by Dwight F. Davis, then Secretary of War, and Curtis D. Wilbur, then Secretary of the Navy. It states in part:

"The draft of the contract and draft of the amended cross-license agreement were submitted to the legal branches of our respective departments and after careful consideration, the latter have made certain suggestions tending to clarify the proposed revision of the agreement and the new form of contract for the Government. As thus amended, they meet with the approval of the War and Navy departments and should be promptly likewise approved and accepted by the owners of patents and the manufacturers of airplanes generally.

"The prompt acceptance of the contract and the cross-license agreement are of importance to the Government, to the industry and also to the public as a means for the continued unhampered development of aviation in the United States.

"We realize that we have been fortunate in the past, due to the early adoption of the principle of cross-licensing of airplane patents. By the cross-license agreement of your Association manufacturers and operators of aircraft have been spared the expense and injury of long drawn out patent litigation.

"Under the amended cross-license agreement the industry can proceed in an orderly and business-like manner to meet the increased demands of aviation, both civil and military, under the changing conditions incident to a rapid development of the art, without dissipating its strength and resources in patent controversies."

Within a few months after Bradley commenced devoting all his time to the work of the Manufacturers Aircraft Association he had enrolled, as members or subscribers to the cross-license agreement, forty-five of the leading airplane manufacturing companies, embodying in that group about eighty-five per cent of the productive capacity of the industry. The machinery for protecting those manufacturers from patent litigation and other forms of interference dealing with patent claims was operating smoothly. In that respect the industry was assured of continued peace. It could present a solid front against the fakers and other irresponsible claimants to patent ownership whenever they might attempt to extort money from the builders.

Moreover, Bradley had organized a patent research division to check and distribute to members a thorough description of all new patents and inventions which might be of value to the industry. This division also provides for the interchange of new and promising ideas. Instead of one company working on the solution of a problem, all of them may tackle it and thereby speed up improvements in airplanes.

In that Bradley has brought into the industry further application of the spirit of cooperation which has distinguished American aeronautics since the war, and which at this time—eleven years later—promises to quicken its growth in the most difficult yet essential field, that of engineering.

The public is fairly sold on flying. The people believe in aviation. They are confident that it will provide a major means of transport. All the auxiliaries to success are being provided—legislation and regulation, airways and airports, trained pilots and surface personnel. But the improvement of aircraft must keep pace with everything else. The machines must be developed to the limit of perfection. How necessary, then, is cooperation among the inventive branches of the industry. One is tempted to predict that the growth of aviation from now on will be in direct proportion to the cooperation of its inventors, determined by the degree of mental effort which the industry as a whole devotes to the solution of technical problems.

With peace assured, with the manufacturers, designers and inventors free to work out their ideas, using the best that others have provided in order to improve upon an idea, the last obstacle in the part of aeronautics has been removed. Flying may now become everybody's business. And aviation should continue to grow up into a major industry.

Part II
The Aircraft Industry in the Depression Years
1930–1940

3. Depression, Industrial Concentration, and the Growing Export Market

With the general collapse of prosperity following the stock-market crash in 1929, sales of the aircraft industry contracted almost as rapidly as they had expanded during the "Lindbergh Boom." From 1927 to 1929 sales had jumped from $21,162,000 to $71,153,000. By 1933 they had fallen to $26,460,000, and literally scores of aircraft companies, especially the smaller new entrants, were forced out of business. As a result of two five-year procurement programs enacted by the government in 1926, military demand had continued to grow somewhat, but the demand for aircraft for private and commercial uses contracted sharply. At the 1929 peak, 5,516 civil aircraft were produced; in 1932, there were only 803 produced. Aeronautical exports also declined between 1929 and 1932.

The Army and the Navy concentrated their orders among a few producers while the five-year programs were in effect. With the severe contraction in demand for civil aircraft, only a small number of producers other than the military contractors survived among the scores of plane-makers who had gone into business during the previous decade. The government, by following a selective procurement policy, was largely responsible for the industrial concentration that developed in the aircraft industry then and has continued to exist ever since.

Holding companies were formed to gain monopoly power. Although related activities of the aviation industry were encompassed in the process, the ownership or control of aircraft manufacturing firms along with air transport companies was the dominant form of integration. Not only did several organizations get practically all the orders for military aircraft, but they also got almost all the government air-mail business.

The interlocked positions of the major air transport companies and the large aircraft manufacturers had been suspect for some time, but it was not until after the Congressional investigation by the Crane Committee in 1933 that steps were taken to break up these combinations. The Crane Committee said that the holding companies had prevented the free development of aviation and had caused a waste of public funds. The result of the Committee's findings was the passage of the Air Mail Act of 1934, which forced the legal separation of the air transport companies from the aircraft manufacturers in an effort to prevent the continuance of certain monopolistic practices that had been in existence since 1928.

At this time the aircraft industry was experiencing serious difficulty, particularly since 1932, when the Army and Navy five-year programs were completed and the demand for civil aircraft had sharply declined. In 1934 another government committee, the Baker Board, was appointed to investigate the reasons for the depressed status of the industry. The report of the Baker Board resulted in the passage of new five-year procurement programs for the Army and the Navy, which got under way in 1935. To protect against further adverse publicity in government dealings with the industry, the Vinson-Trammell Act of 1934 limited profits on sales of aircraft to the Navy to 10 per cent. Legislative action to limit profits on aircraft sales to the Army, however, was not taken until 1939.

Besides the sharp contraction in civil demand and the growth of concentration in the industry with its consequent reactions, another outstanding characteristic of the 1930's, as far as the industry was concerned, was the growth in demand for aeronautical exports. As international relations deteriorated, the industry's exports expanded. Indeed, the ability of the United States to win World War II no doubt was enhanced by its broad industrial base in aircraft manufacturing, made possible by the export market, on which to build upon entering the war.

Elsbeth E. Freudenthal, an author of books on aviation, has provided the most complete account of the aircraft industry's history from 1930 to 1940. The selection that follows describes in detail the effects of the depression, the industrial concentration that evolved, the resulting legislation, and the expanding export market for the products of the aircraft industry.

*The Aviation Business in the 1930's**
Elsbeth E. Freudenthal

I.

Charles A. Lindbergh's flight stimulated the popular imagination as all previous aviation accomplishments had failed to do. Lindbergh himself was modest about his flight, and many flyers agreed with Birger Johnsen's opinion:

> No professional flying man would have selected that as a performance throwing all others into the shade; a good single-handed job, with lots of luck, would have been the expert's verdict.[1]

There were other notable flights before and immediately after Lindbergh's. In 1926 Roald Amundsen, Lincoln Ellsworth, and Umberto Nobile had flown over the North Pole in an airship; in the same year Commander Richard E. Byrd and Floyd Bennett flew from Spitzbergen to the North Pole and back. Clarence Chamberlain and Charles A. Levine flew to Germany in June, 1927. In 1928 Sir Hubert Wilkins and Carl B. Eielson flew over the North Pole, and Byrd flew over the South Pole. In the same year that remarkable flyer, Amelia Earhart, achieved the record of being the first woman to fly the Atlantic and land in Europe. The Pacific was conquered also when Lieutenants Lester J. Maitland and Albert F. Hegenberger of the Army Air Corps flew from San Francisco to Honolulu in June, 1927, succeeding where the attempt had failed in 1925.

A Detroit businessman, Edward F. Schlee, and William S. Brock, aviator, attempted to circle the globe. They got as far as Tokio, but had to stop there, "In deference to a general sentiment against their attempt to fly across the Pacific from Japan, with Midway Island, a tiny speck in the ocean, as the first fueling stop, ..."[2] This item, published in 1928, is significant in view of the present importance of the Pacific islands in the Japanese-American situation: ten years later this "tiny speck" was a new air-defense outpost, where the Army and Navy were constructing a seaplane base to cost over $2,000,000. (And Pan American Airways advertised it as a vacation resort!)

There is little doubt that much progress was being made in airplane

---

* Reprinted by permission of the publishers from Elsbeth E. Freudenthal: *The Aviation Business: From Kitty Hawk to Wall Street* (New York: The Vanguard Press, 1940), edited selection from pp. 90–282. The title supplied by the editor.

[1] Henry Wysham Lanier, *The Far Horizon* (New York: Alfred A. Knopf, 1932), p. 210.

[2] Aeronautical Chamber of Commerce, *Aircraft Yearbook* (New York: Aeronautical Chamber of Commerce, 1928), p. 31.

design and the development of the air-cooled radial engine at this time. However, these developments and flights, although undertaken seriously and in the main for scientific reasons, were commercialized in order to increase the popular impression that aviation had suddenly "arrived." These advances were overshadowed, as were the serious purposes of the flyers, by the popular hysteria. Ballyhoo kept the flames of excitement burning. Lindbergh's personality was capitalized and the picturesque aspects of his solo flight were flaringly publicized. A series of orgiastic receptions to returned flyers was only one of the ways by which the public hysteria was increased.

The public became so airminded that it dug into its pockets for the price of a ride—on Wall Street. Even Lindbergh, the people's hero, felt it necessary to sound a warning against investing in "unsound" projects. The *Aircraft Yearbook,* remarking on the fact that " . . . money, everywhere, seemed to be available for aviation ventures," went on to say smugly (and prematurely), " . . . the 'wild-catting' and exploitation following this wave of enthusiasm was negligible, considering the magnitude and sustained character of the popular public interest."[3]

Wall Street betrayed this confidence in the next eighteen months. No further warnings were heard from Lindbergh as he gradually withdrew from popular interest and became a legendary hero. Lindbergh's flight occurred in May, 1927, in a plane powered by a Wright "Whirlwind" engine. A month previously this company's stock had been selling at 25, and by December, 1927, it had more than tripled in value, going to 94¾ ; in another year it reached 245. In nineteen months, then, the popular interest had sustained an aviation-stock flight from 25 to 245 . . . .

Dominant Groups Take Control

The intense cultivation of aviation in the 1927–1929 period was due, of course, to increasing possibilities of profits. Industries of the same size—corsets and purses—were not eagerly sought after by Morgan, National City or other financial forces. Nor had aviation found an economic function that would cause this sudden interest. Neither was it a result of the fact that the big financial groups had awakened to the limitless possibilities of aviation, for pioneering had always been carried on by individuals or by the government, not by financiers.

[3] *Ibid.,* p. 49.

Besides the fact that the laws passed in 1926 promised subsidies for aviation companies, there were profits also to be made on stock issues. The names of the new holding companies formed in this period of mergers may be unfamiliar, but they were merely continuations of the war and prewar companies. These groups—General Motors, Curtiss-Wright, Aviation Corporation, and United Aircraft and Transport—controlled the industry in all its phases. Not usually cynical, the *Aircraft Yearbook* wrote: "The 'independent' lines, if the companies not included in the four major financial groups can be properly called that, . . ."; and later, "As in the air transport and aircraft manufacturing fields, the influence which the large financial groups exerted upon the development of the engine manufacturing branch of the industry cannot be over-emphasized."[4]

Profits greased the works and were important in hastening the process of consolidation. The consolidations themselves were of importance, for practically no independent company survived this era. The flood of mergers engulfed all the old pioneers and aviation engineers who had managed to carry their own companies through the previous years of erratic development. They could not compete, they realized, with the large combinations backed by powerful interests that were now dominating the industry. So they either sold out to the financiers, as Loening and Boeing did, or, like Douglas and Consolidated, admitted some financial interests.

Loening described the sudden interest of Wall Street in these small independents (many of them capitalized at no more than $100,000) when they began to receive orders totaling several million dollars. His company, like the other independents, had found it impossible to borrow money up to this time, but now, " . . . it began to look as if we would be left out in the cold if we didn't have some hook-up with an airline or a big group."[5] And so Loening's company sold out to Hayden, Stone and Company.

The late Anthony H. G. Fokker, famous during the World War, came to the United States in the early 1920's and formed his own company, The Atlantic Aircraft Corporation. By 1929 he had come to the same conclusion as Loening:

---

[4] Aeronautical Chamber of Commerce, *Aircraft Yearbook* (New York: D. Van Nostrand Co., 1930), p. 22.
[5] Grover C. Loening, *Our Wings Grow Faster* (New York: Doubleday, Doran and Co., 1935), p. 171.

... the Lindbergh boom suddenly expanded aviation activities tenfold ...
The sudden dumping of 400 millions into the industry, six months after a
period in which no aviation company could even get credit, made it imperative
that I join forces with a strong financial ally.[6]

And that is how General Motors acquired 40 per cent (and control) of
Fokker's company.

Due to the pyramiding of companies and the complicated maze
of mutual stock holdings, the lines dividing the main groups were
indistinct and changed frequently. By the end of this period, in 1933,
there were really three groups instead of the four outlined below, for
Curtiss-Wright was definitely included in the General Motors sphere of
influence. These groups dominated the whole industry from 1927 to
1933, and continued to do so from then on.

I. General Motors–North American Aviation Group

At the end of the war General Motors owned one of the main
manufacturing companies: the Dayton Wright Company. Its interests
during this period were as obscure as during the war, and it did not
indulge in spectacular stock transactions like those, for example, of the
United Aircraft and Transport. From 1927 to 1933 General Motors
seems to have acquired stock in many companies, so that it had a finger
in practically all the pies then being so hastily baked. Due to the shifting
relationships within the industry, this was an advantageous policy, for
in acquiring interests in several companies, each of which might own
stock in another, General Motors frequently got majority control.

The main manufacturing interests were held through General
Aviation Corporation (owned by General Motors) and North American
Aviation (General Motors-controlled by 1933). General Aviation was a
merger of the Dayton Wright Company and Anthony H. G. Fokker's old
company. Fokker finally broke away, but his company was really the
nucleus of this group's manufacturing interests.

North American Aviation was the investment company formed by
C. M. Keys in 1928. In this period of feverish financing it started with
an unusually prudent nonwatered issue of stock at $15 a share. But
there was potential watering even here, since an unissued balance of
2,000,000 shares was held under option at $12.50 a share until 1931.

---

[6] Anthony H. G. Fokker and Bruce Gold, *The Flying Dutchman, The Life of Anthony Fokker* (New York: Henry Holt and Co., 1931), p. 14.

By 1933 North American Aviation was a large holding company, having acquired Sperry Corporation, Ford Instrument Company, and Berliner-Joyce Aircraft. In addition, it controlled Curtiss-Wright and owned stock in Douglas and many other companies including even United Aircraft and Transport, which was in the National City orbit. The list of its manufacturing companies was large, particularly taken in conjunction with General Motors' control of Bendix Aviation Corporation (another complex holding corporation).*

In the transport end General Motors' interest was equally widespread. Through North American and its subsidiaries it controlled or owned large stockholdings in Eastern Air Transport, Western Air Express, Transcontinental and Western Air, Inc., Ludington Air Lines, and several other companies later included in the Pan American system. Its interest in Transcontinental Air Transport was a good example of the complex relationships of this period. For Transcontinental Air Transport was formed by Curtiss, Wright and Pennsylvania Railroad interests in 1928. Its backers also included National Air Transport, several members of the New York Stock Exchange, and many other individuals through whom its board was cross-linked with dozens of other boards of directors. By 1933, National Air Transport had passed from this group to the control of United Aircraft and Transport; Curtiss-Wright was in the North American orbit, and Transcontinental Air Transport and Western Air Express had joint interests in Transcontinental and Western Air, Inc.

These General Motors-controlled and related transport companies collected in seven years an average of approximately 26 per cent of all air-mail payments.... Through these and many other complexities the General Motors–North American Aviation interests formed, by the end of this period, a vertically integrated group covering all phases of aviation.

II. Curtiss-Wright Corporation

It is ironic that the names of the Wright brothers and Glenn H. Curtiss should be joined together in this large holding company. Their feud has not even yet been settled, though the merger was effected in

---

* General Motors' interest started in 1929 when it gave Bendix $15,000,000 in cash, Delco Aviation Corporation, and many patents and contracts. In return it got 500,000 Bendix shares. By 1934 General Motors' General Aviation Corporation was a shareholder and General Motors held directly 23 per cent of Bendix stock. Thus General Motors controlled Bendix, even though Vincent Bendix, who had been in aviation from the start, was and continues to be the company's president.

1929. Even so, Orville Wright and Glenn Curtiss had long since severed their connections with the companies that bore their names (Wright Aeronautical Corporation and Curtiss Aeroplane and Motor Company).

Because of its twenty-nine subsidiaries and eighteen affiliated companies, Curtiss-Wright claimed to be the world's largest aviation group. It was most important in the manufacturing field, for its engine-manufacturing subsidiary, Wright Aeronautical, continued to be one of the two engine-manufacturing companies to which the government restricted its purchases. The company had an inflated capital structure which it claimed approximated one-third of the total aviation investment of the country. The severe deflation of aviation securities was shown by the slide in this company's common stock from a high of $30 in 1929 to a low in 1932 of 87½ cents.

By 1933 General Motors had acquired a large interest in this company. Secondary interests also important were Hayden, Stone, and Bancamerica-Blair, the latter represented by J. Cheever Cowdin. Richard Hoyt of Hayden, Stone had been connected with Wright Aeronautical since before the war, and continued in this and many other aviation companies until his death. But C. M. Keys, who gained control of Curtiss Aeroplane in the early 1920's for about $650,000, was out of this company by the end of the inflation. This left it in the General Motors–North American Aviation sphere.

III. United Aircraft and Transport Corporation
(National City-Deeds-Rentschler)

Insiders formed this holding company and gathered huge profits from their stock manipulations of a series of mergers. The prime movers of the group were the men made familiar in the war period: Edward A. Deeds, F. B. Rentschler, the Talbotts, George Mead, and Charles F. Kettering, some of whom had moved into the National City Bank. The first link was through the brother of F. B. Rentschler, Gordon S., who had been a director of National City Bank since 1923. Then Edward A. Deeds appeared on the National City board in 1927, where he still is a director. Rentschler was made president after the National City Company had made huge profits on the launching of this large aviation company.*

---

* Although Deeds and his son, and Rentschler, Mead, and their National City connections were the main factors in this merger, there were also links with other groups: William B. Mayo of Ford was a director, and there were officials of the Standard Oil Company of California. Charles F. Kettering continued to be an important connecting link between General Motors (Morgan-DuPont) and the Deeds group: he was vice-

In spite of pyramiding of companies in this holding group and the million-per-cent profits made by insiders on its securities, UA&T was one of the most successful operating companies. This was due mainly to its large share of government business, for Pratt and Whitney was one of the two engine companies manufacturing for the military services. The merger acquired also such pioneering companies as Sikorsky, Chance Vought, Hamilton, and Northrup. Frequently the experts were left in charge of their companies, which may be one factor accounting for this corporation's success.

In addition to these important manufacturing companies, the merger had a transcontinental line through Boeing (on the west coast) and NAT, which it acquired after a proxy fight. By 1933, this holding company, it was estimated, received one-third of all Army and Navy expenditures. UA&T also received about 45 per cent of all mail payments . . . .

Financially, this company was an outstanding example of the profits made in this period not through technical knowledge but by financial manipulations. As Senator Black said later in his questioning of Rentschler:

"Then it is your judgment that the other assets in the United Aircraft were on the same basis as the purchase by them of this stock from you, which had cost you $253 and which you sold to them in 1928 on a basis which, at the then price of the stock was worth $21,000,000?"[7]

IV. Aviation Corporation of Delaware
(Lehman-Harriman and others)

This fourth important company was political. It was formed on March 1, 1929—just three days before the change of administration in Washington. Harry S. New, former Postmaster General so friendly to aviation companies, became a director, and the following directors were contributors to the 1928 and/or 1932 Republican campaign funds: David K. E. Bruce (Andrew Mellon's son-in-law, who was also treasurer of the company); R. K. Mellon; Matthew C. Brush, and J. M. Franklin of the International Mercantile Marine. There were many other interests. In fact, the directorate, including E. P. Farley of American-Hawaiian

---

president and director of General Motors as well as a director of United Aircraft and Transport. But most important in the UA&T merger was the National City influence.
    [7] Black Hearings: U.S. Senate Special Committee on Investigation of Air Mail and Ocean Mail Contracts, Hearings, Seventy-third Congress, 1933 to 1934, p. 815.

Steamship Company, and Robert A. Dollar of the Dollar Steamship Company, numbered sixty-five men. The Harrimans, interested in aviation since its start, joined with Lehman Brothers as the controlling forces of this company.

At its peak in 1930 this holding company had about eight subsidiaries, including manufacture as well as transport. Its main transport company was described as an "incoherent" collection of 9,100 miles of routes. This company was described more fully in 1930 by its attorney, Mabel Walker Willebrandt of Prohibition fame, as a "holding company organized in an effort to *carry the losses* and promote financially a number of the lines that have air mail contracts. . . ." [Italics mine.][8] As a House committee found: "This description was not in complete accord with the statements used in the prospectus by which the company was sold to the public in 1929 as an aviation investment trust."[9]

A later Congressional committee described American Airways (Aviation Corporation's transport subsidiary), as " . . . a number of widely scattered local lines, which were later pieced together more or less into a jumbled, far-flung network of lines, by means of extensions granted by the Post Office Department."[10]

At the end of 1932 an outsider, E. L. Cord, got control of this important holding company. He had been trying since 1928 without success to get an air-mail contract for his Century Airlines, and in 1932 he made a spectacular offer to carry mail at half the rate then being paid to the mail carriers. Immediately thereafter Cord's Chicago line cut the pilots' pay by 40 per cent. Following this there was a pilots' strike on his line, and Cord's offer was forgotten in the excitement about his labor relations. Even before this offer Cord was known for his low wages. His Century Lines were paying substantially less than any other lines in the country.[11]

However, the strike was settled a few months later and no more was heard about a contract at half rate, for Cord was now bending all his effort to gain control of Aviation Corporation. In the fall of 1932 there was a hard-fought contest between Cord and the Harriman-Lehman

---

[8] U.S. House Committee on Post Office and Post Roads, Hearings, Seventy-first Congress, second session, 1930, p. 38.
[9] Paul T. David, *The Economics of Air Mail Transportation* (Washington, D. C.: Brookings Institution, 1934), p. 92.
[10] Crane Report: U.S. House of Representatives Committee on Post Offices and Post Roads, House Report 2087, Seventy-second Congress, second session, 1933, p. 3.
[11] U.S. House of Representatives Committee on Post Offices and Post Roads, Hearings, Seventy-second Congress, first session, 1932, pp. 42, 153.

interests, which included a proxy battle.* Soon after, Cord was in complete control of Aviation Corporation. Its heavily subsidized American Airways received 27 per cent of the total air mail pay in 1933 ... but carried only 10 per cent of the pound-miles of mail.

Besides the main groups described above, there were other companies, but almost all were linked in some way to these four. There was, in fact, a widespread interconnection, so complex that it is impossible here to trace all the links. Speaking only of the transport end, which was under the same control as the manufacturing companies, a Congressional report early in 1933 mentioned the harm that had been done aviation by interlocking interests:

> Interlocking financial interests have in the past prevented the full, free, and independent development of aviation. They have resulted in the waste of public funds and run counter and do violence to the very purposes for which the subsidy has been provided.
>
> Although the air transport industry is a very young one its intercorporate relationships have rapidly assumed a degree of complexity which would do credit [sic] to long established industries such as the utilities and the railroads.[12]

The means by which these main groups gained control of the industry by 1934 are significant of that period. The "Spoils Conference"† gave transportation to the three large groups so that they controlled 90 per cent or more of the air-mail payments .... In fact, the same

---

* The *New York Times* (November 20, 1932) reported: "The fight will rank as one of the most savagely contested struggles for control in financial history. In the short space of a week half a dozen banking firms, numerous brokerage houses, the American Federation of Labor, the air pilots' union and important political figures had been drawn into the quarrel."

† Editor's note: The "Spoils Conference" to which Freudenthal refers were meetings of leaders of the aviation industry, held in Washington, D. C. between May 15 and June 4, 1930, to divide up air-mail routes. The selected leaders were invited by Postmaster General Brown. The result was that the three largest carriers (United Aircraft, Aviation Corporation, and the North American–General Motors group) emerged with all but two of the twenty air-mail contracts.

The principal criticism of Postmaster General Brown's action was that he had not acted in the public interest when he did not advertise for bids on each route and award contracts on a basis of low bids. On the other hand, Brown contended that he had acted in the public interest, under the authority of the McNary-Watres Act, by inviting only the most experienced companies in aviation to negotiate because the most extensive aviation experience was essential to passenger safety. Brown wanted to establish a network of interconnecting airlines that carried passengers. By making passenger hauling a condition for the award of air-mail contracts he hoped to achieve this aim, and did.

[12] Crane Report, pp. 11, 20.

Congressional committee quoted above reported that 98 per cent of the air-mail system was controlled by holding companies. . . .

They Also Take Manufacturing—and the Profits

Although there was no "Spoils Conference" for the manufacturers, the large companies manufacturing for the Army and Navy did exceedingly well in those years from 1927 to 1933. Their profits soared and they had an enormous share of the available business. The small companies were doomed from their start: on one hand by the limited market for their products, and on the other by the domination of the large groups. Their fate was sealed by the fact that there was little, if any, competitive bidding on contracts.

The production capacity in 1929 was estimated at between 15,000 and 20,000 planes a year. The fact that with this large capacity only about 6,000 planes were actually turned out, shows the extent of the inflation. And the further fact that about half the number of planes produced were carried over unsold into 1930 shows the lack of demand. But in 1930 there still remained more than two hundred small companies, most of which built only one plane apiece before they went out of business. There had been very little commercial demand to justify this expansion of manufacturing capacity before 1929, and after the crash there was practically none. Again the government was the only reliable source of business. To carry out the Army and Navy five-year programs approved in 1926, appropriations totaled over $435,980,000 for the years from 1927 to 1934.

Not only was this a large sum, but it came from a cash customer—the United States government—which was the main support of a highly concentrated industry. The military demand, it was estimated, was confined to about ten companies, which received roughly 90 per cent of this business. Standard Statistics Company commented on this concentration as follows: *"In other words, the other 286 companies manufacturing planes have almost no participation in this stable* [i.e., government] *business."*[13] [Their italics.] Even in 1929, the top year, the commercial demand was controlled about 75 to 85 per cent by the large companies.

Manufacturing was even more closely concentrated than this indicated. For in military-engine manufacture there were still only *two*

---

[13] Standard Statistics Company, *Standard Trade and Securities* (New York: December, 1930).

companies. In airplanes there were only about ten companies participating —but this total included the affiliates of the same two engine companies. Official records, from which the following table was computed, were submitted to a Congressional committee by C. W. Browning, chief accountant of the Navy Department. These figures are not the total sales of all the companies, but they indicate their relative positions.

Two groups, according to these figures, accounted for 71 per cent of Navy business from 1927 to 1933, almost 80 per cent of sales to the Army, and about 94 per cent of the commercial sales. These two—United Aircraft and Transport and Curtiss-Wright—were amalgamations of the companies that had always dominated the industry. All the other companies in the field, even those having some connection by stock holdings and cross-directorships, had to divide among themselves 29 per cent of the Navy business, 20 per cent of the Army orders, and 6 per cent of the commercial business. The production and experimental contracts on Army and Navy orders are combined in [Table I, p. 86].

In the manufacture of planes it was easier to start with small capital and it required a less specialized setup than the manufacture of engines. And it was therefore possible, although it did not often happen, for a small plane manufacturer to get an order, or at least an experimental contract. But there was also some restriction of the field by the Manufacturers Aircraft Association, the patent association formed during the war. This had continued in force, and the government continued to pay the MAA $200 on each plane manufactured, plus a $25 additional charge.[14]

According to the Federal Aviation Commission's report in 1935, the MAA's agreement with the federal government expired in 1928, on December 31, and was then renewed with the Army and Navy, to run to 1933. The government agreed to pay the MAA up to $200 for each plane built in its plants, "and to secure the payment of like sums from nonmembers of the association constructing aircraft for the use of the War or Navy Departments."[15] These departments thus acted as collector for the MAA in this period, for the number of planes constructed in government plants was negligible or nonexistent, as we have noted.

The manufacture of military engines, however, was so completely dominated by Wright and P&W that virtually no other company was

[14] Delaney Hearings: U.S. House Naval Affairs Committee, Hearings before Subcommittee on Aeronautics, Seventy-third Congress, 1934, p. 477.
[15] U.S. Federal Aviation Commission "Report," January, 1935, p. 219.

TABLE 1 *Plane and Engine Sales, 1927–1933*

COMPANIES*	SALES TO NAVY	% OF SALES TO NAVY	SALES TO ARMY	% OF TOTAL ARMY SALES	COMMERCIAL SALES	% OF TOTAL COMMERCIAL SALES	TOTAL SALES	% OF TOTAL SALES
1. UA&T (Boeing, Chance Vought, Pratt & Whitney).	$33,212,890	48.4	$16,971,553	29.3	$28,056,208	48.0	$78,240,651	42.3
2. Curtiss-Wright (Curtiss, Wright, Keystone).	15,707,937	22.9	29,047,653	50.2	26,813,517	45.9	71,569,107	38.7
UNITED AND CURTISS TOTALS	48,920,827	71.3	46,019,206	79.5	54,869,725	93.9	149,809,758	81.0
3. Douglas	4,551,018	6.7	9,886,605	17.1	1,412,790	2.4	15,850,413	8.6
4. Glenn Martin	9,886,605	14.4	none	—	none	—	9,895,605	5.4
5. Great Lakes	2,418,307	3.5	33,686	.1	905,719	1.5	3,357,712	1.8
6. Consolidated Aircraft	2,347,622	3.4	1,960,010	3.3	1,118,231	1.9	5,425,863	2.9
7. Grumman	452,195	.7	none	—	153,492	.3	605,687	.3
TOTAL OF INDEPENDENTS	$19,664,747	28.7	$11,880,301	20.5	$3,590,232	6.1	$35,135,280	19.0
TOTAL OF ALL COMPANIES	$68,585,574	100.0	$57,899,507	100.0	$58,459,957	100.0	$184,945,038	100.0

* The groups include engine and plane companies controlled by the end of this period. Later in the hearings sales of three small companies were added to the Navy's sales (p. 1040), and have not been included in the above. Two of the three were merged in the large holding companies, so that their inclusion in this table would not affect the percentages of the large groups to the total. Source: Compiled from Delaney hearings, pp. 502–503.

given orders after 1926.[16] Rear Admiral Ernest J. King, chief of the Bureau of Aeronautics of the Navy, testified to the concentration of production: "Those are the only two companies in this country which produce engines of the size and power to meet the requirements of military aircraft."*[17] David S. Ingalls, Assistant Secretary of the Navy in charge of aeronautics from 1929 to 1932, described the situation even more plainly:

> The whole difficulty is in the engines, and this is a different kind of field, and there is a reason, because there has been a monopoly in the engine field, *and there is nothing we could do about it.* [Italics mine.][18]

These two companies not only monopolized the engine field but also arranged their products so that some of them would not be in the same classes. In the low-horsepower class only Wright Aeronautical had an engine; in the intermediate class there was only Pratt and Whitney; in the high-power class there were the "Hornet" (Pratt and Whitney) and the "Cyclone" (Wright). Of this last class, Admiral King said, "There you find that the power is about the same and the prices are about the same."[19]

In all ways the situation was so controlled as to favor the large groups. There was the moot question of competitive bidding on contracts. Because of complicated methods of negotiating contracts, the section providing for competitive bidding was frequently evaded and, it was alleged, practically all contracts in this period were let on a non-competitive basis.[20] Summarizing figures on file with the Comptroller General's office, Congressman McFarlane stated, in a minority report of the subcommittee on Aeronautics to the House Committee on Naval Affairs, that since the aircraft act of 1926:

"... the Army has purchased $57,346,098 of which $3,336,634 was by competitive bidding, or *92 per cent* of their contracts during this period *were let without competitive bids;* the Navy purchased

---

* Representative McFarlane stated in a minority report of the subcommittee on Aeronautics to the House Committee on Naval Affairs: "Of the 4,245 engines purchased by the Army since the Aircraft Act of 1926, *2,492 were purchased from Pratt & Whitney, and 1,153 from Wright, 587 from Wright subsidiaries, and only 13 from all other engine manufacturers together.* Since the Aircraft Act of 1926 the Navy obtained *2,149 engines from Pratt & Whitney, 971 from Wright, 2 from Wright subsidiaries and 36 from all others*" (Delaney report, p. 1477; italics mine).

[16] Delaney Hearings, p. 1048.
[17] *Ibid.*, p. 442.
[18] *Ibid.*, p. 950.
[19] *Ibid.*, p. 1046.
[20] *Ibid.*, pp. 772, 780.

$53,026,614 of which $5,901,051 was purchased through competitive bids, or *91.3 per cent of the Navy's aircraft equipment was purchased without competitive bids."* [Italics mine.][21]

It is difficult to determine, therefore, which came first in this particular circle: whether the existence of only two engine companies caused the government to restrict its contracts to them; whether other qualified companies could not get the orders; or whether no other companies existed in this field, knowing it was hopeless before they tried.

Favored manufacturing companies made huge profits in this period. As in most bookkeeping practices, the actual amounts were subject to much discussion. From all reports, however, Pratt and Whitney led the other companies in profits, and even on its own figures it made 33.6 per cent on the Navy in 1929, and in the same year 40.5 per cent on the Army. In considering these percentages, submitted by the company itself, it must be remembered that they were computed after deducting bonuses. From 1927 to 1931 this company paid $1,350,000 in bonuses alone (which means that this does not include salaries and directors' fees). Because of these large amounts, naturally Donald L. Brown of P&W contended that profits should be computed after deducting bonuses and federal taxes.[22]

According to Army audits—which, the Army claimed, were more thorough than the Navy's—Pratt and Whitney's profits on Army orders were 32.7 per cent. However, the Navy audit (figured on cost) showed that Pratt and Whitney's profits on completed business from 1927 to 1933 were 23 per cent on Army orders, 71 per cent on commercial orders, 36 per cent on Navy orders, and a general average of 43 per cent on all orders.[23] The commercial profits (as shown in the following table) were so high because they included all Army contracts in 1929 and Army spare parts contracts in 1930.

Experimental work, given frequently to the smaller companies, brought average profits down. Thus, on Navy business the plane manufacturers averaged 2.8 per cent profits for this entire period compared with an average of 23.5 per cent profit for the two engine companies. Although Boeing's profits reached almost to the level of Pratt and Whitney's—65 per cent in 1930 on Navy work—its average profit

---

[21] Delaney Report: Report of Subcommittee on Aeronautics, Seventy-third Congress, second session, 1934, p. 1488.
[22] Delaney Hearings, pp. 887, 904, 905.
[23] *Ibid.,* p. 503; *New York Times,* February 10, 1934.

was lowered by experimental losses. Grumman was practically the only company to profit on experimental work, showing 70 per cent in 1933. No single company, and certainly no airplane manufacturer, showed the profits on the government orders that P&W did in this period on the sale of engines.

TABLE II *Per Cent of Profits on Costs of Engines and Spare Parts Completed 1927–1933 by Pratt and Whitney Aircraft Company*

YEAR	% ON NAVY ORDERS	% ON ARMY ORDERS	% ON COMMERCIAL ORDERS
1927	40	73	72
1928	40	48	50(*)
1929		—(*)	100(*)
1930—9 months	50	25	33
1931—6 months	31	23	42
1932—5 months	20	25	55
1933—4 months	7	7	43
AVERAGE PROFITS	36	23	71

* The Delaney hearings, p. 496, from which this table is taken, explains the commercial figures for 1928 and 1929 as follows: "Includes Army contracts 1929 and spares 1930—not separate on available records. Figures based on total sales for 1929 and 1930."

Consolidated Aircraft made an average profit of 12.4 per cent on Navy orders in this period, and 11.3 per cent on Army business—far below P&W profits, for example. Nevertheless, because the Army considered the company's profits in two years excessive, Consolidated gave back to the United States Army fifty planes at a dollar apiece. Consolidated's president testified that another reason for returning the planes was that "... unfortunately, we had negotiated our contracts with the Army."[24]

Other averages indicate the large profits made on the government in these years. Boeing, plane manufacturer of UA&T, made 21 per cent on the Navy and 25 per cent on the Army. Douglas Aircraft made 21 per cent on the Navy and 18 per cent on the Army. These were higher than the average for plane companies, but still far below P&W's. Wright Aeronautical, the other engine-manufacturing company, showed a lower average profit than P&W's—5 per cent on the Navy and 10.5 per cent

[24] Delaney Hearings, p. 706.

on the Army. They had been higher before P&W broke into this company's monopoly of engine manufacture.[25]

In transportation also the same groups profited from the government's expenditures. And from the point of view of these large companies, the "Spoils Conference" justified the efforts of Brown, Glover, MacCracken and others. By the end of 1933 these four large groups controlled air-mail routes through which they gathered in over 90 per cent of the air-mail payments .... Indeed, the government was supporting the transport companies. Their revenues from passenger and freight ... were a minor proportion of the sum handed over by the Post Office. Even by 1933 passenger and freight accounted for only about 25 per cent of the companies' revenues; 75 per cent came from the Post Office.

Nevertheless, the companies frequently showed losses—due to the setup of holding companies. The profits made on the government were therefore not generally taxed; nor were they distributed to the theoretical owners of the companies—the stockholders—for very few dividends were disbursed. The expenditures went directly to the officers and directors of the companies in the shape of salaries, bonuses, and directors' fees. Besides collecting from the government, they had made enormous profits on the many involved stock transactions that they engineered; and had conserved at least part of these profits by selling out before the crash.

Sixty per cent of the sales of P&W in one year went to its officers and directors. United Aircraft and Transport, parent company of P&W paid its officers in the four years from 1929 to 1932 compensation totaling $3,554,130. This meant that Charles W. Deeds got his portion, for at the ripe age of 26, without any technical training whatsoever, he was secretary, treasurer, and director of UA&T. His bonuses alone from P&W totaled $151,176 from 1927 through 1931. In addition to these salaries, bonuses, and directors' fees, it must be remembered that Deeds's $40 investment in 1926 in P&W stock was worth over $5,000,000 by 1929. Another member of this group—F. B. Rentschler—gathered in from UA&T and P&W the sum of $1,241,000, from 1927 to 1933; in one year, 1929, payments were over $400,000. This did not include other profits like the 79-for-1 stock dividend of P&W.[26]

[25] *Ibid.*, pp. 800, 1040; *New York Times*, February 10, 1934.
[26] Delaney Hearings, pp. 508–509, 903; Black Hearings, pp. 1708, 1803–1804; *Congressional Record*, April 9, 1934, pp. 6282–6283.

The significance of the government's subsidies was brought out by Senator Black. After noting that United Air Lines (transport subsidiary of UA&T) had received $40,000,000 from the government from 1926 to the date of this investigation, Senator Black asked F. B. Rentschler:

If it [United Air Lines] had not got the $40,000,000, is it your judgment that the bonuses and salaries amounting to over $400,000 to one man could have been paid?

MR. RENTSCHLER: Possibly not.

THE CHAIRMAN: Is it also not true that if it had not been for the subsidies, the stock could not have gone up from a value of $253 to a value of $35,000,000?

MR. RENTSCHLER: Possibly not.

THE CHAIRMAN: As a matter of fact, it would not, would it, Mr. Rentschler?

MR. RENTSCHLER: I say possibly not.

THE CHAIRMAN: That is your best judgment, is it not?

MR. RENTSCHLER: I think you are right.[27]

The Government Pays for All

These individual and company profits were made directly at the expense of the government, for without subsidies the holding companies could not have existed. When the transport subsidiaries of the groups that had been awarded government contracts needed equipment to carry the mails, they bought from the manufacturing subsidiaries, and again the government paid. The important point is that the Army and the Navy, and the Post Office Department, were all paying the same companies, although dealing with different subsidiaries of these large groups.

The fact that P&W's profits rose to 70 per cent in one year indicates not only excessive profits but the monopolistic position of the engine companies. Faced with these profits at a committee hearing, Rear Admiral King of the Navy built up an ingenious argument for permitting them: if the Navy cut P&W's profit, then Wright (which he claimed made only 5 per cent profit) would be forced out of business. From this it followed that the Navy would then be at the mercy of a monopoly, instead of having two competing companies on which it could rely. Representative

[27] Black Hearings, p. 1827.

McFarlane, taking this reasoning at its face value, inquired: "But if we have to subsidize one of them to keep two in the field, we are paying a rather dear price, are we not, Admiral?" Several weeks later Rear Admiral King tried to explain his statement about P&W's profits by saying, "What I meant was this: If the Navy had forced P&W's price to a *very low level* so that its profits were, say, of the order of *15 per cent*, then Wright, to stay in business, would have had to reduce its prices *correspondingly;* . . ."[28] [Italics mine.]

A more plausible explanation was given by David S. Ingalls, Assistant Secretary of the Navy in charge of aeronautics from 1929 to 1932. Noting that profits on planes were lower than on engines, he attributed this to the existence of the Naval Aircraft Factory. Although this had become not much more than a repair station, nevertheless it could, if necessary, build planes immediately. It was therefore a potential threat to the plane manufacturers. It could not, however, threaten the two engine companies. And, in fact, when the Navy in 1938 manufactured entire planes, it had to buy design rights for engines from one of the two engine companies.

On the other hand, in 1926 and 1927, the manufacturing companies were almost completely dependent on government orders. But as the general commercial demand began to develop, that took up part of the production, and in the exceptional year of 1929 commercial sales of P&W were 53 per cent of all sales. That was only a flash in the pan, however, and the fadeout began immediately in 1930. By 1931 and 1932 government orders again accounted for at least two-thirds of the manufacturers' business.

The significance of this dependence is brought out by Douglas Aircraft. Noting that until 1933 approximately 90 per cent of this company's income came from the government, the magazine *Fortune* remarked that as a result Donald Douglas and his staff had " . . . an aeronautical education for which the U.S. had put up some $19,000,000 cash."[29]

For the period 1927 to 1933 the proportion of government business (Army plus Navy contracts) to total sales of the companies was always over 50 per cent. It must be remembered that these are minimum figures in the preceding table, for the transport companies bought planes and

---

[28] Delaney Hearings, pp. 478–479, 1039.
[29] *Fortune*, May, 1935, p. 178.

TABLE III *Per Cent of Sales to Government (Navy and Army) to Companies' Total Sales, 1927 to 1933*

COMPANY	% GOVERNMENT SALES TO COMPANIES' TOTAL SALES
Boeing Airplane Co.	59
Chance Vought Corp.	75
Consolidated Aircraft Co.	79
Curtiss Aeroplane and Motor Co.	76
Douglas Aircraft Co.	91
Glenn Martin Co.	100
Great Lakes Aircraft Co.	73
Grumman Aircraft Engineering Corp.	75
Keystone Aircraft Corp.	77
Pratt & Whitney Aircraft Co.	64
Wright Aeronautical Co.	58

Source: Compiled from Delaney hearings, pp. 502–503.

engines to carry the mails, and so a certain portion of the air-mail subsidy went to the manufacturers . . . .

II. *Clearing the Air (1934 to . . .)*

Cancellation—Climax of a Long-Approaching Storm

On February 9, 1934, Postmaster General James A. Farley telegraphed domestic-air-mail carriers that their contracts would be canceled in ten days. The Army Air Corps was to take over the flying of the United States air mail.

It was no sudden caprice that caused the cancellations, but an accumulation of evidence, some of it gathered in the previous administration. As early as 1932 there had been agitation for the cancellation of the contracts awarded in 1930. A Congressional committee began hearings in March, 1932, on a bill directing the Postmaster General to revoke all contracts, route certificates, and so forth, which had been awarded by him without public advertisement. That this was not carried into law, as *Fortune* remarked, was because:

. . . a Republican Congress made barren soil for any inquiry into the actions of the party's No. 1 Politico, always the Posmaster General.[30]

In the next year, in February, 1933, the so-called Crane Committee of the House of Representatives reported that interlocking interests and

[30] *Ibid.,* May, 1934, pp. 154–455.

directorates had definitely prevented the free development of aviation and had resulted in the waste of public funds. This report, commenting on the failure of the existing legislation (the Watres Act) to function properly, recommended that the rate-making powers of the Postmaster General be curbed. This foreshadowed the Air Mail Act of 1934, as well as another recommendation: that operating and manufacturing companies be separated.*

In the next session of Congress the Crane report's recommendations were reinforced by the testimony before the Senate Special Committee on Investigation of Air Mail and Ocean Mail Contracts under the courageous chairmanship of Senator Hugo Black. This committee brought out the details of the "Spoils Conference" in 1930 and other acts of Postmasters General New and Brown, as well as the huge grants of government money to favored companies.

At the same time Representative William D. McFarlane, a fighting minority of one of the Subcommittee on Aeronautics of the House, focused attention on the aviation situation from another angle: the profits made by the manufacturing companies on government orders. The profits revealed by this committee were so large that the House Military Affairs Committee instituted an inquiry into the profits on Army orders, supplementing the work of the Naval Affairs Subcommittee.

McFarlane's efforts brought out two aspects of the situation: that the manufacturers monopolizing Army and Navy business were subsidiaries of the same large groups that monopolized air-mail contracts; and that the large profits made by these subsidiaries were not directly subject to taxation, since their parent companies filed consolidated income-tax returns. He estimated that the government had lost more than $2,000,000 on the consolidated returns of five companies.[31]

From all sides the situation was being uncovered. Aircraft companies were included in the munitions companies whose activities in the export field were thoroughly investigated by Senator Nye's

---

* The Crane report (page 4) said: "The air mail administrative machinery under the Watres Act has failed to perform its function of carrying out the provisions of air mail legislation in an efficient and businesslike manner." Page 15: "Whatever justification there may be for a large subsidy as a means of establishing the new aviation industry it is time now to look forward to the cessation of such payments and the establishment of the air mail service on a self-sustaining basis." Page 20: "Interlocking financial interests have in the past prevented the full, free, and independent development of aviation. *They have resulted in the waste of public funds* and run counter and do violence to the very purposes for which the subsidy has been provided." [Italics mine.]

[31] *Congressional Record*, April 9, 1934, p. 6282.

committee. Huge profits on aviation stocks by underwriters and insiders, revealed by the Senate Committee on Stock Exchange Practices, added more fuel to the fire of public indignation.

These events and arguments were front-page news spread over the country. The revelations of the "Spoils Conference," of the profits on aviation stocks by insiders, of huge profits on Army and Navy orders—all had brought the same companies, managed by the same men, into the headlines. This conjunction of scandals and inquiries aroused an already disgruntled public, aware of its assigned role of footing the bills. It might envy the man who ran a $40 "flier" in a stock into a $5,000,000 profit. But when one investigation after another strengthened the impression that this profit came out of the pockets of small investors and taxpayers, then anger replaced envy. So the aviation scandals were one element undermining respect for financial institutions and trust in Wall Street.

If the existing economic setup were to continue, an attempt had to be made to restore the general confidence in financial institutions and in the men controlling publicly owned companies. A strenuous effort was necessary to clean up what had begun to seem like the Augean stable of the aviation industry. The most direct way to start was to cancel air-mail contracts which had all been fixed by the 1930 conference.[32] Although the carriers declared vehemently that the Army was not able or equipped to carry the mail, the revoking of their contracts was ordered.

The cancellations brought to a climax this long series of events and focused attention on the air-mail situation. But before the public could digest all the events that led to this action, the newspapers were headlining the inadequacy of the Army to fly the mail. One Army pilot after another, so it seemed, crashed to death. Although ten Army fliers died, only four of this number were killed while actually carrying the mail, and six were training or proceeding to the mail route. Furthermore, the weather conditions over the whole country were particularly bad, as President Roosevelt pointed out:

> I appreciate also that almost every part of the country has been visited during this period by fog, snow, and storms, and that serious accidents, taking even more lives, have occurred at the same time in passenger and commercial aviation.[33]

But the Army accidents were played up so prominently that they

[32] Black Hearings, p. 2389.
[33] Delaney Hearings, p. 1523.

diverted the attention of the country from the main issues,* and President Roosevelt was forced to order the Army to curtail its flights. To some this proved the superiority of the commercial lines and was an acknowledgment by the President of a too hasty act in canceling their contracts. But to a minority it pointed to the fact that there was something not quite adequate in the training of the Army Air Corps. For experts agreed that the Army was not trained to fly across the country or in bad weather. Like all prophets in their own countries, General William Mitchell was to see his criticisms justified a little late.

In considering the cancellations in 1934, the following legal opinion given by Attorney General Cummings is significant:

"There can be no reasonable doubt that the arrangements, understandings and agreements out of which the route certificates subsequently grew [before 1934, and following the "Spoils Conference"] were highly irregular and interfered with the freedom of competition contemplated by the statutes.

"These circumstances and irregularities were such as to impel you to cancel the route certificates . . . .

"While the course you pursued in this respect was amply warranted, it is our opinion that the irregularities referred to are not such as to justify or require criminal prosecution. Such irregularities would, however, be pertinent and vital factors in the event of further litigation."[34]

The Army continued to fly the mail for several months on a restricted basis. Meanwhile the domestic companies were preparing themselves for the spring house cleaning of 1934. For the formulation of laws proceeded with unusual speed. Unlike many previous investigations, this series did result in Congressional action.

Did the Leopards Change Their Spots?
When the air-mail scandal burst, there was no thought of having the government carry the mails permanently. Even though liberal weeklies like the *New Republic* suggested it, the emphasis was on

---

* Immediately upon the cancellation of contracts, Lindbergh wired President Roosevelt protesting this action. Shortly after, Secretary of War Dern appointed Lindbergh, Clarence Chamberlain, and Orville Wright to serve on a committee to study Army operation of the air mail. But Lindbergh and Wright declined this appointment, Wright on the grounds of ill-health.

[34] *New York Times,* June 5, 1938.

cleansing the existing setup of the companies, on separating the wicked from the good, so that they could once again be entrusted with the service. Looking forward to when this would occur, a financial newsletter of that time talked about the "temporarily interrupted progress" of the aviation industry, clearly implying that the same companies would regain control.

While the Army was carrying the mail from February to June, 1934, the companies used the interlude to reorganize in order to be eligible to bid on the new temporary certificates. Obviously the nuclei of the old companies would continue and, if their compliance was legally sufficient, would get the awards. The reason for this was pointed out at the time by Paul T. David, of Brookings Institution: "The bald fact is that an airline cannot be operated without money, and the only substantial amount of money available for airline operation is in the hands of the former mail carriers, . . ."[35]

But there was a very important difference in the requirements for the new companies. After this period of upheaval the aviation industry was separated into two parts—an acknowledgment of a difference that had existed almost since its birth. Hereafter transport and manufacturing were recognized to be—indeed, they had to be—two separate industries. This had, in fact, been the practice under the National Industrial Recovery Act of 1933. There were separate codes for air-transport companies and for commercial aviation (that is, nonscheduled, miscellaneous flying, airports, etc.). The manufacturers were to operate under another code, but this had not yet been passed by the time the NRA ceased, although, as the *Aircraft Yearbook* reported, " . . . the manufacturers have drafted more codes than there are companies in the industry."[36]

To prevent companies and individuals that had participated in the "Spoils Conference" from re-entering the field, strict qualifications were made for the new bidders on contracts. Then the Watres Act of 1930 was repealed and the Air Mail Act of 1934 (48 Statutes at Large, 933), under which the transport companies were legally divorced from the manufacturers, was passed in June. In an effort to break the monopoly of the large groups, the act forbade interlocking directorates, overlapping

[35] David, p. 207.
[36] Aeronautical Chamber of Commerce, *Aircraft Yearbook* (New York: D. Van Nostrand Co., 1935), pp. 16–17.

interests, certain consolidations or mergers, and mutual stockholdings. The amendment to this act in 1935 continued these provisions, and they have again been affirmed in the Civil Aeronautics Act of 1938.*

After the cancellation, companies reorganized, and "black-listed" officers resigned. In many instances names were gravely changed from "Ways" to "Lines." United's transport division became United Air Lines; American Airways of Aviation Corporation became American Airlines. Eastern Air Transport and Transcontinental and Western Air of the North American–General Motors group had a good many changes involving "Inc.," "Transport," and "Lines," and they finally became Eastern Air Lines, Western Air Express, and Transcontinental and Western Air, Inc.

Besides making these name changes, the three large groups complied with the law in the diverse ways discussed below, but all of them showed a certain amount of continuity in their control and/or management. In following these complicated reorganizations and reshufflings, it must be remembered that the central point of all the laws was the effort to break the stranglehold of the main groups while retaining the service built up through years of experience. This fast-growing industry, which had been nursed through its infancy at such large expense, had now to be controlled to serve the larger purpose of the national good....

III. *Manufacture Shifts to a New Role (1934 to ...)*

Aeronautical manufacturers found themselves in 1934 in the unwelcome limelight of public scrutiny. Various Congressional committees were covering, and uncovering, their activities in selling munitions abroad and in profiting at the expense of this government. They played a spotlight on the inside workings of a few large holding companies which had the government at their mercy; they revealed to taxpayers the excessive profits on government orders; and they showed clearly the evasion of income taxes by the filing of consolidated returns. By the end of 1934 the public was well aware of the general practices in this industry, and steps had to be taken in aircraft manufacturing as well as in

---

* But the 1934 and 1935 legislation had one defect, as the Interstate Commerce Commission noted:
"No specific provision is made for policing these prohibitions, nor does the act vest authority in us to pass upon the legality of consolidations, mergers, or acquisitions of control which may have been effected or may be proposed, such as ... we are authorized to exercise in respect of rail and motor carriers." (Interstate Commerce Commission, "Annual Report," Nov. 1, 1937, p. 38).

transport, to restore public confidence. Legislative controls were being formulated, and more were in prospect.

By the end of 1938, aviation companies were again in the limelight. But now they had taken on a heroic cast, for they had become the nation's most spectacular means of defense, to be pampered and cultivated.

This shift in role is a reflection of the heightened world tension from 1934 to 1939, and this country's recent decision that it, too, must arm. As current hostilities spread to involve more countries throughout the world, attention focuses increasingly on aircraft. The romance of conquering the air has changed to the terror of merciless bombing from the sky.

The change in sentiment from 1934 neutrality to 1939 defense-at-all-costs has been of indubitable benefit to the aviation manufacturers. Their sales bounded from $44,000,000 in 1934 to about $150,000,000 in the first ten months of 1939, and by January 1, 1940, piled up to more than $600,000,000.

Whether the country has benefited equally from the change in these years must also be considered, since aviation is now hailed as a vital link in the nation's defense. The industry's activities—manufacturing and exports—must therefore be evaluated against the background of the nation's good as well as against the industry's profits.

Under the Shadow of Censure

Aeronautical manufacturing continued to depend on the government after 1934. When government business lagged, aircraft production slumped; when government buying increased, the industry rode through depressions in which other industries sagged. The *New York Times* said, "Almost since the inception of flying, military orders have been the backbone of the industry."[37] But the government has furnished the flesh and muscles as well.

When the Army and Navy five-year programs of 1927 were being completed in 1932 and 1933, production sagged, and the confusion in the industry was attributed to the lack of a government program. There was no new buying program until the middle of 1934. Then a committee headed by Newton D. Baker came to the rescue of the manufacturers. Admitting that the commercial demand was insufficient to maintain the industry, the Baker Board recommended an increase in the strength of

---

[37] *New York Times,* June 5, 1938.

the Army Air Corps to 2,320 airplanes by 1940. The Vinson Act (48 Statutes at Large, 503), passed in the same year, authorized the Navy to buy 1,200 planes during the next five years.

These figures seem small compared with the 6,000 planes to which the Army's strength will soon be increased, but at that time they called for a sharp rise in military purchases over the preceding years. The result was that by 1936 about two-thirds of the industry's business was accounted for by the military services. Due to these orders the industry had a 50-per-cent increase in the first half of 1938—a startling contrast with the automobile industry, for example, whose new passenger-car sales dropped 50 per cent in the same period. An increasing proportion was due to the government: in the first quarter of 1938 military plane and engine deliveries were up 114.4 per cent and 39 per cent over the first quarter of 1937, whereas commercial deliveries had increased only 5 per cent and 2.2 per cent respectively.

This dependence of the aviation industry on the government is the keynote of its history.* As the Federal Aviation Commission reported in 1935: *"It has always to be remembered that this industry is peculiar in that it has essentially but a single customer."* [Italics mine.][38]

Congress, aware of this dependence of the industry on the government, passed several laws which were designed to diminish, or at least to control, the profits of the companies on government orders. In order to provide a yardstick with which to measure costs (as well as to diminish the government's reliance on private companies), the Vinson Act of 1934 required the Navy to build at least 10 per cent of its aircraft and engines in its own plants. Although this applied only to the Navy, and the President was allowed discretionary powers and modifications of this rule, the *Aircraft Yearbook* recognized this threat to private industry and reported: "Among the disturbing factors in American aviation is an increased tendency in some official circles to consider seriously government manufacture of aircraft and engines...."[39]

---

* Consolidated Aircraft, in the 15 years from 1924 through 1938, sold about 81 per cent of its total of $51,427,721 to the government. As late as 1937 the Navy alone accounted for 80 per cent of its sales in that year. Glenn L. Martin's unfilled orders on September 30, 1938, were 70 per cent for the government. All the business on the books of Bell Aircraft at the end of 1938 was for the Army and Navy, totaling about $3,675,000. The Army Air Corps is Douglas Aircraft's best customer by a large margin. Even though its planes have become almost standard equipment on the commercial lines, from 1935 to 1938 about 72 per cent of its sales were to the government.

[38] U.S. Federal Aviation Commission "Report," January, 1935, p. 160.

[39] Aeronautical Chamber of Commerce, *Aircraft Yearbook* (New York: D. Van Nostrand Co., 1936), pp. 19–20.

This tendency apparently has not increased, for the Naval Aircraft Factory (NAF) in Philadelphia, established after the World War, continues to be the only factory owned by the government. But the Vinson Act has expanded the operations of the NAF, and in 1937 it produced 117 trainers. In 1938 it made a further step forward—for the first time it turned out complete planes, including the engines. Further, at least 20 trainers of an order for 185 training planes were entirely manufactured at the Naval Aircraft Factory. This was not a record of complete independence, for the rights to build the engines were bought from the Wright Aeronautical Company of Curtiss-Wright.[40] An act* passed in April, 1939, however, was designed to develop the facilities of NAF by authorizing funds for continued construction of an engine factory there.

There is no record that the Army has ever manufactured its own planes, although it does carry on extensive experimental work at Wright Field. The Baker Board report in 1934 was partly responsible for the lack of an Army plant. Headed by Newton D. Baker, the board reflected the man who, as Secretary of War, had supported Edward A. Deeds's administration of the Army Air Corps. Baker's board reported that the government should not, by manufacturing its own aircraft, compete with this excellently organized industry.

Shortly after the excessive profits on government orders were disclosed, the Vinson-Trammell Act established a 10-per-cent profits limit on Navy orders. There was no limitation on Army-order profits until 1939. Although it was frequently asserted that there was an implied, unofficial limit of 15 per cent on Army orders, Consolidated Aircraft, for example, made a profit of 34.2 per cent in 1935 on its Army contracts.

There was, of course, opposition to the profits limitation on Navy orders—opposition which gathered momentum through the years. A subcommittee of the House Naval Affairs Committee recommended in January, 1938, that naval aircraft be exempted from the 10-per-cent limit on the ground "that airplanes be considered in the category of scientific instruments . . . ."[41] (This was in line with the practice of the Navy Department in exempting aircraft instruments from the 10-per-cent limit on the basis that they were scientific instruments.) Opposition to

---

* U.S. Statutes, Public 18, sec. 14, April, 1939.
[40] *New York Times*, May 8, 1938.
[41] *Wall Street Journal*, January 17, 1938.

other controlling laws also increased as the industry's strength waxed with its elevation to an important part of the nation's defense . . . .

. . . .

And though the Vinson-Trammell Act limited profits on orders for the Navy to 10 per cent, Congress took five years to pass a similar law for the Army. For it was not until April, 1939, that profits on Army orders were limited to 12 per cent. The Navy's limit was raised to the same amount by this same law. Because of one provision in this law, however, it is expected not to affect the company's profits adversely. For the companies are now permitted to *average* their profits and losses over five-year periods, whereas under the Vinson-Trammell Act the Navy had to consider only annual reports. Since the Army's policy, it is reported, has been to average earnings over a period of years anyway, the law merely improves the outlook for profits on Navy orders. In fact, according to an explanation given by Senator Warren R. Austin (Republican, Vermont), the new averaging provision will benefit the manufacturers considerably:

. . . if a manufacturer earns 15% on the first year's contracts, he must return 3% to the Treasury, but in the event he earns only 9% in the succeeding year, he may either obtain a refund from the Treasury or apply the 3% in computing costs on contracts for the ensuing year.[42]

The limiting of profits on the Navy's orders does not seem to have seriously affected profits in the past. In 1937, for example, earnings of the leading manufacturers were up 75 per cent over 1936. Even through the recession, aviation profits increased: In June, 1938, they were 60 per cent greater than the year before, compared with a drop of about 70 per cent in general industrial earnings. Profits ratios have increased largely in this period: United Aircraft's net to sales went from 3.7 per cent in 1935 to 14.7 per cent in 1938; in the second quarter of 1939 it rose still further, to 19.2 per cent. North American's ratio increased from 18.9 per cent in 1938 to 22 per cent in the first quarter of 1939. Typical of the companies' growth was the increase in North American Aviation's net profit in the first quarter of 1939 to almost four times its sales in the year 1935. As a whole, the industry reported a profit margin of 17.3 per cent for the first half of 1939 . . . .

[42] *Ibid.,* March 15, 1939.

IV. *Political Nationalism and International Profits*
When War Is Called Peace, Exports Rise

In 1934 this country was aghast at the rising tide of nationalism and rearming apparent in Europe. It was convinced of its ability to disassociate itself from what were still called "foreign entanglements." Accordingly, it was shocked at the participation of the aviation companies, along with other munitions companies, in the international arms trade.

The Nye Committee investigation in 1934 left no doubt that the export of aeronautical products was chiefly for war. As the final word on the impossibility of distinguishing between civil and military aircraft, which can no longer be considered debatable, the National Munitions Control Board in 1936 described the interchangeability of all types of aircraft.* This had been acknowledged as early as 1925 when the "Convention for the Supervision of the International Trade in Arms and Ammunition and in Implements of War" at Geneva included aircraft of all types. But the United States did not ratify this convention until ten years later.

However, the year before, on May 28, 1934, this country took a most important step in the control of munitions exports when Congress passed a "Joint resolution to prohibit the sale of arms or munitions of war in the United States under certain conditions." Section I made unlawful the sale of these products to Bolivia or Paraguay, then engaged in the Chaco war.[43]

---

* Its report was prophetic of what was to happen in Europe three years later: "Indeed, it is administratively impracticable to introduce a distinction between civil and military aircraft into the supervision of the international traffic in arms. If an export license is to be required for the exportation of military aircraft, then there must be a similar requirement for civil aircraft. Otherwise each aircraft to be exported would have to be inspected by an expert of the Department of Commerce or by a military expert to determine into which classification it fell. . . . Even inspection by an expert would in many cases be ineffective and inconclusive. . . .

"The fact is that the most harmless civil airplane can carry a few bombs aloft and drop them on an enemy town. A commercial plane used for such purpose might be woefully inefficient from a modern military point of view, but, in areas where strictly military aircraft are scarce, they may be used, and often have been used, for military purposes.

"All in all, it is perfectly clear that an aircraft of any type can be and frequently is, modified for use in actual combat.

"If it is difficult to determine in advance the use to which a completed aircraft will be put, *it is impossible to do so in the case of an aircraft part or an aircraft engine.*" (National Munitions Control Board, "First Annual Report," November 30, 1936, pp. 37–38; italics mine.)

[43] U.S. Proclamations: President Roosevelt 2087, 1933–1936.

Still no specific mention was made of aircraft. But when Curtiss-Wright Export shipped four planes to Peru, this government maintained that the planes were actually meant for Bolivia. Suit was instituted against three Curtiss-Wright companies and certain officers for infraction of the act of May, 1934. Although this suit was not settled until February, 1940, it had an important effect by its example at that time. In 1940 two officers and the three Curtiss-Wright units involved pleaded guilty of violating the neutrality embargo of May 28, 1934. John S. Allard, who was president of Curtiss-Wright Export, and Clarence W. Webster, South American representative, were fined $11,000 each, and the companies were fined $260,000. After the inauguration of this suit in 1935, other laws were passed to lessen the chances of such infractions.

The famous Neutrality Act (Joint Resolution 67, passed by Congress on August 31, 1935) was one expression of this country's desire to remain aloof from the martial fervor of the rest of the world. Under this act the President was to declare specifically those articles of indisputable military use in a list of implements of war. President Roosevelt, accordingly, proclaimed that every type of airplane and airship and their engines, assembled or unassembled, and some parts, were munitions of war. For the first time a President defined munitions, and this government finally placed on record its realization of the fact that all aircraft are of military importance.*

In spite of the weaknesses in this much-discussed Neutrality Act, the inclusion of aircraft in such a list of war implements was an important acknowledgment by this government. When the law broke down in its application to the "civil war" in Spain, where the Republican

---

* The proclamation was worded as follows (U.S.: President: Proclamations (Roosevelt) 2138, September 25, 1935. Italics mine):
"Category III—(I) Aircraft, assembled or dismantled, both heavier and lighter than air, which are designed, adapted, and intended for aerial combat by the use of machine guns or of artillery or for the carrying and dropping of bombs or which are equipped with, or which by reason of design or construction are prepared for, any of the appliances referred to in paragraph (2) below:
(2) Aerial gun mounts and frames, bomb racks, torpedo carriers, and bomb or torpedo release mechanisms.
"Category V—(I) Aircraft assembled or dismantled, both heavier and lighter than air, other than those included in category III:
(2) Propellers or air screws, fuselages, hulls, tail units, and under carriage units;
(3) Aircraft engines."
On February 2, 1936, this resolution was amplified so that Category V (3) above read: "(3) Aircraft engines, assembled or unassembled." (U.S. President: Proclamations (Roosevelt) 2159).

government was unable to buy arms here, and to the Sino-Japanese conflict where no war has yet been declared, a desire to amend the law to accord with the realities of the situations increased.

War in 1934 still meant the declaration of a state of hostilities; the 1938 version was merely the bombing of civilian populations with no declaration except possibly the love of peace. The several undeclared wars in this period demanded large quantities of military aircraft as well as of other munitions. As the international situation deteriorated, American aircraft exports flourished.

Except in the year 1935, aircraft exports surged upward. The decline in that year was due in part to the Nye Committee hearings (which started in 1934 and continued into 1936), the Neutrality Law, and also because exports in 1934 had been extraordinarily large. Exports rebounded immediately, and by 1938 they accounted for 46 per cent of the total production of the aircraft industry (see Table IV). Even when

TABLE IV *Total Production and Exports of Aviation Industry, 1925–1939*

YEAR ENDING DECEMBER 31	AIRCRAFT PRODUCTION	AIRCRAFT EXPORTS	% OF EXPORTS TO PRODUCTION
1925	$12,775,181	$ 783,659	6.1
1926	17,694,905	1,127,210	5.8
1927	30,896,638	1,903,560	6.2
1928	64,662,491	3,664,723	5.7
1929	91,051,044	9,125,345	10.0
1930	60,846,177	8,818,010	14.5
1931	48,539,715	4,867,687	10.0
1932	34,861,185	7,946,533	22.8
1933	33,357,122	9,180,328	27.5
1934	43,891,925	17,662,938	40.2
1935	42,506,204	14,330,843	33.7
1936	78,148,893	23,143,203	29.6
1937	115,076,950	39,404,469	34.2
1938	150,000,000 (estimated)	68,209,050	45.5 (estimated)
1939	225,000,000 (preliminary estimate)	117,081,212	52.0 (estimated)

Source: Aircraft Production: U.S. Bureau of Air Commerce (Department of Commerce), Bulletin, "Progress of Civil Aeronautics in the United States"; 1937 figures, *Wall Street Journal,* June 13, 1938; the 1938 and 1939 figures are estimated. Aircraft Exports: Compiled from U.S. Bureau of Foreign and Domestic Commerce, "Foreign Commerce and Navigation of the United States," and "Aeronautical World News."

all exports from the United States declined in 1938, aircraft exports increased 73 per cent over the year before .... Some of the rise was undoubtedly due to the superior quality of American products. It was also the result of a limited world supply. The sudden rise in exports late in 1936, for instance, was attributed partly to the withdrawal of large producing countries from foreign markets, leaving them open to American manufacturers.

The activities of certain countries, such as Italy in Ethiopia, and both Germany and Italy in Spain, used up their surpluses. Or they stored them for a future day "of need." By 1937 and 1938 the United States accounted for over 45 per cent of aircraft exports from all the principal producing countries of the world. Export sales of Great Britain, France, Germany, and Italy in 1938 totaled $66,258,542[44]—which was less than the $68,209,050 exported by the United States alone. With the opening of the European war late in 1939, the proportionate increase in American exports became even more pronounced.

In the years from 1935 through 1938 our aeronautical products were widely distributed over the world .... While the number of countries to which we shipped was as large as for the period from 1925 to 1934 ..., the relative amounts bought by each showed a marked change.

The fact that the demand from various areas shifted in this period, from 1935 to 1938, as compared with the earlier one, was due to increased world tension. For the turbulence in Europe and the comparative peacefulness of Latin America were both reflected in their proportions of aeronautical imports from the United States .... Contrary to its large purchases up to 1935 ..., Latin America thereafter showed a notable decline in its proportion, whereas Europe's percentage of our aircraft exports increased.

This changing demand was indicated also in the ten largest purchasers (see Table V, below). Three American countries (Mexico, Colombia, and Peru) and one European country (Germany) dropped out from the list of the largest purchasers from 1925 to 1934. In view of her extreme nationalism, it was to be expected that Germany's imports of aircraft would decline. No doubt her shortage of acceptable currency was a large factor as well in her straining effort to be independent. The positions of these four countries in the list of largest purchasers were

[44] *New York Times,* April 23, 1939; July 23, 1939.

TABLE V *Ten Countries Purchasing Largest Amounts of U.S. Aircraft Exports, 1935–1938 (in thousands of dollars)*

COUNTRY	AIR-PLANES*	ENGINES	PARTS	PARA-CHUTES	TOTAL	% OF ALL AIR-CRAFT EXPORTS
China	$12,406	$ 3,359	$ 4,269	$ 28	$ 20,062	13.8
Japan	7,174	1,094	7,189	29	15,486	10.7
Argentina	9,462	1,151	2,456	194	13,263	9.1
Neth. Indies	7,259	544	2,524	154	10,481	7.2
U.S.S.R.	3,686	577	5.408	2	9,673	6.7
Netherlands	4,567	2,194	2,402	—	9,163	6.3*
United Kingdom	2,437	1,214	2,912	4	6,567	4.5
Canada	2,412	1,152	2,980	18	6,562	4.2
Turkey	4,489	279	965	87	5,820	4.0
Brazil	3,331	502	1,235	36	5,104	3.5
	$57,223	$12,066	$32,340	$552	$102,181	70.3

* Includes seaplanes, amphibians, and gliders. Canada was the only country of gliders, to the extent of $3,600.
Source: Compiled from U.S. Bureau of Foreign and Domestic Commerce, "Foreign Commerce and Navigation of the United States."

taken by four others: Turkey, the United Kingdom, the Netherlands, and the Netherlands East Indies. It is worthy of note that purchases by the Netherlands East Indies were even larger than those by the mother country.

China and Japan headed the list of largest individual countries (see Table V, above) purchasing in this period. This was reflected in the large increase in demand from Asia . . . , which accounted for 40 per cent of our exports in 1938 as compared with an average of only 23 per cent in the earlier period. Force was given to the arguments of the anti-old-Neutrality Law group by the enormous increase in 1938 of Japan's purchases, bringing her not far under China. But the Neutrality Law was not applied to the Sino-Japanese conflict, since Japan had not declared war, but merely waged it. Therefore the National Munitions Control Board, established by the law under the State Department, could not refuse licenses for exports of munitions to Japan.

Licenses for export of *all* arms, munitions, and implements of war granted by the National Munitions Control Board under the Neutrality Law amounted to only $176,890 in the first three months of 1939. On the other hand, aeronautical exports to Japan in the same period totaled over $1,000,000. The difference in these figures is due to the fact that the list of munitions proclaimed under the Neutrality Law does not include many aircraft parts and accessories. Therefore Japan could buy aeronautical parts here without applying for permission to the State Department, whereas licenses for finished planes and engines had to be obtained from the State Department.

That the licenses were so small was due to an appeal by Secretary of State Hull. For in the summer of 1938 the Department of State requested aircraft manufacturers not to export to nations bombing civilian population. At that moment this request could apply only to Japan. Although the *Christian Science Monitor* could get no statement on their policy from seven aircraft companies to which it telegraphed after this appeal, United Aircraft replied, "We are not selling Japan any aeronautical supplies."[45] Nevertheless, it was later reported that all the aircraft companies, except United Aircraft, had agreed to co-operate.[46] Six months after the State Department's request, United Aircraft announced its support of this policy, and claimed that, except for propellers, it had always conformed to Secretary Hull's appeal. But, it may be noted in passing, propellers are as important to a plane as an engine. Furthermore, the Japanese government as far back as 1929 was one of this company's largest propeller customers.[47]

Whatever the role of United Aircraft, the companies did not immediately or unanimously comply with Secretary Hull's request. As recently as February, 1939, Lockheed Aircraft reported contracts to deliver planes to Japan.[48] Furthermore, there were large exports to Japan of aeronautical products that do not come under the State Department's control. Japan's purchases in the first quarter of 1939 were smaller than those of Great Britain, France, and the Dutch East Indies, but still high enough to rank Japan as the fourth largest customer.

Contrasting sharply with this situation was the prohibition that had such an adverse effect on Republican Spain. When Spain was torn by war, this situation did not come under the Neutrality Act, since it was technically a civil war. But immediately after the struggle started, the Department of State refrained from, and thereby discouraged "any

---

[45] *Christian Science Monitor*, June 24, 1938.
[46] *New York Times*, January 15, 1939; January 20, 1939.
[47] Pynchon and Co., "The Aviation Industry," September, 1929, p. 62.
[48] *New York Times*, February 17, 1939.

interference whatsoever in the unfortunate Spanish situation."[49] And on January 8, 1937, Congress passed a Joint Resolution prohibiting the export to Spain of arms, ammunition, and implements of war.

This effectually cut off the Loyalist forces from the supply of planes available here, whereas Franco was able to buy from the "Axis." Official figures for Italy alone (quoted in the *New York Times*) showed that 6,011 men of the Italian Air Force were sent to Spain, and that almost 130,000 tons of explosives were dropped.[50] Although there were two shipments from the United States, other planes that were bought and paid for here could not be shipped to the Loyalists. One exporter told this writer that he was awaiting the outcome of the government's unsettled suit against Curtiss-Wright Export for shipping planes allegedly for Bolivia. (The suit was settled in February, 1940, when two officers and the company pleaded guilty to the government's charges.)

Though the Neutrality Law prevented the shipment of vitally needed planes to Loyalist Spain, it did not prevent the shipment of arms to Japan in its undeclared war on China. And because of these and other contradictions, a shift occurred in the national sentiment. It was a far cry from the revulsion that caused the passage of the Neutrality Act in 1935 to the popular demand for its revision in 1939. A large factor was the question of delivering large numbers of aircraft to the French and British governments. But even before the current war was declared, it became apparent that this country's policy toward aeronautical exports might well turn the scales for one side or another. For this country and Canada constitute the safest aircraft factory in the world.

Exports Boom in a Warring World

Although the flow of munitions to Europe was interrupted for a brief time in the fall of 1939, this was merely a welcome breathing spell to the aviation industry. Through heightening world tension, declarations of war, placing embargoes, and then lifting of embargoes subject to the new law, aircraft trade boomed.

Because of the mounting public dissatisfaction with the Neutrality Law,* the arms embargo was repealed in November, 1939. The

---

* Laws, proclamations, and joint resolutions amending the original Neutrality Act were passed each year, but they were all generally referred to as the Neutrality Law.
[49] National Munitions Control Board, "Second Annual Report," November 30, 1937, p. 74.
[50] *New York Times,* June 11, 1939.

legislation had not, it was seen, applied successfully to changing world conditions, nor had it effectively kept this country from being involved with the rest of the world.

When in September, 1939, a state of war was declared to exist between Germany, France, Poland, the United Kingdom, India, Australia, and New Zealand, President Roosevelt was forced to ban the export of arms, ammunition, and the implements of war to these countries. Canada was added to the list shortly after. A special session of Congress was called to consider repeal and a new law, and in the meantime shipments were held up. Arguments in favor of repeal were based on the general sentiment in this country favoring the Allies, combined with the knowledge that it would be exceedingly difficult to control shipments of arms. It was also apparent that a strict embargo would be harmful to the upswing that munitions industries were already reflecting from the war.

If continued and enforced, the embargo would have hit the aviation industry particularly hard, for it had been rolling up orders from France and Great Britain since the early part of the year. Actually, however, the embargo hurt the industry's future expectations more than it did the contracts then in force. In some orders already placed, provision had been made that in case of war the company would make delivery in the United States and would receive payment of the balance of the contract. At the time war was declared, contracts for the French and British orders in production by Douglas, North American Aviation, and Lockheed had been so worded, it was reported, that the companies were to be paid "for materials ordered, labor expended and planes completed in full or in part."[51]

The new Joint Resolution on neutrality enacted by Congress after the arms embargo kept the machinery of the old law: the National Munitions Control Board was to license and register munitions companies, and these were to be defined in accordance with President Roosevelt's proclamation listing arms, ammunition, and implements of war. In addition, the new resolution included provision for what was known as the "cash-and-carry" system. The aviation industry had already taken care of the "cash," as we have seen; and it was not involved in the "carry" part of the new law, which imposed restrictions on the merchant marine. Indeed, the stock market rose strongly the day the new law was

---

[51] *Ibid.*, September 17, 1939.

enacted, led by the aviation issues, with Curtiss-Wright as the most spectacular performer.

The lifting of the embargo and the new act were expected to benefit most American industries, but the aviation industry was the chief beneficiary. United Aircraft, Curtiss-Wright, and Douglas were reported to have received orders from France and Great Britain totaling $160,000,000 immediately after the embargo was repealed and the new law enacted. All companies benefited from this demand, which came not only from the Allies, but from countries, which, at the moment of writing, are classed as nonbelligerents.

In proportion to their size, small companies also flourished. An unnamed "neutral country" gave Republic Aviation Corporation a

TABLE VI *Licenses Granted for Aeronautical Exports, November 30, 1937–1938 (in thousands of dollars)*

COMPANY	1936 AMOUNT	1936 % OF TOTAL	1937 AMOUNT	1937 % OF TOTAL	1938[1] AMOUNT	1938[1] % OF TOTAL
United Aircraft Corp.[2]	$ 2,854	13.18	$ 3,932	10.53	$ 4,584	5.22
Curtiss-Wright Corp.[3]	3,307	15.26	3,929	10.51	11,092	12.62
North American Aviation, Inc.	39	.18	866	2.32	9,907	11.27
Aviation Corp.[4]	625	2.89	549	1.47	1,596	1.82
Douglas Aircraft Co.[5]	2,865	13.23	4,499	12.05	5,811	6.61
Consolidated Aircraft Corp.	314	1.45	1,274	3.41	130	.15
Martin, Glenn L., Co.	2,200	10.16	6,316	16.91	10,767	12.25
Lockheed Aircraft Corp.	508	2.34	2,942	7.88	24,049	27.37
Boeing Airplane Co.	8	.03	60	.16	36	.04
Grumman Aircraft Engineering Corp.	none	—	205	.55	171	.20
Republic Aviation Corp.[6]	197	.91	105	.28	none	—
Brewster Aeronautical Corp.	none	—	none	—	384	.44
TOTALS						
Above Companies	$12,917	59.63	$24,677	66.07	$68,527	77.99
All Companies	$21,664		$37,347		$87,872	

[1] 1938 is without deducting revocations which will be published in the next year's annual report.
[2] Includes United Aircraft Corp. and United Aircraft Exports.
[3] Includes Wright Aeronautical, Curtiss-Wright Airplane Co. and Curtiss-Wright Export Corp.
[4] Includes Aviation Mfg. Corp. and Stinson.
[5] Includes Northrop in 1936 and 1937.
[6] Formerly Seversky.
Source: Compiled from annual reports of the National Munitions Control Board of the U.S. State Department; Categories III (1, 2); V (1, 2, 3).

$4,000,000 order, raising its backlog to $10,000,000, which is roughly equal to its annual production capacity. But the larger companies maintained their dominant positions in the export field. Licenses granted by the National Munitions Control Board to munitions exporters showed that twelve companies in the following table received over 78 per cent of the aircraft licenses granted in 1938.

These figures indicate the domination of export trade by the same large companies which previously had been shown to dominate domestic trade also. This table is, however, an understatement, since the figures are for licenses granted, and not for actual total export sales. For many foreign purchasers have agents in this country, who buy here. Their purchases are, therefore, reflected in the domestic sales of the companies, not in the companies' export licenses. Aviation Equipment and Export, for example, is said to be the middleman for China's purchases. Much, if not all, of the Soviet Union's purchases are made through the Amtorg Trading Company.

Lockheed, one of the smaller plane companies, was an exceptionally large exporter, showing a higher proportion of exports in 1938 than of domestic sales. This was due to the fact that in 1937 Lockheed advertised the ease with which its new transport plane could be converted into a military bomber. As a result of this frankness, its business boomed: Lockheed's total sales of $2,000,000 in 1936 swelled two years later to $27,000,000 worth of orders from Great Britain alone.

To add to the rosy picture of booming sales, the profits margin on exports is likely to be even larger in the future than it has been in the past. A report from Los Angeles about the plants of Douglas, Lockheed, Vultee (of Aviation Corporation), and North American Aviation, stresses the wartime spirit of the industry:

... although there is an obvious effort on the part of the company officials to minimize the boom atmosphere in the industry there is a "war-time" spirit that cannot be mistaken.[52]

The only fly in the ointment is the fear of peace. This industry has not yet had to meet the danger of world peace, and the fears expressed by Standard Statistics as early as 1937 have not materialized: that "... any trend toward better international relations would thus reduce

[52] *Ibid.*, November 9, 1939.

earning power substantially."[53] In fact, orders and profits have increased and aircraft stocks are now in the forefront of war stocks.

Because they are in a commanding position in the market, aircraft manufacturers, according to the *Wall Street Journal*, ". . . have taken precautions to protect themselves against loss in the event that current hostilities should no longer demand their products." From an article on November 4, 1939, this paper describes some of these precautions more fully:

Liberal advance payments are being offered by the purchasers; in some instances they cover the cost of plant expansions now underway. Should hostilities end before delivery of the new orders, the contracts provide, it is understood, that *all the manufacturers' costs* on the undelivered portion will be liquidated. Ample deposits to cover this contingency will be maintained. Another factor for the protection of the companies is that advance payments apply, in most instances, to the products delivered last, while the first delivered planes and engines will be paid for when turned over to the purchaser in this country. [Italics mine.][54]

Even before the present war was declared, terms of payment were favorable to companies in this seller's market. Frequently the manufacturers got large down-deposits, amounting to 20 per cent or 30 per cent; "progress payments" were received while the work was going on, and the balance was to be paid on delivery at American ports. Pressure of war needs is now so great that France and Great Britain are reported to be taking options on orders to be delivered in 1941.

The large backlog of United States government and foreign orders has raised the question of whether this government's needs will be fulfilled if the war continues. Even before the war started, it was estimated that 87 per cent of the actual contracts in the first part of 1939 (before the United States began to buy for its new program) were from the French and British air ministries, with miscellaneous orders from the Netherlands and other countries. In November, 1939, the huge backlog of orders, amounting to $533,000,000, was more than 50 per cent due to export orders.

Since the summer of 1939, the Army and Navy Munitions Board had been considering the question of whether foreign orders conflicted with domestic production schedules. In November, 1939, it was

[53] *Standard Trade and Securities,* April 7, 1937.
[54] *Wall Street Journal,* November 4, 1939.

announced that the control exercised by the National Munitions Control Board directly through its licensing system, and indirectly by the Army and Navy, was functioning satisfactorily in respect to this problem. Meanwhile, the Senate in October voted down a proposal that no licenses should be issued for export until a minimum of 3,000 planes had been produced for the Army and Navy. This leaves the control in the hands of the National Munitions Control Board. It may, however, be difficult to insure delivery of domestic orders first, because of the fact that some of the export contracts, it is reported, " . . . provide for penalties to be assessed against the manufacturer if deliveries are not made on time in accordance with guaranties."[55] Even this is softened by a maximum which limits the penalty.

Control of aircraft exports will probably be made more difficult by the fact that profits on this business are very high. That the industry has been dependent on this government up to now is not being taken into consideration. Furthermore, in exports, too, this government's business accounts for a large part of the profits. Although this may at first seem an exaggeration in view of the industry's large quantities of exports, the fact is that in exports, as well as domestic trade, government business is the important factor. The government fosters the development of military planes, and various costs are charged off . . . before the profits limit is applied. When these same models are exported, prices are very high, and the profits on the actual exports—amounting to as much as 20 per cent—are in addition to the profits already realized on the production for this government.[56]

Formerly the Army and Navy prohibited the export of military planes and engines for a certain period of time after their first production. In order to prevent the newest models from being shipped abroad, they were held back for as long as a year. Recently, however, there has been a change in this official policy, as in many others, to permit the manufacturers of certain unannounced types to make quicker delivery abroad. This important question involves international spies and the possibilities of keeping the details of a new military plane secret once it has been put into production, flown over this country, seen by many people, and photographed frequently. As in many problems affecting aviation, there is a reported difference of opinion between the various government departments involved. The United States Aeronautical Board

[55] *Ibid.*
[56] *Fortune,* September, 1938, p. 94.

is said to have pursued the policy that release of models for export should be settled in each individual case, depending, for one thing, on the purchaser. The State Department, on the other hand, insists that when a type has once been released to any one foreign country, it should be available to all countries. In other words, if a certain type has been exported to Sweden, it must therefore be allowed to be exported to Japan. This and other similar questions, it is reported, will go to President Roosevelt for settlement.[57]

The question of priority between domestic needs and the needs of other countries has still to be settled. If this war continues and/or other wars start, and their participants have enough acceptable cash, the problem will become more acute. Control by this government to insure its own supply is the only factor that will stop the upward surge of exports.

[57] *New York Times,* November 11, 1939; November 13, 1939.

Part III
World War II
1940–1945

4. Conversion to Wartime Production

The aircraft industry had actually begun its wartime expansion before the United States' entry into World War II. On May 16, 1940, President Roosevelt made what appeared at that time to be an unrealistic request of the industry: "I should like to see this nation geared up to the ability to turn out at least 50,000 planes a year. Furthermore, I believe that this nation should plan at this time a program that would provide us with 50,000 military and naval planes." There followed a series of steps to attempt to implement the President's request.

To achieve a gigantic production expansion in a short period of time was an immensely difficult task. Facilities of existing plants had to be expanded; new facilities had to be produced; nonaircraft producers had to be brought into the industry; qualified personnel had to be recruited; new production processes had to be developed; new legislation had to be passed; and countless other problems had to be overcome.

There was not much choice but to expand the production of existing aircraft models. To get from the drawing-board stage to actual production in quantity usually took several years, but there was no time for delays. Existing plants were enlarged, branch plants were built, nonaircraft producers were licensed to produce products developed by the aircraft industry, and producers subcontracted work with nonaircraft producers.

A revolutionary change in the technology of production was needed if large-scale production was to be realized. A shift from the "job shop" method to the assembly-line technique was the result. This shift, of course, necessitated greater standardization of parts and job processes than was previously known to the industry. How extremely difficult the task was is suggested by the complexity of the product itself. For example, the 18-foot nose of the B-29 alone had over 50,000 rivets and 8,000 kinds of parts, and these parts were procured from over 1,500 subcontractors. When Ford was licensed to produce the Consolidated B-24, it was necessary to break down the assembly process into approximately 20,000 drawings before an assembly line could be set up at Willow Run. Only then could there be sufficient specialization so that aircraft could be produced by the lesser skilled personnel on whom the industry was forced to rely for the rapid production expansion.

A Harvard University study group was given the task of analyzing the problems encountered in accelerating aircraft production in the United States during World War II. The purpose of the study was to discover the implications of this then recent experience for a sound peacetime defense policy for the aircraft industry. An important selection from this study is now presented.

Conversion to Wartime Production Techniques*
Tom Lilley et al.

The Wartime Production Programs

The decisions made in Washington during the latter half of 1940, just after the wartime mobilization began, set the basic pattern for the entire wartime expansion of the aircraft industry. Despite changes in detail, expansion in the later periods followed the broad outline of the original decisions. Before discussing technical methods of manufacture, the production programs resulting from these government decisions will be reviewed, first for engines and then for airframes.

The Manufacturing Plan for Engines

Early in 1940 there were three producers of engines suitable for military combat use. Two of them, the Wright Aeronautical Corporation, in Paterson, New Jersey, and the Pratt & Whitney Aircraft Division of United Aircraft Corporation, in East Hartford, Connecticut, had been aircraft engine makers for a period of years. Each was expanding its plant as a result of French and British orders. Although the early 1940 expansion seemed large at the time, it looks small in retrospect.

The Allison Division of the General Motors Corporation, long a builder of aircraft engines on special order, was carrying out the final production engineering on its 1,000 horsepower V-1710 engine based on an anticipated low rate of output. It also had under way a plant expansion, based on the size of orders foreseeable at the time.

None of these early expansions took the plants far in the direction of the line production methods that were ultimately used, but they gave invaluable preliminary experience with the problems of planning expansion; they furnished the machine tool makers with greater knowledge of the product and its production characteristics; and they brought some new suppliers into relationship with the engine companies.

At government-industry conferences held in Washington in 1940, a decision was made to encourage the development of military engine designs by other nonaircraft companies. With respect to this endeavor, certain companies, including automobile engine builders, promised great things in short periods, but none delivered a new engine in the periods allotted. Later, one company did deliver a promising engine, but the needs of the war had changed and it was not pushed.

Although new designs were solicited, the government decided that

---

* Reprinted by permission of the publishers from Tom Lilley *et al.: Problems of Accelerating Aircraft Production During World War II* (Boston: Division of Research, Harvard Business School, 1947), pp. 32–41.

the production effort should be concentrated on proven engine models. For engines of military size, this meant the products of Wright and Pratt & Whitney. Allison's liquid-cooled engine had passed its type test; but it was not yet proven and had not been developed for high-altitude work. Consequently, the Allison engine was supplemented with the Rolls-Royce Merlin engine, a high-altitude, liquid-cooled engine urgently desired by the British Purchasing Commission.

It became clear in mid-1940 that the volumes needed would greatly exceed the expansions then under way at Allison, Pratt & Whitney, and Wright. Both within the government and in industry strong differences of opinion developed as to the proper program for expansion. The general principles decided on were to disperse centers of production and to bring into the program outside companies with a demonstrated competence in volume production involving similar processes. Nevertheless, in each instance these principles were modified to meet the wishes of company managements.

Allison, whose foreseeable expansion at the time was the least of the three, obtained approval of its plan to handle the expansion in or near its home plant in Indianapolis and to draw in men from other General Motors divisions as managerial help might be needed. The Wright management preferred to handle all the final assembly work itself. It was prepared to increase its subcontracting greatly, but hesitated to give to any other company the whole responsibility for producing a Wright engine, although it cooperated fully later when licensees were named. The Pratt & Whitney management offered to license its designs. It believed that there were definite limits to its ability to handle greatly increased manufacturing commitments and preferred to turn over the volume production of established models to others. The problem was complicated at Wright and Pratt & Whitney by the necessity of making early deliveries of trainer engines as well as the combat engines considered herein.

After some discussion, upon finding the Wright management firm in its preference to accept the responsibility for final assembly of its engines, the government authorized the company to build a large branch plant to make R-2600 engines but required that the plant be located in the inland area. Lockland, a suburb of Cincinnati, was chosen, although the company had suggested Philadelphia. In connection with this plant Wright proposed to use five major subcontractors, to be known as "cooperating companies," for the production of major subassemblies.

These were: the Ohio Crankshaft Company (crank-shafts), Otis Elevator Company (crankcases), Hudson Motor Car Company (pistons and rocker arms), Eaton Manufacturing Company (propeller shafts), and Graham-Paige Motors Corporation (master and articulated connecting rods). Wright retained for itself gear making, cylinder making, and magnesium casting—the processes which it considered the most difficult. Certain other production processes, together with assembly and testing, were also retained.

Shortly after this plan was formulated, the need for R-2600 engines increased. In November 1940 Mr. Knudsen's office brought the Studebaker Corporation into the R-2600 production program on a licensee basis. This decision was made over the objection of Wright, which proposed a further expansion at Cincinnati in order to avoid making the same engine in two plants. In June 1941, before Studebaker produced any R-2600 engines, its assignment was changed to the production of Wright R-1820 engines for the B-17 program. The government asked Studebaker to make this change instead of Wright because Studebaker was considered more able to change course in mid-stream.

The only other licensee for Wright aircraft engines ever named was the Dodge Division of the Chrysler Corporation. Wright itself made further expansions at Cincinnati and Paterson, and built a second large branch plant at Wood-Ridge, New Jersey. In addition, Continental Motors Corporation manufactured the Wright Whirlwind engine for use in tanks.

The production pattern for Pratt & Whitney engines was quite different. This company preferred to use licensees, although in 1942 it was required to assume the responsibility for a branch plant in Kansas City because no satisfactory licensees were available. The Pratt & Whitney R-2800 engine was licensed to Ford in August 1940 and the R-1830 to Buick in October 1940. Other licensees entered from time to time; ultimately Chevrolet, Nash, Continental Motors, and the Jacobs Aircraft Engine Company, in addition to Ford and Buick, each produced one or more Pratt & Whitney models as licensees. Concurrently, Pratt & Whitney expanded its East Hartford plant until, with its three smaller "feeder plants," it produced a peak output which was third largest in the industry. This plant manufactured a diversified group of models, whereas the two plants with larger peak outputs were new plants specializing on one or two models.

The contrasting policies of Pratt & Whitney and Wright are reflected by the following figures summarizing production, in horsepower, from 1940 through 1944:

	PRATT & WHITNEY		WRIGHT	
Prewar Plants	162,163	35%	108,278	32%
Branch Plants	7,083	1	133,972	39[1]
Licensee Plants	298,976	64	96,998	29
	468,222	100%	339,248	100%

Looking at this history with the benefit of hindsight, most informed observers have concluded that the use of licensees was a wise choice. The relative increase in the administrative burden of the Wright company was far greater than that of Pratt & Whitney, and the consequent dilution of Wright management, was probably one of the causes of the greater expansion in the use of Pratt & Whitney engines. For example, one reason that the Pratt & Whitney R-2800 displaced the Wright R-2600 in the C-46 transport model was to relieve the pressure on Wright; and the development of the Wright R-3350 was delayed by the concentration of the Wright management upon current production problems.

The licensee arrangement could, however, be used only to the extent that satisfactory licensees were available, and the supply was definitely limited. Pratt & Whitney's experience in 1942, when it was given the Kansas City branch, is evidence of this limitation. It is confirmed by the instances of refusal on the part of licensees to take over the responsibility for other models or plants.

The results of the engine production plan are shown in Exhibit I. Perhaps the most emphatic way of stating the importance of the licensees is to point out that 48% of a five-year total horsepower output (1940–1944) was produced by licensee plants which were in production only a few months more than three years. In the peak year, 1944, they delivered almost 60% of the horsepower output. In contrast, the three home plants accounted for 38% of the five-year output, while branch plants accounted for only 14%. It is significant, however, that the home plants produced all but a negligible quantity of the military engines delivered before Pearl Harbor, despite the fact that the licensee and branch plant program was originally set up in 1940.

---

[1] Includes Wood-Ridge plant.

EXHIBIT 1. *Total Horsepower Delivered, Principal Engine Plants, by Years:*[1] *1939–1944 (Thousands of horsepower)*

MANUFACTURER	NO. OF PLANTS	1938	1939	1940	1941	1942	1943	1944	TOTAL FIVE-YEAR PERIOD 1940–1944 AMOUNT	%
Pre-War										
Allison	1	13	50	1,260	7,365	25,071	36,273	35,982	105,951	10.8%
Pratt & Whitney	1*	1,956	3,080	7,500	18,265	40,196	53,096	43,106	162,163	16.5
Wright	1	2,346	3,204	6,963	19,868	30,012	28,929	22,506	108,278	11.0
Total	3	4,315	6,334	15,723	45,498	95,279	118,298	101,594	376,392	38.3%
Branch										
Pratt & Whitney	1	—	—	—	—	—	2	7,081	7,083	0.7%
Wright	2	—	—	—	757	24,557	41,640	67,018	133,972	13.6
Total	3	—	—	—	757	24,557	41,642	74,099	141,055	14.3%
Licensee										
Packard	1*	—	—	—	61	11,056	20,661	38,406	70,184	7.1%
Licensees of:										
Pratt & Whitney	4	—	—	—	539	31,610	111,680	155,147	298,976	30.4
Wright	2	—	—	—	—	8,540	34,508	53,950	96,998	9.9
Total	7	—	—	—	600	51,206	166,849	247,503	466,158	47.4%
Total Output	—	4,315	6,334	15,723	46,855	171,042	326,789	423,196	983,605	100.0%
PERCENTAGE OF TOTAL HORSEPOWER DELIVERED, BY YEARS										
Pre-War Total		—	—	100.0%	97.1%	55.7%	36.2%	24.0%	38.3%	
Branch Total		—	—	0.0	1.6	14.4	12.7	17.5	14.3	
Licensee Total		—	—	0.0	1.3	29.9	51.1	58.5	47.4	
% of Total Five-Year Output:		—	—	1.6%	4.8%	17.4%	33.2%	43.0%	100.0%	

[1] Includes an allowance for spare parts delivered.
* These plants had one or more "feeder" plants in nearby cities.
Sources: Company data and Aircraft Resources Control Office, Report 15.

EXHIBIT II. Pounds of Airframe Accepted, by Plants: 1940–1944 (In thousands of pounds; spares excluded)

PLANTS	1940	1941	1942	1943	1944	TOTAL 1940–1944	RANK[1]
MAJOR PRE-1940 PLANTS							
EAST COAST							
Bell—Buffalo	141	3,421	7,296	18,409	13,910	43,177	17
Chance Vought—Stratford	124	1,701	2,635	9,790	14,702	28,952	22
Curtiss—Buffalo	4,318	8,817	19,260	26,985	35,834	95,214	7
Grumman—Bethpage	514	1,382	10,257	26,259	35,355	73,767	11
Martin—Baltimore	1,723	6,040	19,402	36,583	32,909	96,657	5
Republic—Farmingdale	383	572	3,494	19,328	25,057	48,834	14
MID-WEST							
Curtiss—St. Louis	53	463	2,629	3,925	2,057	9,127	30
WEST COAST							
Boeing—Seattle	1,346	5,225	31,912	57,798	70,074	166,355	2
Consolidated-Vultee—San Diego	428	8,904	37,222	66,968	67,180	180,702	1
Douglas, Santa Monica	4,148	9,294	10,211	24,016	28,372	76,041	10
Douglas—El Segundo	507	1,431	4,338	13,423	4,485	24,184	25
Lockheed "B"—Burbank	3,013	11,595	20,303	25,660	35,977	96,548	6
North American—Inglewood	3,638	6,669	17,494	24,338	28,283	80,422	9
Total Major Pre-1940 Plants	20,336	65,514	186,482	353,482	394,195	1,019,980	
MAJOR NEW PLANTS—AIRCRAFT COMPANY MANAGED							
NEAR HOME PLANTS, WEST COAST							
Boeing—Renton	—	—	—	—	6,686	6,686	31
Douglas—Long Beach	—	34	20,757	47,400	55,798	123,989	3
Lockheed "A"—Burbank	—	287	12,179	35,536	35,568	83,570	8
REMOTE FROM HOME PLANTS, EASTERN							
Bell—Atlanta	—	—	—	192	9,668	9,860	29
Curtiss—Columbus	—	—	1,419	5,898	20,162	27,479	23
Republic—Evansville	—	—	64	7,238	19,757	27,059	24
Curtiss—Louisville	—	—	—	164	4,107	4,271	33

[1] The plants are ranked on the basis of the total poundage accepted in the five-year period, 1940–1944.

EXHIBIT II (Continued)

PLANTS	1940	1941	1942	1943	1944	TOTAL 1940–1944	RANK
REMOTE FROM HOME PLANTS, MID-WEST							
Boeing—Wichita #2	—	—	—	4,185	34,728	38,913	18
Consolidated-Vultee—Fort Worth	—	—	1,033	28,272	40,722	70,027	12
Douglas—Tulsa	—	—	186	11,908	17,669	29,763	21
Douglas—Oklahoma City	—	—	—	5,627	40,692	46,319	15
Douglas—Chicago	—	—	—	239	6,038	6,277	32
Martin—Omaha	—	—	1,376	19,639	9,298	30,313	20
North American—Kansas City	—	—	5,003	19,715	39,047	63,765	13
North American—Dallas "A"	—	1,920	9,982	11,661	20,752	44,315	16
North American—Dallas "B"	—	—	—	1,415	20,996	22,411	26
TOTAL MAJOR NEW PLANTS—AIRCRAFT COMPANY MANAGED	—	2,241	51,999	199,089	381,688	635,017	
MAJOR NEW PLANTS—NON-AIRCRAFT COMPANY MANAGED							
EAST COAST							
Eastern[2]—Linden	—	—	83	5,111	10,642	15,836	27
Eastern[2]—Trenton	—	—	20	7,652	24,361	32,033	19
MID-WEST							
Ford—Willow Run	—	—	557	29,951	92,568	123,076	4
Goodyear—Akron	—	—	—	2,074	11,594	13,668	28
TOTAL MAJOR NEW PLANTS— NON-AIRCRAFT COMPANY MANAGED	—	—	660	44,788	139,165	184,613	
TOTAL MAJOR NEW PLANTS	—	2,241	52,659	243,877	520,853	819,630	
TOTAL ALL MAJOR PLANTS	20,336	67,755	239,112	597,359	915,048	1,839,610	
TOTAL ALL OTHER PLANTS	2,775	13,609	36,717	56,829	46,073	156,003	
GRAND TOTAL—ALL PLANTS	23,111	81,364	275,829	654,188	961,121	1,995,613	

[2] Eastern Aircraft Division of General Motors Corporation.
Source: Compiled from unpublished data furnished by the Statistical Control Office, Air Technical Service Command, Wright Field.

The Manufacturing Plan for Airframes

The over-all government production plan for airframes differed from the plan for engines in three important respects. First, in 1940, when the plan was initiated, many more companies were actively engaged in airframe production than were engaged in engine production. During the war, the home plants of these companies carried a larger portion of the total war production load than did the home plants of the engine companies. Second, many more new branch plants were constructed during the war. Third, only a few important airframe assembly plants were managed by nonaircraft companies in a manner analogous to the licensee arrangement for engines. The output of these plants was relatively insignificant compared with that of the engine licensee plants.

In 1940 thirteen major airframe plants, managed by eleven different companies, were in active production, compared with only three major engine plants. The thirteen aircraft plants which were in production in 1940 produced over 50% of the total poundage of airframe output in the five years 1940–1944, compared with 38% produced by the three engine home plants (see Exhibit II).

When the over-all manufacturing plan for airframes was developed in 1940, the decision was made to rely primarily on plants managed by peacetime producers of aircraft. One or more sizable production programs were planned for each of the thirteen pre-1940 plants listed in Exhibit II. Meanwhile, construction of a number of branch plants was started. Sixteen major new branch plants were constructed during the war. These plants were responsible for over 30% of the total poundage output in the years 1940–1944, and in the year of peak production, 1944, they were responsible for approximately 40% of total output. This record differed radically from that of the less important branch plants manufacturing engines.

The branch airframe plants, like the branch and licensee engine plants, did not get into production in appreciable quantities until 1942. Thus for both products the going concerns of 1940 carried practically the entire production burden in the pre-Pearl-Harbor period.

The most striking difference between the airframe and engine production programs was the relatively small reliance placed on licensing arrangements for the assembly of completed airframes. Only four major airframe assembly plants were operated by companies which had not been in the business prior to 1940. As shown in Exhibit II, these plants accounted for less than 10% of total aircraft poundage in 1940–1944.

The four plants did not get into production in significant quantities until 1943 and 1944. By 1944, however, they were making a sizable contribution to total airframe production. In that year, one of them, the Ford Plant at Willow Run, achieved a poundage output larger than that of any other plant and almost 10% of the total output of all plants.

Companies other than the prewar aircraft manufacturers carried a much more important part of the airframe production load than the figures would have indicated, but they did so primarily by acting as subcontractors of the aircraft assembly plants and as suppliers of purchased parts and components. By the latter part of the war, the percentage of work subcontracted by aircraft assemblers was near 30%. In many individual plants the percentage was far higher.

The major reasons for the difference between the airframe and engine production plans can be traced to the nature of the products themselves. The special characteristics of airframes required manufacturing techniques quite different from those employed by most other industries in peacetime, while engine manufacture could more easily utilize the normal production techniques of the metal-cutting industries. Hence, while peacetime producers of automobiles supplied the majority of the engines delivered in World War II, no attempt was made to use these manufacturers to a comparable extent for assembly of completed airframes.

The officials responsible for determining production plans realized, however, that if the peacetime airframe industry attempted to carry out all wartime airframe production, an almost insuperable load would be placed on the managements of the airframe manufacturing companies. To try to lighten that load, as well as for other reasons, the device of subcontracting was used more and more extensively during the war.

The Time Required to Reach Quantity Output

Statistical information has been obtained with respect to the dates when important steps were taken in all major engine programs and in a majority of the major airframe programs. . . .

Analysis of the number of months which elapsed from the first informal go-ahead received from the government to the acceptance of the thousandth airplane demonstrates that, even under the best of circumstances, it takes many months to reach any appreciable scale of airframe production. The fastest program for which data are available required 19 months from go-ahead to the thousandth acceptance. Most programs required between two and three years, with a median of 31 months for one- and two-engine aircraft, and 33 months for four-engine bombers. In general, the fastest progress was made on post-Pearl-Harbor programs for developed one- and two-engine models which had previously been in production in home plants . . . .

Substantial time lags were also involved in accelerating engine production. During the first year and a half of the mobilization effort, prewar plants, which were in production on established engine models, were the only important sources of military engines. The licensee plants, however, did outstanding work after getting under way. Subject to . . . qualifications . . . , the figure of 15 months from a firm go-ahead to a war production rate of 500 engines per month is typical for established models produced by such licensees. An important element in this speed of getting started was the ability of licensees to tool up rapidly. Longer periods were experienced by branch plants and by all plants concerned with engine types that were going through final engineering development during the war.

Production Processes

The wartime production record clearly indicates that, even in the case of the most successful programs, long time spans were required to obtain quantity output of both engines and airframes. The reasons for these time lags cannot be adequately understood without some background knowledge of the nature of these products and their manufacture. Hence the following paragraphs will describe briefly the processes used in manufacturing airframes and engines and the vast changes made in these processes during the war.

The Nature of the Product and Its Manufacture

Airframes

As aircraft have become increasingly complicated mechanisms, the task of designing and manufacturing them has grown in magnitude and difficulty. One result of this complexity has been an increasing degree of specialization among the companies fabricating and assembling these products. The wartime manufacture of airplanes was divided among producers of airframes, engines, propellers, instruments, landing gear, and an ever-increasing array of other specialized parts and equipment. Thus, the airframe manufacturers, which assembled all the components into completed aircraft, were relieved of much designing and manufacturing responsibility.[2] Their responsibility included meeting government performance specifications for the completed product, however, and hence required a considerable amount of joint engineering work with the manufacturers of components.

The assembly of an airplane can be divided roughly into two types of work: the building of the airframe shell, which requires the unique processes described below, and the installation of equipment in the airframe.

A military airframe is, in reality, an extremely complex metal shell. It is made up mainly of a framework composed of parts known as spars, stringers, bulkheads, frames, and ribs, and an outside covering known as the skin. The framework and skin are made principally from sheet metal, although a relatively small number of parts are fabricated from forgings, castings, extrusions, and bar and tube stock. Most of the metal used is aluminum alloy. Military airframes are made up of a vast number of parts; for instance, the B-25 contains 165,000 separate parts, not counting 150,000 rivets or the engines, instruments, and other equipment. In contrast, there are roughly 5,000 parts in a medium-price automobile.

The fabrication and assembly of the sheet-metal portions of an airframe present some very difficult production problems. One reason for these difficulties is that a relatively complex series of operations is required to translate airframe engineering information into tooling before manufacturing begins.[3] The problem is one of building large, sheet-metal structures to close tolerances of weight, strength and curvature. Consequently, ordinary dimensioned drawings, suitable for the metal cutting industry, are not sufficient guides for building the necessary tooling.

Assembling the sheet-metal parts of an airframe is entirely different from assembling machined parts into a product. The tolerances established in designing machined parts are such that many parts are interchangeable, and assembly can usually take place by simply putting the parts together without the necessity of fitting or postassembly

---

[2] During the war, many airplane components such as engines and instruments were purchased directly from their respective manufacturers by the government and supplied to the airframe manufacturers as Government Furnished Equipment (GFE). For a medium bomber such as the B-25 there were as many as 750 GFE items produced by many manufacturers located throughout the United States.

[3] The term "tooling," as used herein, includes all types of jigs, dies, and fixtures used in the fabrication of parts and in subassembly and assembly operations. The tooling ranges from dies used to form simple aluminum alloy parts to the huge fixtures used for assembly of complete aircraft wings.

machining. Mating surfaces are characteristically large enough and parts are rigid enough so that they can be positioned satisfactorily without intricate holding devices. In the case of airframe manufacture, there are few such mating surfaces except at major joints such as the joint between wings and fuselage. In assembly, numerous large and frequently flexible parts must be held in proper relationship to each other as they are riveted together. It is the determination of the contours—the setting of jig-locating points in positions so that parts can be assembled properly—that introduces into the production of airframes elements that are peculiar to the industry.

In order to reproduce in physical form the curved surfaces designed into the airplane on paper, it is necessary to resort to the laying out of templates on metal sheets by means of a process known as "lofting" or "master layout." This technique has been adapted largely from the "lofts" of the ship-building industry where somewhat similar problems are encountered. "Loft lines" are obtained by passing sections through a portion of the airplane at uniform spacing in both horizontal and vertical planes so that a series of contours results. When these contours are cut out of sheet steel as templates and assembled in the same relationship as the sections passed through the structure, the result is a skeleton representation of the structure itself. If plaster is then filled in between the templates, and, when set, worked down to the outside contours an accurate plaster "mock-up" is obtained from which tools can be made.

A related method consists, in effect, of building a mold surrounding the contour. If "female" templates are cut out of the steel sheets, laid out as above, and locating points in the form of wood or steel docks are fastened in the proper positions, it is possible to develop a jig within which the desired structure can be assembled. In peacetime jigs built up in this fashion for the assembly of the first experimental units of a new model were frequently satisfactory for the small orders which sometimes followed, and were commonly referred to as experimental tooling.

The basic dimensions and reference points of specialized airframe tooling are established by this type of transition from engineering data into temporary jigs and other tools.[4] As the volume of production increased during the war, many changes were made in these tools. Temporary assembly jigs were broken down into smaller sections,

---

[4] Other airframe tooling, especially tooling used in the machining of certain parts, was much simpler and more closely allied to the tooling used in other industries (e.g., tooling used for machining forgings).

strengthened through the use of heavy steel members, simplified by the removal of unnecessary portions of the template detail, and rendered more suitable for higher production through better location of control points and greater accessibility. These changes were, however, variations to meet the needs of increased volume. The translation of engineering data into tooling still followed the general pattern outlined above.

Engines

The aircraft engines of World War II had the common characteristics of being multicylinder, reciprocating engines designed to produce their rated output in a minimum of space and with a minimum weight. The manufacture of such products requires processes quite different from those used in making airframes.

Engine manufacturing processes are generally similar to those of the metal-cutting industries. Most of the parts are shaped and finished by the removal of metal from partially formed blanks. Thus the problems of engine manufacture are associated with processes calling for forges, foundries, and machine shops almost to the exclusion of such airframe problems as handling and forming sheets and making large structures. The assembly of engines is a relatively simple problem compared with airframe assembly. For engines, it is the design of tools, jigs, dies, and fixtures for the machining of parts which presents the chief difficulty.

Some conception of the multitude of closely fitted parts in a high-output aircraft engine is given by consideration of the R-2800, which was in the middle-size range at the end of the war and has about 13,000 pieces, many of which are alike. There are about 1,400 individual designs of parts, most of them moving parts or in contact with moving parts, and almost all calling for working to close tolerances and extremely high finish.[5] The desire to achieve maximum performance with minimum weight accounts for the manufacture of engine parts and the assembly of the engine. Even the lowly stud that serves to hold together such parts as crankcase sections is especially designed for weight saving, and has "locator points" so that the goal of equal tension on each stud can be reached by measuring its stretch in tenths of thousandths of an inch. Some gears are ground so that under load conditions they will bend into the

---

[5] The T-33 (I-40), a jet engine of about twice the power, has about 6,900 parts, of which about 800 are individually designed. The number of parts in a turbine type of engine of similar power would be between those in the reciprocating and in the jet engines.

desired shape. Minute scratches in the finish of a part cause rejections because the high stress in operation may bring a failure, much in the way that a scratch on a sheet of a glass enables it to be "cut" as desired.

Such examples emphasize the generally recognized fact that aircraft engines require very high standards of quality in manufacturing processes, compared with such mass production industries as the automobile industry. What is not generally recognized is the extent of the resulting difference in manufacturing methods. It is not alone a question of great care in conducting production operations. The number of operations is greatly increased, and inspections become more frequent and more severe. For instance, under conditions of volume production, the fork connecting rod of one of the military aircraft engines, weighing 4¾ pounds, requires 90 operations to machine the forging to final dimensions and surface finish. One hundred inspections take place. A conventional connecting rod for an automotive engine, weighing 2½ pounds, requires but 25 operations and 30 inspections.

One further result of the requirement of precision is the large proportion of manufacturing effort that is consumed by rejections. Such rejections occur at all the stages in the manufacturing process, even after assembly. The testing of a completed automobile engine is accomplished by a brief "run in." By contrast an aircraft engine as it leaves the so-called "green" assembly line, fully assembled, is connected to a bank of delicate measuring devices in a test cell and run for a period of hours on a schedule of outputs which taxes its capacities to the full. This is the "green run." Following this test, the engine is almost completely torn down and each part is inspected. Any defective part is replaced and the engine reassembled on the "final" assembly line. Even if its green run is perfect in all respects, the engine is put back into a test cell for a "final run." If a part is replaced, a "penalty run" is required. Furthermore, even after the experimental stage has been passed and regular production has gone on for some time, a significant percentage of parts is rejected after final assembly, thus wasting all the man-hours that have been expended to make the parts and to assemble them into engines. This loss is an indirect but inevitable result of the military necessity to get maximum reliability and maximum performance in combat.

Thus, in summary, engines as well as airframes are complex products, and, as a result, their manufacture is far more difficult an undertaking than the manufacture of most articles used in volume during peacetime. Although the production techniques used by the mass production industries can be more readily adapted to engines than to airframes, the differences between aircraft engines and such products as automobile engines are sufficiently great so that the production methods of the automobile and other similar industries had to be substantially modified before they could be used in engine manufacture.

Wartime Changes in Production Processes

The processes used in manufacturing any product depend not only on the product itself but also on the volume of output. The vast increase in airframe and engine output between 1940 and 1944 required far more than a mere duplication of the processes and tooling used in the earlier year. It required a revolutionary approach to the basic methods of production . . . . In order to make this analysis easier to follow, the method of producing airframes and engines in 1940 will first be contrasted with the very different processes in use when production reached its peak in 1944.

1940 Job Shops

Although they dealt with very different operations, the airframe and engine builders of 1940 were similar in that their processes were adjusted to the existing small-scale demand for their output. Their products were "handmade," parts were produced in "lots" (or "batches"), and the plant was a "job shop."

"Handmade" Products—By using the term "handmade," production men imply that parts are not interchangeable and hence a certain amount of finishing work is required in assembly to fit them properly with others. In some cases when machined parts were used in engines and airframes in 1940, the type of fitting that would typically occur during assembly consisted of such operations as grinding, lapping, or reaming. In other cases, selective assembly was practiced: parts were matched in relation to size. For instance, a shaft that was slightly oversize might be matched with an oversized bearing. A major reason for this fitting and selection was that many parts were machined without adequate jigs or fixtures. Thus the term "handmade" also implies that the parts of the product are made by methods that rely on the skill of the individual machine operator.

Both the fabrication and the assembly of the sheet-metal parts of an airframe in the prewar years could also be characterized as "handmade" in many respects. Because of small volume of output and the frequency of change in design, the key characteristics of prewar aircraft tooling were simplicity, inexpensiveness, and flexibility. Such temporary qualities of tooling meant that relatively skilled shop workers were required.

The processes for forming sheet aluminum were not fully developed in 1940 so that the degree of shrinkage of formed parts was not well known. As a result, parts reaching the assembly floor varied in dimension to such an extent that much filing, bending, forcing, and reforming were necessary. Also, because of these variations, a great deal of drilling was left until the two pieces to be riveted together could be held in the proper relationship.

Production in "Lots"[6]—Another characteristic of small-volume aircraft production in 1940 was the manufacture of parts in small lots or batches. By producing in this manner, manufacturers made the most efficient use of general purpose machine tools, presses, and other factory equipment with small volumes of final output. In "lot" production a machine that is capable of handling various types of jobs, such as a milling machine or a drop hammer, is set up for a needed production operation and a "lot" of parts is run off. Perhaps a month's needs will be processed in a few days through the particular operation. The existing setup is then torn down, and another job is set up and run.

Such a scheme of production fits well into the small-volume manufacture of a variety of products, since it permits setup and capital costs to be absorbed in an efficient manner. Even under war conditions, lot production is the most feasible plan for producing some sheet-metal and machined airframe parts because of the wide diversification of parts and the relatively small production runs on any one operation.

Prewar assembly of both engines and airframes was handled on a lot basis. There was little attempt to break the complete assemblies down into even major subassemblies. Nor was there much attempt to establish flow through progressive assembly operations. Rather, airframes and engines alike were usually erected in one position on the assembly floor.

"Job Shops"—A "job shop," such as that operated by the average prewar airframe and engine manufacturer, was a general purpose shop. Its keynote was flexibility. It was usually made up of general purpose equipment, so arranged that similar kinds of equipment were grouped together. It could handle a variety of production assignments, as well as produce experimental parts or assemblies as required. But it was geared to intermittent production in lots which, together with the equipment

---

[6] Often referred to as "job lot" production.

arrangement, caused the flow of production to be sluggish. The sheet-metal job shop of the prewar airframe builders and the machining job shops of the prewar engine makers were well suited to the low-volume needs in the period prior to 1940 and probably will be well suited to their needs in the postwar period.

1944 Line Production
In order to make possible the rapid increase in rate of output required by the war, the aircraft companies began to grope for a new manufacturing technique as early as 1940. This new technique was "line production," well known in many branches of American industry but new to most of the aircraft manufacturers. Line production is characterized by a controlled flow of the product through work areas in which balanced operations have been laid out in a progressive sequence. By 1944, all major airframe and engine companies were applying these basic principles.

The most dramatic evidence of line production in 1944 was the arrangement of equipment in both airframe and engine plants so that a progressive sequence of operations could be carried out. This arrangement of equipment constituted the first element needed to achieve quantity production. Channels were established so that production could flow without the back-tracking so characteristic of job shop work. Plant layouts at home and branch airframe plants quickly assumed the outward characteristics of line production by their provision of assembly lines, although it took several years in most cases to approach a really steady flow. The assembly department received the most attention because it was the bottleneck operation in the process of making airframes. It is significant to note that most Midwest branch plants were designed as long, slender buildings to accommodate progressive assembly lines. On the other hand, engine companies concentrated on parts manufacture since this constituted a more difficult problem for them than assembly, and their plants tended to be square. Progressive machining operations became the rule. Special purpose, multistation machines and arrangement of other equipment to form short production lines for parts were characteristic of engine production in 1944.

Mere physical rearrangement of the old job shop could not alone make possible the meeting of wartime schedules. Controlled flow was the second important element needed to achieve the peak production of 1944. Steady flow along the final assembly lines required careful production control in the assembly, subassembly, and fabricating departments. Scheduling assumed new prominence. In order to supply assembly lines with the thousands of parts entering into aircraft production, an enormous amount of detailed clerical work was required. It was necessary to schedule and follow up each part in accordance with the over-all production schedule. When assembly lines were first established, production was sporadic, particularly in the case of the airframe plants. A great deal of pressure was brought to bear toward the end of each month to meet the schedule for the month, with the result that airplanes were turned out at a greater rate during the last few days than was called for on the schedule. This end-of-month rush often depleted available supplies of certain parts and components so that very little if any output could be attained in the first few days of the next month and deliveries of spare parts were affected. Then, as parts were expedited out of the fabrication or subassembly departments, pressure was again applied to assembly, and the rate of output increased. Continual development of production control techniques ultimately smoothed out the process.

The third essential element in the peak production year of 1944 was the careful balancing of operations in each production line. The key to steady output from the special purpose equipment of the engine manufacturers was close balance of the various operations performed in a progressive sequence. Likewise, in the assembly lines of the airframe manufacturers, the various feeder and final assembly lines were so geared together that each production line turned out the right number of components to maintain balance with the others. In both cases assemblies and processes were broken down and arranged in balanced operations, usually in accordance with time standards.

The attainment of the above basic principles of line production had to be realized in spite of frequent changes in design and in schedules of finished units and spare parts. Changes were particularly disruptive in connection with the activities of tooling up, laying out the plant, and controlling production and materials. But such changes had their most profound effect when line production techniques were introduced. Prior to the war, standardization of design and steadiness of scheduled rate had been considered fundamental prerequisites to line production. The success of the mass production industries had been built in large measure on their ability to call a halt to changes prior to large-scale output so that carefully developed plans could be put into effect without serious interruption. Obviously, a rigid approach of this sort was impossible in aircraft production during the war. The fact that the aircraft industry was ultimately able to introduce a high degree of flexibility into production procedures, and thereby to make effective use of line production techniques in spite of change, constituted an outstanding contribution to production management.

* * *

In summary, many of the changes in engine and airframe manufacturing processes between 1940 and 1944 could be classed as differences in kind, not just differences in degree. While techniques were borrowed from other industries, the special characteristics of airframes and engines made it impossible to adopt the established techniques of any other industry without revisions. To meet wartime production goals, the manufacturers of airframes and engines were not just forced to do, on a vastly greater scale, a job that they had already been doing in peacetime. They had to do an essentially different job which neither they nor others had ever done before.

5. Wartime Performance of the Industry

The wartime performance of the aircraft industry was one of the greatest production feats of all times. On January 7, 1942, President Roosevelt requested that aircraft production be increased to 125,000 units in 1943. Although the industry did not produce that many aircraft in 1943, in terms of airframe weight it produced more than the equivalent because of the greater concentration in production of larger, heavier aircraft in 1943.

The sharp rise in efficiency of production, expressed in terms of increases in pounds of airframe weight produced per worker, and the spirit of co-operation between thousands of firms that contributed to this production feat, were remarkable. Co-operation among prime contractors, subcontractors, and licensee firms was facilitated because there was hardly any necessity to compete with one another; the demand for aircraft was usually well in excess of any one firm's capacity to supply the product.

The incentive of higher wages increased the number of workers in the industry, and the expectation of larger profits facilitated both expansion and co-ordination of the business enterprises. In addition, there was an observable patriotic dedication which unquestionably furthered the accomplishment of the task confronting both labor and management.

Reginald M. Cleveland and Frederick P. Graham, the editors of the Aviation Annual of 1945, *describe the remarkable performance of the aircraft industry up through 1944, the peak production year of World War II, in the following article.*

Aviation Manufacturing Today in America*
Reginald M. Cleveland and Frank P. Graham

The first year of war for the American aviation industry was the year of promise. By the same token, 1944 looms as its year of abundant fulfillment. The aviation manufacturers pledged themselves after Pearl Harbor to become the arsenal of democracy's air power, and that pledge is being splendidly redeemed.

The price of its redemption has been high. The industry's financial security was the first casualty of its incredible expansion, and even this sacrifice was but a single installment. The balance is being settled now only because American aviation workers, those in shirt sleeves and overalls alike, are persevering at tasks no longer fresh or stirring.

Like the fighting forces they serve, they have always done the difficult immediately and asked only a little longer to do the impossible. The "impossible," in their case, was the tenfold increase in their industry's production and the "little longer" required for its attainment was less than two years. United States wartime plane output is doubly historic. Even as early as 1943, American aviation was the greatest single industry in the world, and the weapons which rolled from its production lines were the greatest single factor in winning the most devastating war ever fought.

The stabilization of production in mid-1944, only twenty-eight months after the President's demand for 125,000 planes a year, offered the final proof of aviation's real accomplishment on the home front. It is lamentably true that there were some for whom the industry's triumph spelled only a chance to point a decrying finger at every cutback in specific production quotas. They were the noisy few who had forgotten that the goal was the attainment of output sufficient to permit the word cutback to have a practical meaning. The vast majority of aviation workers, loyal to their fighting sons and husbands overseas, know that it is backlogs, not cutbacks, that may endanger final victory. And those same men and women are unstintingly laboring to bring about the greatest cutback of all, the end of the war.

They are not unaware that the coming of peace may challenge their industry's very existence. Every aircraft manufacturer in the nation has been grappling with postwar problems since 1943. Some progress has been made in their solution, but no one expects that the vast

---

* Reprinted by permission of the publishers from Reginald M. Cleveland and Frank P. Graham (eds.): *The Aviation Annual of 1945* (Garden City: Doubleday, Doran & Co., 1944), pp. 75–89.

machinery for making swords can be turned to beating out plowshares, as it were, without painful economic dislocation. Aviation production must be cut not less than 90 per cent during the first two years of peace. The manner in which this reduction is made, now being blueprinted, is related to the whole American economy. Its success or failure is of the same magnitude as was the earlier problem of conversion to war.

But it is important that no preoccupation with the challenge ahead obscure our gratification at the near-miracle of the industry's past and present performance. Only searching hindsight into how its war job was done will provide the true measure of aviation's potential ability to meet any tests, including the unprecedented problem foreseen after victory.

Let us look at the current production picture first in terms of production statistics.

The 1943 aircraft production total was 85,946 planes; the 1944 quota is better than 110,000 planes, and there is every reason for confidence that the quota will be met. These figures have erroneously been taken to indicate only a 25-per-cent increase in production between the second year of war and the third. To correct this miscalculation it is necessary to remember how much the manufacturers' definition of "an airplane" has changed within that same year. The typical airframe (less its engine) of 1943 weighed a little over four tons; a similar hypothetical craft of 1944 would weigh better than five. In terms of pounds of airframes accepted (the only logical index of production) the 1943 total is 741 million, the 1944 quota approximately an even billion. Thus our 1944 production will be again a third as great as it was in the preceding year, a circumstance which should effectively answer those who aver that the war is won. It is not even all over but the fighting; there is still a production battle ahead.

The altered character of 1944 production has been dictated by the new emphasis on the most needed combat types, all of which are heavier than their predecessor models—of the 163,000 planes built between 1941 and 1943, only 105,000 were tactical types; most of the remainder were lighter training aircraft. The virtual cessation of the training-plane-building program in March 1944 has meant that floor space and personnel used by trainer manufacturers are now freed to undertake construction of larger planes. Moreover, in factories where current and "super" warplanes were once constructed side by side, the weightier and more powerful new plane has entirely superseded the earlier model.

Thus the numbers of planes being produced in 1944 are only slightly higher than those built in 1943—a monthly rate of 9,000 compared to 7,172—but their total weight is up to 50 per cent greater.

A unique compilation of statistics released by the War Production Board early in 1944 dramatizes the present trend. The WPB calculated plane output for 1941–44 on the basis of the sizes, types, and proportions produced in 1942, the year when the 125,000-plane goal was established. The Board estimated that the aircraft produced in 1943 were the equivalent of 122,000 1942-type planes, and that more than 100,000 planes due to be made in 1944 would be the equivalent of about 167,000 1942-type aircraft. In short, the WPB made plain the fact that the industry's productive capacity had not only achieved the presidential goal but had substantially exceeded it.

The figures above apply to the industry's over-all output in terms of twelve-month periods. If that output is totaled June 1940 (the date when war-plane construction for our Allies began) to December 1943, three and a half years encompassing its full war expansion, the resultant figure is even more significant. Consider that the United States war expenditures over a similar length of time were announced by the Treasury at two hundred billion dollars. Aircraft supply contracts, not including armament or instruments, were valued at forty-eight billion, fully one quarter, when those factors are included, of the whole cost of war. The following table shows the distribution of contracts in leading war-production areas for the 1940–1943 period:

(Figures are expressed by thousands of dollars)

Hartford	$1,892,996
Buffalo	2,641,750
Nassau County	2,100,057
Newark–Jersey City	3,070,137
Baltimore	1,660,678
Chicago	1,338,165
Indianapolis	1,373,574
Kansas City	1,201,613
Wichita	1,303,910
Dallas–Fort Worth	1,553,793
Los Angeles	6,139,819
San Diego	2,631,092
Detroit	3,372,895
Seattle–Tacoma	1,881,983

These figures and those on the foregoing pages are at the moment one of the most important sets of statistics in the world, because they mean that we in America have the tools and the know-how to hold global aerial supremacy for the duration. Beside them, however, we must put another set of figures, one which describes not how many planes are being built but how well we have learned to build them. These are the computations that will be studied long years after the war is over. They are the figures which measure what has been learned—from aviation's gigantic effort—about the business of making goods—in other words, about manufacturing. Subject of perhaps the greatest lesson of all has been production efficiency, literally increased ten- to twenty-fold in the past three years.

One example pointed up by analyses from official sources concerns the labor force required to construct our incredible total of aerial weapons. Throughout 1943, the number of United States aviation workers rose to 1,500,000; yet during the ensuing year—despite the projected increase in their production quota—only a few hundred thousand additional men and women were to be added to the force. For the average monthly weight output per employee, which was twenty-eight pounds in 1941, is now close to 125 pounds. In other words, while an aircraft builder could have easily lifted with one hand the "pieces of airplane" he processed each month in 1941, the 1944 yield from his monthly labor will be well over two thirds his own weight.

This instance is only one proof of the industry's efficiency. A similar calculation, recently made public by the Aircraft War Production Council, describes the changing relationship between mass production and man-hours needed to turn out a single unit. The AWPC cited the case history of a typical fighter plane from the first to the thousandth production model. Every doubling of the total number built meant a cut of almost 75 per cent in man-hours required. The same time and effort expended to construct the first plane built twenty planes, once a thousand units had been produced. Here is the Council table in full, with the center column indicating design changes incorporated in the aircraft without interruption to its assembly line:

```
   1st plane—Model "A"—157,000 man-hours
  10th plane—Model "A"— 59,000 man-hours
  13th plane—Model "B"— 59,000 man-hours
  90th plane—Model "B"— 50,000 man-hours
 100th plane—Model "C"— 26,500 man-hours
 700th plane—Model "C"— 19,500 man-hours
1000th plane—Models "C" to "F"—7,800 man-hours
```

The production history of one four-motored bomber type mentioned by the AWPC demonstrates the same point. The first aircraft required 200,000 man-hours for construction; the 1000th plane took 22,500, and the 2000th only 13,000. In this case the amount of labor which went into building one of the earliest units is now sufficient to produce sixteen airplanes.

Another criterion of production efficiency is the price of the finished article. It may seem strange that cost should be introduced as a measure of wartime manufacturing, for dollars-and-cents economy is rarely recognized as a military consideration. Yet despite the fact that making airplanes has been incomparably more important since 1941 than making them cheaply, virtually every plane built in 1944 cost the taxpayer from 20 to 40 per cent less than the same plane constructed two years before. Had the AAF made its 1943 and 1944 plane purchases in 1942 (or had their matériel been manufactured by the methods of that year), the bill would have been higher by some fifteen billion dollars.

The Army Air Forces recently revealed the story of its B-24 Liberator purchases between 1942 and 1944. In March of the earlier year the AAF ordered twelve hundred B-24s at a price of $238,000 apiece. Exactly two years later forty-five hundred additional B-24s were contracted for, each to cost $137,000. The saving involved is roughly $100,000 on every airplane, a total of close to half a billion dollars for the later order.

Because Consolidated Vultee is at once the largest producer and one of the most efficient producers of airplanes in the world, the B-24 does not represent an entirely typical case. All war matériel will not be proportionately reduced in price; some aircraft costs may even rise again as cutbacks affect production rates. But the know-how which is represented by the efficiency practiced today in aviation manufacturing can never be lost. The industry has mastered new methods and systems by which far fewer man-hours and fewer dollars will build far more airplanes than ever before. This is a net gain for aviation so great that it deserves to be termed revolutionary. No matter what economic or political trends develop, the war-won knowledge possessed by the industry about the physical job of producing aircraft is a positive profit of the highest importance. Like the fighting forces, aviation manufacturing has carried out a great research with conspicuous success.

Aviation's Empires of Production

The technical empires of American warplane production can be numbered only by the score. The high degree of their interdependence, which we will describe more fully later, only enhances their individual accomplishments. The details of each major company's facilities and production have been withheld from the public at various times to make our enemies' intelligence task more difficult, but it is interesting to review, in a general way, the nature of each large aviation manufacturer's contribution to our air power.

In the summer of 1944 fifteen airframe builders were turning out twenty-three types of combat aircraft. The Boeing Company was building both Fortresses and Superforts at an ever-accelerating rate, while the vast Consolidated Vultee (Convair) empire turned out both Liberators and Fortresses primarily for the AAF and lesser numbers of Catalina and Coronado patrol bombers for the Navy. Lockheed's "plant A," once the Vega Aircraft Company, performed a major share of Fortress production, simultaneously turning out Ventura Navy search planes.

North American had greatly increased its output of Mitchell medium bombers, and Martin was constructing redesigned Marauders on a somewhat smaller scale, alongside Navy Mariner patrol aircraft.

The only light land-based bomber in production was the Douglas Havoc, but Douglas was beginning large-scale construction of the Navy's new carrier-based TBD torpedoplane, successor to the famous Dauntless. Other Navy shipboard bombers in quantity production included the TBF Avenger, built by Grumman, and the Curtiss Helldiver.

Lockheed, North American, and Republic dominated fighter-plane production. Lightnings were built in record-breaking quantity, with Mustangs and Thunderbolts not far behind. Curtiss-Wright's Warhawk production, which has mounted to ten thousand units since 1938, was first rumored suspended after that figure had been reached; actually, the plane was redesigned and limited production resumed. At Northrup production of the Black Widow P-61 night fighter began. Hellcat fighters for the Navy were being built at Grumman, and the new F7F was being readied for production. Vought Sikorsky was turning out Corsairs, as was the new Goodyear plant near Akron.

Prime contractor for transport aircraft was Douglas, whose many divisions were producing Skytrains, Skytroopers, and Skymasters (two- and four-engined DC types) literally by the thousands. The Curtiss-Wright factories were turning out Commando transports as well as combat aircraft, and considerable numbers of Consolidated's bomber output were being modified for transport use.

Six prewar "middleweight" airframe manufacturers—Beech, Cessna, Fairchild, Fleetwing, Stearman, and Ryan—completed training-plane contracts in 1944, then turned to making subassemblies for combat and transport craft. Most of these companies held limited contracts for trainer and light transport plane replacements.

Observation, liaison, and ambulance craft were being built by the prewar lightplane companies, Taylorcraft, Aeronca, and Piper, and a similar plane, the Sentinel, was in production at Convair. These and several other lightplane makers, including General Aircraft, joined with the Waco Company in producing gliders on a large scale.

Among the power-plant manufacturers, Pratt and Whitney and Wright Aeronautical continued to hold their dominant position. They built tens of thousands of engines in the 1200–1800-h.p. range, and thousands of even larger units. The newest P & W plant at Kansas City was completed in May 1944. Its output was rated at three million horsepower per month, and the plant manufactured only the model 2800-C, 2100-h.p. radial-power unit. Production of the 1200–1500-h.p. Allison in-line engine pioneered during the early months of the war continued high throughout the year. The Ranger inverted in-line engines built by Fairchild were also mass-produced. Substantial quantities of smaller engines were produced by Jacobs, Continental, and Lycoming, and some of this output was used to power heavy gliders.

The Hamilton Standard propeller, with hydraulic pitch controls, and the Curtiss Electric propeller were the two principal types of airscrews produced throughout the year. Perhaps the outstanding engineering accomplishment of the year among airscrew manufacturers was the development, by Curtiss-Wright Propeller Division, of the first practical method of quantity production of hollow steel blades for combat use. The C-W Division built half again as many units during 1943 as during 1942.

Other major propeller manufacturers likewise greatly increased both research activities and production. Prominent among these were the Aeroproducts Division of General Motors and the American Propeller Corporation, a subsidiary of the Aviation Corporation. Both organizations located in Ohio, bringing mass propeller production to the Middle

West for the first time. There were fourteen other United States firms engaged in propeller design and assembly throughout 1943-44.

Titans in the instrument field were Sperry Gyroscope, RCA, Western Electric, Kollsman, Pioneer, and Bendix. Their output of the fully automatic devices—pilots, gun sights, bomb sights, engineering and navigation aids, and other devices—still must remain one of the untold stories of the war. However, together with a number of smaller although no less enterprising instrument manufacturers, these companies developed electronic research to the status of a full-fledged science.

Here are the big names—and the big jobs—of recent aircraft production. This brief recital of their current assignments, however impressive, tells only part of their story. Some of the missing chapters have recently been written, and they make significant reading to students of both aviation and manufacturing. For the industry's trade secret (if a state of mind can be called a secret) is contained in their pages, and paradoxically, it is identical with that of the fighting forces; in a word, teamwork.

While armies and navies studied the integration of their many components into a single striking force, aviation on the home front labored over the integration of its component industries into one superior production force. Teamwork between titans of industry, like that between generals and admirals, is now more than a password or principle. The men who run American aviation today think not in terms of how many planes can be rolled out of one plant; they consider first the potential of all the mines, mills, factories, and assembly lines which may be involved. They know that the sequence of building aircraft begins far behind the production line and sometimes thousands of miles away from it. Wherever the flow raw materials and parts to manufacturing is dammed, the flow of airplanes similarly falters. And so it does no good to tool an aircraft factory for its job until the whole team, the industries-in-partnership with wartime aviation, is ready to make its contribution. Conversely, the value of their output may be negated unless aviation manufacturing is set up to absorb at once what each produces.

These principles are not stated here because they are new but because they have a vast new meaning. Intricate timing of production schedules between a dozen major industries has been established. This teamwork literally involves millions of men and billions of dollars' worth of factories. It is no less significant than the intricate timing of an invasion operation; it is only less dramatic, somehow, to read that a precision gear made in Buffalo today will be installed in a subassembly at Detroit tomorrow and become part of a plane aloft over California ten days hence than it is to peruse the reports of cruisers supporting tanks or parachutists aiding the artillery.

Teamwork within the empire of airplane building first made news in 1942, when competition-as-usual between manufacturers ceased utterly. Through the medium of the regional war-production councils each company literally opened its files to the others. Every tool and jig, every scrap of technical knowledge about plane production, became the common property of the entire industry. This might be termed a sort of horizontal co-operation, by which the existing aviation industry was unified for the immense task ahead. By the summer of 1943 many companies were making aircraft designed by their former competitors; the Flying Fortress, for instance, was being built by Convair and Vega as well as Boeing. Moreover, scores of factories were in the unique position of being run by one management yet producing parts for another. Two of the many examples were the Fairchild plant, turning out bomber control surfaces for Martin, and the Newark Brewster factory, where Consolidated Catalina fabric-covered parts were made.

Intermanagement teamwork extended at once to other manufacturing industries. Ford began the Willow Run plant to build Liberators, and Goodyear Tire and Rubber erected a factory to turn out V-S Navy Corsairs. The Kaiser and Higgins "booms" occurred, and the Higgins plant, after one false start, began high production of Curtiss Commandos. In Grand Rapids, Michigan, fifteen furniture makers united to form a single glider-producing company.

This horizontal teamwork is more than a war phenomenon, and its influence has pervaded far beyond the confines of the aviation industry proper. The National Aircraft War Production Council, formed in May 1943, by merging the several regional councils, has led to a significant liaison between government and management. During its first year the NAWPC engaged in fifty-four activities, forty-seven of which were primarily direct services to federal agencies. Only the remaining seven had to do with the internal organization of the national council itself. Virtually every phase of aircraft manufacturing, from determination of congested production areas for President Roosevelt to arranging gasoline rations for aircraft workers, is represented in the NAWPC's annual report. Besides numerous conferences with Army, Navy, and WPB officials, the council dealt with Selective Service, the National Housing Administration, the War Food Administration, the Director of Canadian Aircraft Production, the Department of Labor, the Foreign Economic Administration, the U.S. Office of Education, the Veterans' Bureau, the Securities and Exchange Commission, and the Truman Committee.

However, the true measure of the War Production Council's success lies less in its individual operations than in the industry's decision to perpetuate the form of the Council into peacetime. This decision was announced in Los Angeles on April 26, 1944, when two new regional manufacturing divisions of the Aeronautical Chamber of Commerce, patterned closely after the East- and West-coast AWPCs, were established. This move, marking the final re-organization of the Chamber, will make it the greatest single force within the industry. Thanks to the war expedient of the councils, the Chamber has at last achieved a unity.

Turning back again to the production record of the current year, this encouraging harmony between the industry's leaders, tremendously significant though it is, should not be regarded as a panacea for management's multifold problems. The plants of prewar large companies had mushroomed uncontrollably by the middle of 1943, and new projects, despite their acreage, ran into temporary but very real difficulties. Monthly products totals were sometimes below the calculated output of the industry as a whole.

Aviation production engineers, who for the first year of war had concentrated on multiplying the efficiency of individual assembly lines and even individual operations, now attacked the over-all problem. They looked first at the old established companies, distended as to be almost unrecognizable. Here they found a multitude of departments side by side, each tooled and qualified to do a particular operation, each with its own executives. The overwhelming majority of men and women who served each department were working at their unquestionable peak capacity, delivering the volume of work which the engineers themselves had determined and sometimes exceeding these quotas. Yet the age-old phenomenon of mass-production efficiency was still evident; in the departments where thousands of similar units were produced by simplified methods the amount of work which one employee could do was more than the same person might turn out by the obviously less streamlined methods of a smaller shop. The answer was plain: reorganize the plans so that there were no more comparatively small shops. At first glance this conclusion does not appear to be very helpful, for floor space was critically short and new manpower likewise low. Organizing only "big" departments might seem to require both extravagantly.

But it did not work out quite that way. First, the planners reviewed the function of each department to choose those which performed operations peculiar to aviation production. Studies of this nature had been made before, first to help the personnel office set up its training program, later to find and break whatever bottlenecks developed. But the most recent survey was even more comprehensive. The engineers were trying to find which departments performed such involved and precise work that only the prime contractor or another company with equal aviation experience was capable of supervising its operations. Surprisingly, the planners found only three such departments: experimental engineering, final assembly, and, in the case of airframe manufacturers, flight testing. All other steps in aircraft production could be assigned to companies with relatively limited background in the field.

These, then, were the only activities which had to be carried on at the established plane-building centers. These were the big departments essential to proper organization of an aircraft manufacturer. Regardless of the floor space and manpower problems, they could not be delegated to newcomers.

But what of the departments whose locations and workers were gobbled up by expansion of such essential activities? Here, too, the engineers had the answer—subcontracting, on a scale never before considered. They had been subcontracting between one another, as has been mentioned, for some time. But throughout the fall of 1943 and into 1944 this subcontracting assumed the proportions of a pooling of tools, skills, and workers. The factories best equipped to do a particular job did an increasing share of the whole industry's work along those lines, and accordingly reaped the efficiency of ever-greater production. And non-aviation contractors who had hesitantly accepted small orders of aviation parts when the war began confidently expanded in their new line. Once assured of a high, steady demand for a product (usually a subassembly) which they themselves had learned to make efficiently, they became in effect one big department of the prime contractor who took their output. Moreover, new subcontractors by the score joined the aviation industry. Some, like those in the southern California area, went into large-scale aviation-parts manufacture because they were geographically located close to their customer. Others, hundreds of miles distant, shifted from making many items (some for aviation companies, others non-aviation material) to manufacturing a single unit or several units, thus increasing their efficiency tremendously. In short, the subcontractors as a body did the work of those prime contractors' small departments which had been dispossessed when the final big plant expansion was completed.

This classic pattern was first described in detail by the AAF Matériel Command in November 1943, when the production of Lockheed Lightnings was ordered increased. In its announcement of the new program the AAF said:

> When Lockheed was first called upon to step up production of Lightnings, the situation was anything but encouraging. The Burbank plant was already working at capacity and could not accommodate additional personnel, even if workers had been obtainable. Expansion of plant facilities was also out of the question, not only because of the manpower shortage but also because of the time element involved.
>
> Accordingly, a study was made to find which components of the plane could be farmed out to other aircraft-structure manufacturers without interrupting the flow of such parts at Burbank. Meanwhile, one of the first components was subcontracted to a local firm to establish a *modus operandi*. It was decided that, although the first contract would not aid the local manpower situation, it would be helpful in relieving the pressure at Lockheed and in making possible the adoption of a standard operational procedure.
>
> The local firm contracted to make the leading edges for the P-38 and made plans to go into immediate production. Inasmuch as Lockheed had previously manufactured such principal components in its own plant, no outside liaison organization existed as far as aircraft structures were concerned. It was highly necessary that one be established, since the shifting of principal aircraft components to another plant involves close engineering liaison, the transfer of tooling and a certain amount of fabricated parts in the early stages, the computing of flow time both for fabrication and shipments, and the scheduling of critical parts. Moreover, it was felt that experience with a local organization would be of value before reaching out East.
>
> Negotiations are now being carried on for other items.
>
> Prominent among these is the complete power-plant subassembly. It is intended to place this unit with an Eastern firm experienced in sheet-metal fabrication and assembly. This subassembly will consist of the engine, engine mount, and all accessories. All pertinent mechanical devices will be thoroughly

tested so that when the unit is received by Lockheed it can readily be attached to the airframe.

It is estimated that the power-plant assembly, if contracted for elsewhere, would save Lockheed in the neighborhood of five thousand employees. The next component under consideration is the wing center section, of high importance also.

It is apparent that when these schedules of subcontracting are in full operation, Lockheed at Burbank will be more of an assembly plant than it is at present.

Under the new setup, AAF officials believe the plant will be able to double the output with less effort than is now being expended to produce at the present rate. In fact, they have so much confidence in the plan that they are now working out similar arrangements with other local airframe manufacturers.

Their confidence has evidently not proved misplaced, for many production empires have undergone similar reorganization since the "Lockheed plan" was introduced. The net effect of the new and broader system was twofold. First, it put the aviation industry more nearly on a truly mass-production basis. The earlier efforts in this direction, those during the first year of war, had produced a mass of airplanes; the methods of that frenzied transitional period had varied from the most advanced to the almost primitive. For instance, some planes were put together on mechanized assembly lines by highly skilled labor with simple hand tools; in other cases the workpieces were moved by hand from one highly modern and complex tool to the next. The subcontracting was then equally haphazard, for no one knew the capabilities of manufacturers without aviation experience. Actually, airplane manufacturers did not characterize this large-scale production as a mass operation at all until 1944, preferring to use their own phrase, quantity production. They then maintained correctly that aircraft can never be built with the minimum of human attention needed on a prewar automobile assembly line, for instance, but the aviation industry has now successfully wedded the old conception of mass production to its own precise needs. The result as we have seen, is ever-rising output and efficiency.

The second impact of this new and close teamwork fell largely on prime contractors, the powerful "big-name" plane producers. Before the war each of their plants was an independent unit, capable of turning raw materials into finished products. Today the firms retain their identity; their familiar names are gloriously and globally known. But none is an airplane builder, or even an engine, propeller, or instrument producer in the strict prewar sense of the word. They are primarily designers and assemblers of these products. Their development departments perform almost all engineering functions—experimental and production—for all of their subcontractors. These vendors, in turn, serve as the manufacturing departments for the prime contractors. Finally, the big plant assembles and tests its product, whether it be a power unit or instrument or a whole plane.

This decentralization of actual manufacturing operations had not been completely carried out by mid-1944. Unless the war is longer and bloodier than appeared likely then, the trend may never reach its fullest expression. However, the length of vendors' pay rolls is roughly twice that of the big-name builders. For every worker under the prime contractor's direction there are another two, nominally under other management, actually making his product by his methods.

Prime contractors and the firms to whom they farmed out a goodly share of their work were not the only companies in wartime aviation. The vendors had their own subcontractors, and sometimes these latter factories, too, split part of their contracts with other plants. That is why the schedules of so many hundreds of factories suddenly had to mesh. The price of unco-ordinated production anywhere could no longer be adjusted by dollars-and-cents penalty payments. It could be measured only by unbuilt airplanes, and these in turn spelled lost Allied lives.

Thus the whole structure of the aviation industry acquired a vertical dimension. The teamwork between big-name companies, the horizontal co-ordination of prime contractors' quotas and methods, had been supplemented by a more comprehensive co-operation. The pattern of subcontracting reached ever closer to general industry; small machine shops as well as vast ore refineries were drawn into the aviation manufacturers' design for victory. Now the problem is to direct the varied output of a dozen industries into a score of narrowing channels, one for each important warplane type. The channels flow to prime contractors' assembly lines, where the multitude of airplane parts built elsewhere can be checked, put together, tested aloft, and finally delivered to the fighting forces.

The Army of the Production Empire

The planners whose work has just been described were the generals of the production battle. They represented both government and management. The misjudgments they did not make could have cost the fight, but they alone could not have won it. Fashioning of the final victory was done by the hands of millions of American workers. Out of their willingness to stay on the job has come the near-miracle of aircraft production. The great majority of these men and women are not working for wages alone; their hours are too long and their duties often too arduous to make this supposition just. They are grateful for good wages, and in the main they are receiving them. But the typical aircraft worker of today recognizes how heavily his son or brother (or her husband or sweetheart) depends on home-front output, and he is determined not to let the fighting forces want for what he makes.

It is regrettable that the multitude who hold their place on the production line should be sometimes represented to the public by those who do not. These have been wildcat strikers and irresponsible labor leaders and other distasteful demonstrations. The relatively few participants have seen their names in the newspapers, while the workers who stayed on their stations more rarely receive public mention. It is these other millions who are the heart and backbone of the industry. They have mastered new and repetitive tasks, and they have done them day in and day out for many months without stint or letup. Some 49 per cent are women, only a few of whom were oriented to manufacturing before the war. These workers and the men with whom they toiled shoulder to shoulder are the Americans who physically made and put together, piece by piece, each one of the 200,000-odd warplanes constructed in this country since Pearl Harbor.

Finding the number of such men and women needed has been the aviation industry's greatest single problem since the fall of 1943. The real crisis occurred on the Pacific coast. During the first six months of that year manufacturers there employed 150,000 men and women—to net only 12,000 new workers.

Reasons for the incredible turnover were not clear, but it was evident that the manpower problem was only secondarily a question of insufficient reserves. Primarily it was a question of holding a higher percentage of employees on the job. A survey by Convair pointed out that of every hundred workers leaving their stations,

15 were drafted;
14 were too ill to continue;
 4 stated that they could not find adequate housing;
18 were dissatisfied with working conditions;
 7 were dismissed; and
43 gave "personnel conditions" as the cause for termination.

Consider the first group, the 15 per cent who were drafted. Actually, Selective Service has been entitled at various times to call some 40 per cent of all engineering personnel, and almost 25 per cent of the toolmakers and inspectors, disregarding for the moment the percentage of eligibles outside the supervisory group. No permanent blanket deferment can be issued for these men, but the subsequent draft laws applying to men over twenty-six have aided immensely in keeping intact the ranks of engineers and other white-collar workers.

The group of employees leaving their jobs for reasons of health cannot be expected to decrease. It may, if the war prolongs itself, grow even larger as workers become fatigued. But the measures taken to safeguard their health are far more comprehensive today than they were a year ago. Safety engineers, staff doctors, nurses, and dietitians are actively helping the men and women who build our airplanes to eat correctly, rest sufficiently, and to observe every safety precaution on the job. Consciousness of the hazards of carelessness away from the plant as well as within it is spreading, and the results have been most encouraging.

The workers who cannot find a place to live are in the minority, despite the wide publicity they have received, according to the Convair report. Several new housing projects, two on the West coast, involving fourteen thousand units have alleviated this national problem somewhat, and the virtual ending of the plant construction program should further aid in its solution. With fewer "floating" labor groups, definite housing plans have been inaugurated by several far-seeing boom municipalities. They know, at last, how many men and women will be in residence for the duration, and this stabilization of the demand for housing is a long first step toward answering it.

The 61 per cent of employees who resigned because they were dissatisfied with working or personnel conditions present the most serious challenge to manpower planners. The so-called "Buffalo plan," first established in the northern New York critical labor area in 1942, was imported to the West coast a year later to guide this pool of workers to stable employment. Co-operation between the War Manpower Commission and the War Production Board is the cornerstone of this plan. The WMC pledges to help find and distribute labor, while the WPB agrees to hold area production quotas to the maximum which the available labor force can hope to turn out. Establishment of a Production Urgency Committee, on which the WPB, Army, Navy, and federal transportation, petroleum and food administrations are represented, is the first step. Then a second and interlocking committee, consisting of WMC and Selective Service officials, is designated. The two organizations join with regional plant managements to make a labor survey of the entire area, while the production committee rates the contracts of various factories according to the urgency with which their output is needed; on the West coast, bombers rated highest, fighters second, trainers last. The United States Employment Service was brought into the picture as soon as the committees had completed their research. All employers agreed to hire only through USES, and the USES officials agreed to refer applicants to various companies only in the order of their urgency rating. Thus an aircraft worker would be directed first to bomber manufacturers, then—only if he failed to find a job at any bomber plant—to fighter builders, and finally to those companies constructing training planes.

There was a second phase of the program which contributed to adjusting "personnel conditions." This was an outright morale-building effort within the factory. Music, lunch-hour entertainment, and the personal appearance of battle heroes using the company's product were the principal means of increasing the employees' satisfaction with their job. Because so many workers' tasks were repetitive by nature, breaks in the routine provided by such devices were wholeheartedly welcomed, and the program is now organized on a national scale. There is no frivolity in this bringing of music and vaudeville onto the production line, for so much of the worker's time is at the mercy of factory routine that he may overlook his need for recreation, unless diversion is provided for him.

Recognition of the relationship between production quotas and available manpower, together with the morale-building program, had materially relieved the labor situation on the West coast by the spring of 1944. The thirty-one prime contractors there had received eight billion dollars' worth of new orders during the six months from October 1943 to March 1944, a substantial increase over the value of their contracts before the manpower crisis, and they were confident that the workers to carry them out would be available "with only minor headaches," as one official put it.

The same story was repeated elsewhere with increasing frequency. Rigid controls similar to those first used on an area basis in the West went into effect in November at Akron, Detroit, and Hartford; and upstate New York, part of New Jersey, and several Midwestern regions similarly adapted the California plan to their needs with good results. In virtually all these once critical areas more pessimism is now felt toward the postwar employment problem that the current manpower situation. However, the psychological threat represented by unrealistic headlines manifests itself sporadically. Military advances are sometimes misinterpreted by workers as invitations to absenteeism. It is only human for a hard-pressed worker to let up when victory seems to loom in sight; his foremen and supervisors and even executives are subject to the same impulse. Moreover, political events sometimes play up to it. Nevertheless, we must recognize this outlet for optimism as what it is: a trap within which production can become surely ensnared. We have the materials and manpower to produce more aircraft faster and more easily than ever before; the only possible limiting factor is the will of the industry as a whole to send them aloft. That will, which has not faltered in the face of far more deadly challenges, must not and shall not waver because the defeat of Germany and Japan begins to brighten the horizon.

6. The Industry's War Record and Postwar Recommendations

The leading role played by American air power in winning World War II is a fact accepted by both sides in the war. It depended on the rapid expansion of productive capacity and production that was achieved by the aircraft industry.

At the end of the war there remained the problems of disposing of surplus aircraft and of developing a policy to insure capability for air superiority in future wars. After World War I available surplus aircraft, on which the country relied, stifled the aircraft industry's development for many years. Domestic five-year programs were of vital assistance in maintaining an industrial nucleus, however, and a demand for aeronautical exports provided an even larger industrial base from which to expand the production of aircraft. Without this base, both the outcome of World War II and the time of it could have been very different.

With the lessons of the World War II experience in mind, various groups recommended unanimously, when the war was over, that the United States actively foster the development of new aircraft for defense, maintain a powerful modern air force, and maintain a high level of productive capacity in the aircraft industry. In the event of a future war, they observed, there would not be sufficient time for the country to develop the air superiority necessary to win.

The following report by the Aircraft Industries Association of America at the end of World War II calls attention to the importance of the role of air power in winning the war, surveys the wartime accomplishments of the aircraft industry, and develops recommendations for a broad defense policy pertaining to the aircraft industry in peacetime.

Aircraft Manufacturing in the United States*
The Aircraft Industries Association of America

The end of World War II makes it possible to present the story of the aircraft-manufacturing industry as a great deal more than simply an annual report. No schoolboy, in this or any other country, is not fully aware of the impact of air power upon our modern way of life. Its devastating effect on modern warfare is told in other chapters of this volume. Its seeming omnipotent power is attested to more graphically and significantly than by any other group by the statements of defeated Axis leaders.

Reichmarshal Hermann Goering, at Augsburg, Germany, on May 11, 1945, said: "The American Air Force made the Allied offensive successful. It was a complete surprise that you could develop a fighter-bomber to fly from England to Berlin and return."

Field Marshal von Rundstedt, on May 5, 1945, said: "The unheard-of superiority of your Air Force made all movement in daytime impossible."

One after another they attested to the overwhelming power of our air forces: Field Marshal Albert Kesselring: "Allied Air Power was the biggest single reason for Germany's defeat." Field Marshal von Kluge: "Every movement of the enemy is protected by its Air Force. He paralyzed all our movements."

And Emperor Hirohito, in his dramatic acceptance of our surrender terms, described the atomic bomb as the principal reason for his capitulation. It was this terrible weapon, delivered on the wings of American bombers, that shattered Japanese hopes of survival and brought to an end nearly seven years of war's carnage.

It was the production of aerial weapons for this greatest of all victories that comprised the wartime role of the aircraft-manufacturing industry. While it was the tremendous courage, skill, and intelligence of our sky warriors that paid off in this crushing defeat, it was equally the knowledge, experience, and hard work of the aircraft industry that provided an overwhelming preponderance of warplanes that made this great victory possible.

It can easily be said that more miracles were wrought in the aircraft industry than in any other producing for war. The reason for this is quite simple: miracles had to be wrought in order that the job be done; there was no alternative. The details of that miracle can be given in a number

---

* Reprinted from Reginald M. Cleveland and Frank P. Graham (eds.): *The Aviation Annual of 1946* (Garden City: Doubleday, Doran & Co., 1945), pp. 87–100.

of ways, but the most obvious and easily understood examples are the total production figures. From January 1, 1940, to August 14, 1945, a total of 300,317 military aircraft was produced by the aircraft-manufacturing industry. Just how many airplanes is that? Well, it is 16,680 complete squadrons, for example, although that number of squadrons was never assembled. It is also one airplane for every 434 men, women, and children in the United States. If parked nose to tail, they would reach a distance equivalent to that between New York and London: more than three thousand miles. The total weight of this gigantic production is more than the combined weight of all the battleships produced for the United States Navy since Pearl Harbor!

This astounding performance is one of the greatest chronicles in the annals of modern industry. Contrary to popular opinion, this great production miracle started even before President Roosevelt's request for sixty thousand airplanes in his message to Congress on January 6, 1942. The industry had already undergone a tenfold expansion made necessary by foreign orders for military types. During 1942 it tripled, and in 1943 it doubled its output. In 1944 it increased production again by nearly 15 per cent. The end of the war in Europe brought extensive reductions in production schedules, and output continued to decline through V-J Day.

In 1938 the industry was operating a total of fifteen air-frame, engine, and propeller plants. By 1940 these had increased to forty-one, and in 1943 the industry expanded to a total of eighty-one factories plus five plants operated in Canada, a total of eighty-six in all. The gross value of these facilities increased from $114,000,000 in 1939 to $3,906,000,000 in December 1944.

One of the greatest bottlenecks solved by the industry in its meteoric expansion was that of manpower. From a working force of only 48,638 in 1939 the industry managed to hire, train, and employ up to a peak of 2,102,000 in November 1943. Mobilization of this giant working force required every known technique of personnel recruiting. Women were urged to leave their kitchens; retired workers came back into the labor market; executives, bank clerks, and laborers worked on night shifts while holding down their normal positions in the daytime. Boys and girls worked after school and during summer vacation. Sound trucks, bands, free shows, special offices in downtown districts, drives to reduce absenteeism, and appeals of all types were used to meet the manpower shortage which persisted up to the date of surrender.

One of the significant surprises of the war has been the magnificent skill, patience, and tenacity of women in war work. During one period (July 1944) 36.9 per cent of the workers in prime contracts were women. At the peak, in November 1943, more than 486,073 women were employed by the aircraft industry. Many changes were wrought by the advent of women. Women personnel councilors were hired, special rest and recreational facilities were installed, and even nursery facilities were added.

Women proved entirely capable in most jobs, the full equal of men in others, and actually superior in certain types of work. Among these latter were tedious and monotonous jobs in which long hours of continuous work of a completely repetitious nature prevailed. The efficiency of women, in terms of output vs. hours, was far higher in all classes than men. Their patriotism and full faith and belief in the efficacy of their job was superior to men's. Fewer interplant transfers were made by women than by men. Men excelled in the heavier types of work as well as those requiring mechanical knowledge, such as subassembly and, particularly, final assembly.

The production job of the industry is difficult to tell in all its manifestations. It was a great deal more than simply building additional plants, hiring additional workers, and thereby producing additional quantities of planes.

Two teams considerably altered this fundamental production equation: the production and engineering teams. It is significant that the output per employee increased from twenty-one pounds in January 1941 to ninety-six pounds in August 1944. At first glance it might appear that this increased output came simply from the employee working harder and putting in longer hours. Although this might conceivably have affected the output, its effect would have been infinitesimal. The principal reason for this increased output was the design, installation, improvement, and perfection of production tools as well as the redesign of airplane parts for speedier fabrication. Thousands of special jigs, dies, fixtures, and special tools were literally "invented" on the job, built in quantity and installed in each of the plants. While the burden of this tooling rested upon production and tooling engineers, many hundreds of thousands of man-hours were saved by suggestions and ideas from the workers themselves. Attractive prizes and war bonds were offered and suggestion boxes placed throughout the plants. Continual effort to simplify production techniques, devise machines requiring less skill to operate, and install systems which speeded production was made and vastly increased output per man-hour achieved.

While maintaining and frequently exceeding accelerated production schedules, the industry introduced into the production line a record total of 150 separate types of military aircraft, and of these basic types more than 417 separate and distinct models and additional thousands of detailed engineering changes. The magnitude of this scientific achievement, as reported by Army and Navy records, is fully realized only when it is considered that it takes an average of four years to design, develop, and produce a new military airplane.

Because of its predominant size and variety of jobs, the Army Air Forces accounted for the larger share of these totals, utilizing 255 models of 97 basic types in 21 separate tactical categories. Naval aviation's role in the war required 162 models of 53 types in 17 different tactical classifications.

Whereas model changes in autos, refrigerators, and other family conveniences are largely for improved style and appearance, aircraft-model changes are "styled" by hard, practical requirements of mass production, combat performance, and field maintenance.

The replacement of machine guns with wing cannon characterizes the modified combat airplane as a "new model." New models also result from the addition of armor plate, rockets, a larger engine, improved oxygen, radio, radar equipment, et cetera. Model changes are made as answers to specific questions, each modification requiring hundreds of thousands of engineering man-hours and millions of dollars in research, planning, testing, tooling, and production engineering.

One type of radial-powered fighter plane had reached the model series "N" and was undergoing constant refinement even as its quantity production continued on schedule at the time of the surrender. The first production model of this plane cost 260,000 engineering man-hours. It has since undergone 189 master changes and 3,000 minor engineering changes at an engineering man-hour cost of nearly three times that expended to bring the first model to its production stage.

These refinements have paid off in increased speed, longer range, and greater combat efficiency. The 417 models of 150 separate aircraft types designed and developed by the aircraft industry for war represent 417 major engineering production problems solved in the face of steady increases in wartime production output.

One tangible result of increased production output and efficiency is the fact that the cost of military aircraft dropped sharply and continuously as their production increased. The cost of a giant, four-engine, long-range bomber dropped from $15.18 per pound to $4.82 per pound, a saving of more than $500,000 on each airplane. The cost of a single-seat fighter plane dropped from $7.41 per pound to $5.37 per pound, a saving of more than $20,000 on each airplane.

The aircraft industry in its prewar years was one of the most competitive in the nation. Companies jealously guarded their new designs, production methods, and "trade secrets." When war came they had only one competitor: enemy aircraft production.

Following Pearl Harbor it was suggested that an aircraft "czar" be appointed, as in the last war, to take complete charge of the tremendous aircraft-production job ahead. But experience during the last war, together with the patriotic unity of the aircraft company leaders, pointed up sharply the disadvantages of such an arrangement. In April 1942 the West Coast manufacturers—Boeing, Consolidated-Vultee, Douglas, Lockheed, Northrop, North American, and Ryan—formed the Aircraft War Production Council for the purpose of setting up a panel for the discussion of mutual problems and for the distribution of know-how among the member companies in order that the fabulous job ahead might be expedited.

This tremendously successful co-ordinating group worked so well that the East Coast manufacturers formed a similar group a few months later, and in April 1943 the two groups were merged into the National Aircraft War Production Council. The smooth teamwork of these councils, composed of the manufacturers themselves, was the greatest single weapon against bottlenecks and production delays.

The record of this group fills tons of volumes, but such accomplishments as the following are typical: by March 1944 more than a million engineering man-hours had been saved by the pooling of research and production technique. More than nine thousand technical reports were exchanged by the West Coast Council alone. A North American landing gear went into the Northrop P-61 Black Widow. A Vultee dive brake went into the North American P-51 Mustang. A Boeing power plant went into the Consolidated B-32 Dominator. Lockheed furnished 380,000 square feet of aluminum alloy sheet to Vultee during a crisis. More than 20,600 items were exchanged plus 45,000 items furnished to companies outside the Council.

Aircraft companies made available their patented products and their engineering know-how to auto, refrigerator, and typewriter firms to help produce planes and engines.

Here is a brief summary of the pooling of production by the major manufacturing units of the nation:

B-29 Superfortress: made by Boeing, Bell, Martin
B-17 Flying Fortress: Boeing, Douglas, Lockheed
B-24 Liberator: Consolidated-Vultee, Douglas, Ford, North American
Corsair: Vought, Brewster, Goodyear
Wildcat: Grumman, General Motors
Avenger: Grumman, General Motors
Helldiver: Curtiss, Fairchild (Canada), Canadian Car & Foundry
P-38 Lightning: Lockheed, Consolidated-Vultee
Pratt & Whitney engines: Pratt & Whitney, Nash-Kelvinator, Buick, Chevrolet, Ford, Continental, Jacobs
Wright engines: Wright, Dodge, Studebaker, Continental
Hamilton Standard propellers: Hamilton Standard, Frigidaire, Nash-Kelvinator, Remington-Rand

Bear in mind that these are simply production of completed articles. Literally hundreds of thousands of firms participated in the production of parts, subassemblies, equipment, and supplies. Even basement workshops were utilized. Aircraft production was truly a national effort.

On V-J Day approximately nine billion dollars in production contracts for the Army Air Forces was canceled. This included more than thirty-one thousand airplanes, spares, and equipment in the amount of seven billion dollars. The net effect of this cutback was the cancellation of approximately 90 per cent of existing contracts. Further contract cancellations followed, bringing the total to approximately 95 per cent of the total. The effect of these cancellations was to lay off approximately 1,100,000 workers, completely close numerous huge plants, and place millions of square feet of facilities and millions of dollars of special tooling into the surplus pile.

The effect of unemployment caused by aircraft-contract cancellations, as in other war industries, was of national concern, but the effect upon the surplus problem was of particular interest to the industry. A total of well over one hundred thousand airplanes is expected to be declared surplus, plus fifty thousand or more spare engines and similar or larger quantities of instruments and equipment. An index to the salability of these airplanes can be gained from the fact that only about 30 per cent of the first forty thousand planes declared surplus were sold or leased. This figure is of particular significance when it is realized that the first types released were the popular prewar lightplane designs of the Grasshopper type. These found a wide and ready market and comprised approximately 90 per cent of the twelve thousand surplus sold. With the bulk of these disposed of and the future surplus declarations due to be nearly 100 per cent combat types, the true magnitude and gravity of the surplus aircraft-disposal program is made clear.

The Surplus Property Board, established for the purpose, is duty bound to realize as great a money recovery on these airplanes as is practical and reasonable. This, at first sight, seems the economic course to follow. It is, however, the short view. The long view presents an entirely different picture.

A graphic example of the long-range danger of holding on to surplus material is provided by the debacle of the Liberty engine following World War I. With thousands of these engines available following the Armistice, they were placed in warehouses. As late as 1932 they were still carried on the Air Corps stock lists and used in operational aircraft, this fourteen years after the Armistice! The effect of this policy resulted in a complete stoppage of experimentation and development on American liquid-cooled engines in so far as this surplus worked as a huge "blanket," stifling all incentive to develop a new design with foreknowledge that it would have no market. The final, long-term result of this policy was that when World War II broke out twenty-one years after the first the United States trailed so far behind the other nations of the world in liquid-cooled engine development that it has not yet fully caught up, even after an extensive and concentrated research and development program on the type.

With Liberty-engine-equipped observation machines operable in the United States up until 1935, incentive for their design and development was nil, and we entered World War II far behind other nations in long-range reconnaissance types, wholly neglected in the peace years due to the surplus policy following World War I.

A third example is the 30-caliber Colt Browning aircraft machine gun, thousands of which were stocked and used up until 1943. While 50-caliber-machine-gun and .20-mm.-cannon development lagged, due to this surplus of 30-caliber machine guns in the United States, other nations—notably Sweden, France, and Poland—forged ahead on aircraft-cannon development, and the German Air Force adopted it shortly afterward.

From the long view, then, the policy of "holding on" to our surplus aircraft constitutes a serious, a grave, and a potent menace to the technological progress of the industry. Small research and experimental contracts are not the solution to the pressing need for keeping ahead of the rest of the world in the science of aviation. This war has taught us that the production line is as essential to an air force as are bombers and fighters in action against the enemy. It is a four-year chasm that must be bridged between an experimental prototype and peak production on a medium bomber. Quantity production of a long-range super-bomber is nearly six years of effort in the future from the original experimental airplane. These chasms can be and must be bridged in peacetime. They cannot be bridged in wartime, for there will be no time in a next war.

Of immediate concern to the industry is the disposal of facilities, tools, and production equipment owned by the government. Of the total of $3,721,000,000 of facilities expansion inaugurated between July 1940 and June 1944, a total of $3,428,000,000 (or about 92 per cent) was federally financed. Prewar privately financed facilities were valued at $114,000,000. Thus, of the total present facilities, the government owns nearly 90 per cent. The disposal possibilities of this vast investment are many. For example, the government may desire to dispose of the total by lease, by sale, or by gift. It may decide to set aside as "stand-by" certain portions of it. It may merely rent or lease certain plants to the present occupants or to possible "foreign" occupants. The importance of an early activation of a broad policy for the disposal of surplus facilities is indicated by the delay in reconversion to peacetime production now being experienced. In most cases the announced "postwar" civilian planes are slightly modified wartime models, the basic structure of which is identical. Since complete assembly lines for the production of these types consist of government-owned tools and equipment, the manufacturers cannot proceed with construction until some disposition is made of these tools. Once a satisfactory arrangement is made for this equipment the assembly lines can proceed as they did before V-J Day.

On the government side of the picture, however, is the necessity for disposal to be carried out along democratic lines, i.e., all interested parties must be given an equal opportunity to participate in the sale of government equipment. The surplus disposal problem, both aircraft and facilities, then, is a complex problem which can be solved only through the establishment and execution of a broad, over-all policy. Military and government leaders have agreed with industry spokesmen that the primary thought in such a policy must be the maintenance and strengthening of the aircraft industry, which constitutes the broad base upon which air power and its two largest components, air force and air commerce, are built.

On the subject of a national air-power policy, upon which the future of the aircraft-manufacturing industry rests, there is some startlingly convincing history. When we entered World War I we were lost in a wilderness of unpreparedness. There were no combat military aircraft in the United States capable of surviving the most cursory aerial battle. We had not developed military aircraft because we had been thinking of the airplane almost solely as a vehicle of commerce in time of peace. In the brief eighteen months of our participation in World War I we tried desperately to make up for years of unpreparedness, but we failed dismally. The record of that debacle is too well known to bear repetition here. But the first searchlight pointing the way to newer, higher ground came in 1925 when the nine-man "Morrow Board" filed its report. This report, filed on November 30, 1925, became a charter for American aviation and resulted in the Air Commerce Act, the Army Air Corps five-year program, and the Naval Aviation five-year program. Here, for the first time, was a national air policy which provided the long-needed impetus that brought a virtual rebirth to aircraft design and manufacture in this country. This report placed the responsibility for military-aircraft procurement with the Army, for naval-aircraft procurement with the Navy, and for commercial-air-transport regulation with the Department of Commerce.

Within a few years American airplanes were among the finest in all the world. Our military planes established scores of world's records, and our transport systems were born, nurtured, and matured as the backbone of the world's air-carrier system. We moved into the 1930's at the high point of our leadership in the air.

In 1934, when American air power seemed destined for rapid expansion, the aircraft-manufacturing industry was set back on its heels by the abrupt cancellation of the air-mail contracts. This, at a time when Hitler was assuming his post as Chancellor of Germany, when Japan was marching in China, and when Italy was expanding its air force to an unprecedented size!

With the military program interrupted, the aircraft industry expanded its foreign sales, plus the small volume of commercial sales in this country. Toward the end of the thirties export amounted to nearly 70 per cent of the total business of the industry. Then came the Arms Embargo Act, cutting off export outlets and, again, rocking the industry back on its heels. It did not commence its recovery until President Roosevelt's executive order permitting the production and delivery of foreign aircraft was enacted. Then, with the signing of the Lend-Lease Act on March 11, 1941, the way was cleared for quantity production of military aircraft for Allied nations. From a production of 2,141 military aircraft in 1939 the output jumped to 6,086 in 1940 and to 19,290 in 1941. Most of this production was for foreign delivery.

It can now be generally known that it was this foreign business that revitalized the American aviation-manufacturing industry, that expanded its facilities, increased its personnel, introduced its mass-production techniques, and provided it with the know-how to roll into high gear when we entered this air war and the demand came for unheard-of quantities of airplanes.

No American must miss this essential fact: as in the last war, we were given time at the outbreak of this war to prepare ourselves for victory. In both wars it was the production of planes of foreign design and the production of planes for foreign delivery that laid the foundation stone for our eventual domestic air force. Time has allowed us to make grave errors in national military thinking in the past two wars. If there is a next war, there may be no time.

General H. H. Arnold, Chief of the Air Forces, Washington, February 27, 1945, said: "Air power is the weapon with which the aggressor in this war first struck and with which future aggressors will strike. The range, speed, and destructive capacity of a powerful air force is such that, given sufficient air superiority, the aggressor can by sudden action disrupt the life of the attacked nation and make difficult the taking of defense measures. Moreover, in this field which the present war has shown to be subject to revolutionary advances, we can only dimly visualize the possibilities of such sudden action in the future. The lesson is too plain for the next aggressor to miss: the United States will be his first target. It is of the utmost importance that our first line of defense, in the air, must be ably manned and fully supplied with modern equipment. The United States must be the world's first power in military aviation."

It is difficult, if not impossible, to separate the problems of the aircraft-manufacturing industry and our national air power as a whole. The industry is an essential part of our air forces and our air commerce. This war has shown how our air power is an essential part of our national life. Obviously there is an inescapable responsibility on the American people and their government to make certain that air power is not lost in the shuffle of reconversion of the aircraft-manufacturing industry.

The seriousness of the need for a sound national air policy to protect our leadership in air power was recognized in a study, "Preserving American Air Power," prepared by Harvard University recently. Excerpts applicable to the immediate problems of the industry include:

> The principle of retaining military power as peace insurance so long as we must live in the midst of an armed world is now generally recognized. How to assure this power, especially in such a rapidly developing field as aviation, is an unanswered question we dare not neglect. Today America not only has the world's largest air force but, to supply the equipment which makes this force possible, has organized a gigantic industrial structure dwarfing even the peacetime automobile industry. These national assets will, however, become liabilities if inadequate planning leads to disorderly contraction.

The Harvard study of air power lists the following seven key questions, which serve to indicate the difficulties involved in preserving our future air power and help to stimulate thinking which ultimately will lead to answers and sound action.

    1. What size peacetime air force should be adopted to meet our military needs and still be economically feasible?
    2. What government policies should be adopted to stimulate a healthy rate of technical progress?
    3. How can a properly balanced and rapidly expansible nucleus of productive capacity be maintained in peacetime?
    4. To what extent should plans for any future wartime expansion rely upon the peacetime aircraft companies and to what extent should such an expansion involve conversion of automobile and other non-aircraft industries?
    5. What role should civil aviation and exports play in supporting our peacetime military-aircraft industry?
    6. What plans for transition from war to peace should be made to assure the preservation of an industry adequate for tomorrow's tasks?
    7. How should the air forces and the government civil agencies concerned with aviation be most effectively organized?

It is not within the province of this chapter to suggest some of the considerations that should enter a discussion of these very pertinent problems, all of which bear directly on the manufacturing industry. However, of particular bearing on the future of the industry and its responsibility to technological leadership of this nation is the necessity for the preservation of the skilled research and development teams and facilities created during the war.

General Arnold, in Washington, on February 27, 1945, said:

"The first essential of the air power necessary in our national industry is pre-eminence in research. There must be a strong and healthy aviation industry building thoroughly modern aircraft and equipment and developing, testing, and experimenting with advanced designs for tomorrow. Segments of industry must be capable of, and ready for, rapid conversion to quantity production."

The aircraft industry, together with the Army, Navy, and government agencies, heartily endorses the objectives outlined in eight separate bills introduced in Congress to encourage and co-ordinate the scientific-research efforts of the nation. The development of jet propulsion and supersonic air speeds has created aeronautical problems that only a vastly expanded, well-integrated, and thoroughly competent research effort can approach successfully.

However, these proposals are only a partial answer to the problem of a sound national-defense program. While drawing upon the lessons of this war as evidence of the importance of research, it is important, too, to draw upon this war experience as evidence of the importance of design, experiment, application, test, production, and development as essential elements in technological progress. Only by including all of these elements in a technological program can this nation provide weapons of the highest quality in sufficient quantity to comprise an effective national-defense and international peace-keeping force under the terms of the United Nations Charter, Article 45 of which reads: "In order to enable the United Nations to take urgent military measures, Members shall hold immediately available national Air Force contingents for combined international enforcement action. The strength and degree of readiness of these contingents and plans for their combined action shall be determined, within the limits laid down in the special agreement or agreements referred to in Article 43, by the Security Council with the assistance of the Military Staff Committee."

However, the research program provided by these bills cannot be advanced as a cure-all for the problem under which our responsibilities of Article 45 would be fulfilled. For instance, a program such as is contemplated might produce a new airfoil section, giving promise of greatly reduced drag and consequent increase in speed. However, this basic profile must be applied through design, fabrication, test, production, and development to the airplane before it possesses utility value. Pure research may reveal a new application of electronic theory, but that development must be evolved into new tubes and control units in a radar instrument installed and in service before it justifies its promise.

Research alone cannot provide jet-propelled airplanes, robot bombs, or pilotless missiles. In the words of Dr. J. C. Hunsaker, chairman, National Advisory Committee for Aeronautics, in Washington, on January 26, 1945: "There are no official NACA designs for aircraft or engines." The application of the results of research is the job of the private aircraft-manufacturing industry, which must be provided with military contracts in order that the fruits of basic research can be fully realized. Nor can experimental contracts or orders for small "pilot" quantities provide the intensive development necessary for the realization of the maximum potentialities of a new design. A new experimental airplane of superior performance cannot be recognized as an essential part of our national defense until it has been thoroughly tested, changed, improved, produced in quantity, and developed through lessons learned from this procedure.

The production phase is essential to the development of a new design as well as to the fulfillment of its maximum tactical qualities. This lesson was brought home to the Germans in the failure of their jet- and rocket-propelled fighters introduced in the last six months of the war. Their research on these new inventions had progressed considerably further than our own, but their laboratories were far, far ahead of their production lines. Untested, under-developed, and available only in small quantities, these new weapons were of little consequence in the course of the war. But had their jets been tested in field exercises and developed on the production lines, the war might have easily taken a different course.

The first lesson of this war is that there is no substitute for time in the research and development of a new airplane. The time required to develop a new weapon essential to the national security tends to increase with progress of the science. Whereas our standard four-engined bomber of 1940 required 150,000 man-hours of research and test, our latest super-bomber required 1,500,000 man-hours. Tomorrow's long-range bomber will require 15,000,000 man-hours of time to create and develop.

The second lesson of this war is that quantity production is essential to effective air power. One Superfortress might wipe out a city block, but it was one thousand plane raids that destroyed Nazi war plants and five thousand plane raids that wiped out cities and broke the back of the Wehrmacht. The use of the atomic bomb in Japan might be advanced as the death knell of the aircraft, but it was 1000-plane fighter raids that cleared the way for strategic bases and 1000-plane bomber raids that destroyed enemy fighter production and dispersal areas that cleared the way to the Japanese homeland and enabled the bomber to penetrate into the target for the dropping of that deadly bomb.

The third lesson of this war is the fact that far, far greater expenditures of time and money are required for the development of a new design than for its original research. Research that produces a new plastic for the fabrication of an airplane part may cost only fifty thousand dollars, whereas the incorporation of this new method into jigs, dies, tools, production development, and refinement may require five million dollars. Research that produces a new type of oscilloscope may cost only twenty thousand dollars, yet the design and development of a successful blind-landing-detection radio set that will work and that can be produced in quantity may cost millions.

It is clear, then, that the establishment of a national research program must be integrated with a far-reaching program of production and development. Any program that misses this great lesson will fall short of our essential goal: an effective air force to defend the nation and preserve our hard-won peace throughout the world.

Captain Carrol L. Tyler, Director of Research, Bureau of Ordnance, United States Navy, recently put these points succinctly when he told the Woodrum committee:

> I am driving at this to bring home the point that research is not an end of itself; that it is a very vital and necessary preliminary step in the provision of adequate weapons and devices. However, research is only a step which must be followed by development, production, installation, training, and finally, use.

It is interesting to note that few leaders have stepped out on a limb with predictions of the future size of aircraft-manufacturing business. One of the prophets with the courage of his convictions is William A. M.

Burden, Assistant Secretary of Commerce for Air. He had this to say on the size of the military air establishment in the future:

"In looking toward the future it is well to begin with the outlook for the manufacture of military airplanes. Contrary to popular estimation, commercial aviation-air transport, private flying, and the manufacture of commercial aircraft is not likely to grow to such gigantic proportions that military sales will assume negligible importance in the postwar period. On the contrary, if the United States should decide to maintain a 20,000-plane air force, as compared to the four thousand military planes it had in 1940, annual sales of military aircraft would be twice the commercial sales which can be hoped for even eight to ten years from now.

"The 20,000-plane figure is, of course, the boldest of assumptions, for the military market is impossible to forecast with even reasonable exactness. The number of military aircraft that are manufactured each year will depend on the size of our air force, and that, in turn, will depend on the nature of the peace and the attitude of the public and Congress toward military expenditures in the postwar period.

"The Armed Services are fully aware of the catastrophic effect of the Japanese surrender on the industry accompanied by the almost complete cessation of military purchases. However, the airplane is so firmly established as a major weapon and future invention holds promise of such increasing development that the air forces will clearly absorb a far higher proportion of whatever military budgets are approved than was true before the war. Moreover, the rate of technical progress in the next fifteen years promises to be far more rapid than the last fifteen. The Services realize the vital necessity of keeping their equipment up-to-date by replacing a substantial portion each year. This factor will tend to raise annual purchases to a high proportion—at least 20 per cent—of the total air force approved. Thus, although we hope and expect a peace which will permit our armed forces to be kept at a minimum, there is no question that aviation will receive an appropriate share of our postwar military budget."

On the question of air transport, Mr. Burden predicts an expansion that will mean "a big industry, employing perhaps 90,000 to 100,000 persons, but it will not, because of the great number of miles which a high-speed, modern transport airplane can be flown in a year, require any vast number of airplanes."

Dr. Warner, president of the Interim Council of the Provisional

International Civil Aviation Organization, has estimated that six to eight hundred large passenger aircraft of forty to sixty passengers and three hundred smaller two-engine airplanes of 20-to-30-passenger capacity will be able to do the job. Such a fleet would have six times the seating capacity of the prewar fleet of 300-odd 20-passenger, twin-engine airplanes and would be carrying about eight times the traffic.

Expansion of domestic air transport is already in progress. The award of foreign, overseas routes, orders for new equipment and their production, all point to a brilliant future for air commerce.

Thus, from many considerations, military aircraft, surplus disposal, research and development, military procurement and commercial aviation, the American people have grave decisions to make. Experience has shown that we cannot solve any of these problems which confront us by attacking them in segments. The first requisite is a redelineation of American air-power policy. We must take the Morrow Board policy and reappraise it in the light of recent developments of tremendous importance, especially the advent of economically sound air commerce. The industry is convinced that we need another Morrow Board. Like the other one, it must be selected from a group of experienced and understanding men. But, far more important, it must become the sounding board for public opinion. The many questions involved must be examined in public in order that the full impact of public opinion may be brought to bear on basic policy.

This is the long-term viewpoint. Meanwhile the surrender of Japan has brought the aircraft industry's reconversion problems to the fore. This requires certain immediate steps:

    1. A reaffirmation of the policies set forth in the Army, Navy, and Air Commerce acts of 1926 and other pertinent legislation.
    2. A specification as to the strength and composition of the armed forces which we are obligated to provide for the United Nations Charter.
    3. A program of uninterrupted procurement and replacement.
    4. A long-term program of industrial research and development.
    5. An expanding program of development of air commerce.
    6. A courageous disposal of war surpluses.

We Americans, as the world's greatest air power, have the opportunity to make air power synonymous with peace power. Here is a responsibility of a high order. Fortunately, the answer lies not in some new theory but in the past history of United States aviation, a sound public policy.

It is appropriate to end this chapter with a quotation from the second annual report of General Arnold, who is perhaps closer to the problems and promises of air power than any other man:

In two World Wars the aggressor has moved first against other peace-loving nations, hoping that the United States would remain aloof or that other nations could be defeated before this country's power on land, sea, and air could be brought to bear against him. Luckily, in each war there has been time for the mobilization of such power and the United States has been the determining factor in the defense of civilization. The lesson is too plain for the next aggressor to miss: the United States will be his first target.

There will be no opportunity for our gradual mobilization, no chance to rely on the efforts of others. It is of the utmost importance that our first line of defense, in the air, must be manned and fully supplied with modern equipment. We must be able to provide time for other parts of the national-defense machine to mobilize and go into high gear. The United States must be the world's first power in military aviation.

The United States aircraft-manufacturing industry stands ready to play its part in that tremendous mission: the preservation of democracy and our national way of life.

Part IV
Postwar Developments and the Korean War
1945–1955

7. The Consequences of the Postwar Contraction

After World War II the contraction in demand for the aircraft industry's products was severe and reminiscent of the contraction after the First World War. By the end of 1945, the Army and the Navy had canceled 18,267 contracts totaling $21,578,462,000 in value. Industry sales declined from a peak of $16,047,000,000 in 1944 to an estimated $1,200,000,000 in 1947. By December, 1945, only 16 airframe plants remained of the 66 that had been in the industry one year earlier.

The disposal of surplus war products was a pressing problem. Bombers and fighters with reciprocating engines were, for the most part, made decidedly obsolete by the development of the jet-engine aircraft. Hence, there was a recognized need for replacement of the technologically inferior World War II models.

While there was a cutback in demand for military aircraft, the demand for commercial aircraft, both for transports and light airplanes, was growing. Still, revenue from commercial production remained a small part of the total. The demand for new transports was depressed by the availability of surplus military transports, but the light plane industry experienced a strong demand. Flying had become a familiar experience to many service personnel during the war, which contributed to its postwar popularity; after a couple of years, however, the demand for light airplanes fell drastically.

The general contraction following the war's end, in most cases, forced the automotive manufacturers, licensee companies, subcontractors, and others out of the aircraft industry. By 1949 the producers in the industry were essentially those of the prewar period. Moreover, the geographic location of the industry had changed appreciably from what it was in wartime back to what it had been before the war.

When the Korean War erupted in June, 1950, the techniques of subcontracting, licensing, and the use of branch plants were again employed. Also, the locational pattern of the industry was shifting back to resemble more closely that of World War II.

In a detailed description of the aircraft industry's history from 1945 to 1955, William Glenn Cunningham, an economic geographer, discusses the impact of the postwar contraction on the industry and its location.

181

*Postwar Developments and the
Location of the Aircraft Industry in 1950**
William Glenn Cunningham

I. *Postwar Developments*

The overall picture of the aircraft industry during the two-year period from 1944 to 1946 presented a striking contrast to that of the preceding four years, 1940 to 1944. In place of the unprecedented expansion and feverish activity of the earlier period, these years were characterized largely by contraction, retrenchment, and reconversion. It has been described as "a spectacular expansion in reverse."

It is not to be inferred that all progress was lacking during this period of demobilization. A few individual companies expanded in size; many new ones came into being. Startling technological innovations and phenomenal performance records became almost commonplace. The period saw the rebirth of civil aircraft manufacturing, and production, which had fallen to nothing in 1943 and 1944, rose to 34,874 airplanes in 1946, nearly five times that of the greatest war year.[1]

Decreased Production

The tremendous decrease in military plane production, however, more than offset any other gains and dominated the developments of this period. The most significant of these was the rapid reduction in total employment figures for the industry. The peak of 2,101,600 was reached in November, 1943, and was followed by a gradual but steady decrease until the end of the war in Europe. By VE Day (May 8, 1945) it had fallen to 1,464,200. Thereafter the rate of decrease accelerated and by VJ Day (August 14, 1945) only 519,900 remained on aircraft factory payrolls. A steady reduction continued until a low of 138,700 was reached in February, 1946.[2]

Expansion of production facilities had practically ceased by the end of 1943, and output, following reduction of new orders, commenced to drop a few months after the peak in employment was experienced.

---

* Reprinted by permission of the author from William Glenn Cunningham: *The Aircraft Industry: A Study in Industrial Location* (Los Angeles: Lorrin L. Morrison, 1951), pp. 145–178, 185–187. The title supplied by the editor. Photographs appearing in the original text have been omitted.

[1] U.S. Bureau of the Census, Industry Division, *Facts for Industry, Complete Aircraft,* Release, February 5, 1947, p. 1.

[2] *Aircraft, Engine and Propeller Production,* p. 11, and *Monthly Labor Review,* July, 1946, p. 136. It should be noted that the continued reduction in aircraft employment was not a product of decreasing military output during the entire period. A reversal in trend was experienced not long after the war, military output increasing from 1946 to 1947, civil plane output falling from 34,874 units in 1946, to 15,616 in 1947. *Aviation Week,* February 23, 1948, p. 22.

Airframe production fell after March, 1944; engine production, after June, 1944; and propeller production after January, 1944.[3]

Several months before the cessation of hostilities the government began the cut-back and occasionally the cancellation of contracts. The industry as a whole anticipated and planned for the termination of the bulk of the military contracts and prepared for conversion to a peacetime economy. As early as July, 1944, spokesmen for the industry outlined before the Murray War Contracts subcommittee of the Senate Military Affairs Committee, a program for achieving a balanced production as war needs slackened.

Among the factors to be considered it was suggested that:

1. The aircraft industry has a relatively small postwar market awaiting it. Aircraft cutbacks should, therefore, be effective first for temporary manufacturers such as the automobile industry, which have substantial postwar markets waiting for them.
2. Problems of the creator of the original design should be given some consideration in the decision as to which manufacturer is going to be cut back first—the licensee or the basic manufacturer.
3. Present production status of the manufacturer.
4. Local manpower situation.
5. Meeting of production schedules.
6. Contributions to the progress of aviation.
7. Needs of the aircraft industry to prepare for postwar development and production.
8. Orders for aircraft that are becoming obsolete should be cut back before orders for aircraft of more advanced design and of greater tactical usefulness.[4]

There is evidence that many of the above points were incorporated in the policy followed by the government. In general it was in the plants of the nonaircraft companies that production ceased first, and with one exception, the major aircraft companies were still making deliveries, although in greatly reduced amounts, by December 1945.

The conspicuous exception provided by the early termination of the contracts of the Brewster Aeronautical Corporation has been explained as follows:

---

[3] *Aircraft, Engine and Propeller Production,* pp. 5, 7, 8.
[4] Aeronautical Chamber of Commerce, *The Aircraft Industry Prepares for The Future* (Washington: 1944), p. 21.

Termination of the Navy's fighter plane contract with Brewster Aeronautical Corporation makes the company the first privately owned aircraft plant to be cleared out of war work, ... Selection of Brewster to bear the brunt of the Navy's plans for the reduction of fighter plane production was not unexpected in view of the fact that the company is the smallest producer of Navy fighters, and that relations between the Navy and Brewster have had a long, trying history, involving strikes, management changes, and a plant seizure, all of which combine to make a dismal record.

The Navy order cancelling its contract with Brewster noted that the company has no other Navy contract or any prospects of any, and in addition, production costs were said to be higher than at either of the other two companies producing Corsair fighters—Chance Vought Division of the United Aircraft Corporation and Goodyear Aircraft.[5]

The year 1944 also saw the cessation of military deliveries from Aeronca, American Aviation, Bellanca, Brunswick-Balke-Collender, Budd, Cessna, Fleetwings, Globe, Higgins, Howard, McDonnell, St. Louis Aircraft, Taylorcraft, and Warner Aircraft Engines as well as the Downey (Los Angeles) plant of Consolidated Vultee, the St. Louis plant of Curtiss, the El Segundo (Los Angeles) plant of Douglas, and the Burlington, North Carolina, plant of Fairchild.[6]

Still further reductions were made early in the following year.

On April 18, 1945, the Army Air Forces announced that because of changed strategic and tactical requirements, its over-all aircraft production is being reduced by about 15 per cent measured in airframe weight during the remainder of the year. . . .

The cut-back with respect to the B-24's—the famed Liberator bombers—will result in the discontinuance of aircraft production at the Ford Motor Company operated Willow Run plant in Detroit after July of this year. . . .[7]

Ford actually ceased the manufacture of airplanes in June, 1945; General Motors in September, and Nash-Kelvinator in October. In the

---

[5] "Where Brewster," *Business Week,* May 27, 1944, pp. 31–32. See also Agnes E. Meyer, *Journey Through Chaos* (New York: Harcourt, Brace & Company, 1943), pp. 262–268.

[6] *Aircraft, Engine and Propeller Production,* pp. 50–53.

[7] United States Congress, Senate. War Contracts Subcommittee of the Committee on Military Affairs. *War Plants Disposal: Aircraft Plants, Progress Report On The Preparation of Joint Hearings On The Disposal Of Surplus Aircraft,* 79th Con., 1st sess., S. Rept., 199, Part 2 (Washington: Government Printing Office, 1945), p. 1. Hereafter cited as *War Plants Disposal : Aircraft Plants, Progress Report.*

engine field production ended in the Studebaker plants in June, 1945, in the Chevrolet plants in August, and in those of Buick, Dodge, and Ford in September.[8]

By December, 1945, production had ceased in all but sixteen of the sixty-six airframe plants in operation in January, 1944. Engine plants in operation were reduced from twenty-three to five, propeller plants from six to one, and glider plants from fourteen to one. Only one modification center remained in operation, that of Lockheed in Dallas with an employment of only 235.[9]

Effects of Decreased Production on Locational Pattern
This shrinkage necessarily altered materially the wartime pattern of aircraft manufacturing activities as major and minor aircraft centers disappeared with their units of the industry. Several types of organizational changes were involved. In some instances cessation of activity following the closing of modification centers or branch plants; in others, the withdrawal of nonaircraft companies from the field; in still others, the liquidation of aircraft companies or their conversion to nonaircraft products.

The Elimination of the Modification Center.
As the scarcity of labor and facilities and the need for interior location became things of the past, the usefulness of the special center for modification came to an end. All necessary modification could be handled adequately in the original assembly plant. The customary procedure in the factories, after release of the wartime pressure, was to create a separate "Modification line" through which the completed planes were sent if modification for a special function or set of conditions was required.

Wartime aircraft centers whose existence was based entirely on the presence of modification centers and which disappeared as centers with the cessation of this activity include Denver, St. Paul, Cheyenne, Phoenix, Tucson and Birmingham.

The Withdrawal of Nonaircraft Companies
from Aircraft Manufacture.
With very few exceptions the automobile, refrigerator, furniture and other companies that had manufactured airframes, engines, propellers or gliders under license or of their own design, withdrew from such activities and again turned their attention to their peacetime products.

---

[8] *Aircraft, Engine and Propeller Production*, pp. 162–163.
[9] *Ibid.*, pp. 54–56, 130, 148–149, 174–175, 204.

The exceptions are found in Goodyear Aircraft Division, which, in addition to the continued production of several aircraft parts, operated on a small scale in developing a light personal plane; and in General Electric Company, Aircraft Gas Turbine Division; and Westinghouse Electric Corporation, Aviation Gas Turbine Division; each of which was occupied in the development and production of turbo-jet engines. Aeroproducts Division of General Motors Corporation remained as a producer of propellers.

Among the wartime aircraft centers which disappeared or were reduced to a bare fraction of their former importance as a result of the reconversion or closing of nonaircraft company facilities were Trenton; Cleveland; Toledo; Dayton; Akron; South Bend; Flint; Milwaukee; Grand Rapids; Saginaw, Michigan; Lansing; Deep River, Connecticut; Muncie, Indiana; Iron Mountain, Michigan; Greenville, Michigan; Memphis; Fort Wayne; Binghampton, New York; New Orleans; and Chicago.

The Closing of Branch Plants.
A few of the branch plants and feeder plants of the aircraft companies were closed before VE Day. Most of them were closed within a few months after the end of the war. Three outstanding exceptions are found, namely, the Columbus plant of Curtiss Aircraft Division, which became the main plant of the company, the Fort Worth plant of Consolidated Vultee, and the Wichita plant of Boeing.

The shut-down of branch plants and feeder plants eliminated from the list of aircraft centers the cities of Atlanta; Cincinnati; Evansville; Omaha; Kansas City; Oklahoma City; Tulsa; Louisville; Allentown; Beaver, Pennsylvania; Burlington, North Carolina; Nashville; Hutchinson, Kansas; Providence; New London, Connecticut; and Springfield, Massachusetts. It contributed to the elimination of Chicago and New Orleans.

The Dissolution of War-born Companies.
With the termination or cancellation of contracts several of the aircraft companies organized during the war or the earlier period of the Defense Program, were liquidated in one manner or another, among them, Columbia Aircraft Corporation, Globe Aircraft Corporation, American Aviation Corporation, American Propeller Division of Aviation Corporation, and a number of small glider companies. Although not eliminating any major or minor aircraft centers these losses reduced somewhat the activities of New York, Fort Worth, and Toledo.

The Dissolution of Prewar Companies.
In like manner a few of the aircraft companies in operation before the war went out of existence as contracts were terminated or cancelled. Examples are Brewster Aeronautical Corporation, Culver Aircraft Corporation, Fleetwings, Inc., St. Louis Aircraft Corporation, Howard Aircraft Corporation, and the Naval Aircraft Factory. Wichita, Philadelphia, Chicago, St. Louis, and New York were the centers affected by these liquidations.

Conversion of Prewar Companies.
Five other prewar aircraft companies, although remaining in existence converted largely to nonaircraft products and were no longer counted among the units of the aircraft industry. Interstate Aircraft and Engineering Corporation of El Segundo (Los Angeles), produced aircraft parts but also soft drink dispensers, water softeners and vacuum cleaners. Timm Aircraft Corporation, also of Los Angeles, was a producer of miscellaneous aluminum products. Kinners Motors, Inc., later Gladden Products, Glendale, California (Los Angeles) produced hydraulics and industrial motors. Spartan Aircraft Company of Tulsa built aluminum house trailers while Southern Aircraft in Dallas produced stoves and other durable goods.

Postwar Expansion

Not all changes in the industry were negative however, nor were all developments of the postwar period the product of shrinkage. New airframe, engine, and propeller companies came into existence; nonaircraft companies entered the field; and airframe companies temporarily branched out to include the production of engines and propellers. Several aircraft companies bettered their positions by changes of location and a few new branch plants were operated for a time by airframe companies. Since February, 1946, total employment in the industry has shown a gradual, irregular increase, with a noticeable acceleration from mid-1948 to mid-1949.

New Aircraft Companies
Current directories[10] (January, 1950) listed nearly sixty new aircraft companies located in all parts of the country. Many of these will undoubtedly enjoy only brief careers but many may survive, grow to

[10] *American Aviation Directory, Spring-Summer, 1950; Aircraft Yearbook for 1949; Aviation Week,* February 27, 1950.

significant size and contribute toward the alteration of the postwar pattern of distribution.[11]

Largest of the new airframe manufacturing companies in 1950 was the Chase Aircraft Company, Inc., in West Trenton, New Jersey, with approximately 1,200 employees. Originally a producer of gliders, the company soon turned to the manufacture of assault transports. Also prominent was the Texas Engineering and Manufacturing Company with 120 employees in aircraft manufacture. This company, occupying a portion of the former North American plant at Dallas, produced a personal plane, the Tempco Swift. A smaller producer of personal planes, Mooney Aircraft, Inc., was located in Wichita.

Among the many other new airplane companies listed (most of them with personal planes in limited production or in the late development stage in early 1950), were six in Los Angeles, and one in each of the cities of New York and Rochester, New York; Deep River and Danbury, Connecticut; Wilmington, Delaware; DeLand and Melbourne, Florida; Houston and Tyler, Texas; Wichita and Coffeeville, Kansas; Afton, Wyoming; Douglas, Arizona; Hemet, California; and Longview, Washington.

Rotary wing aircraft appealed to established companies and new ventures alike, and twelve new producers of helicopters were listed. In addition to the Sikorsky Division of the United Aircraft Corporation, two other airplane manufacturers, Bell Aircraft Corporation and McDonnell Aircraft Corporation were among those active. Three new companies in production were located in Morton, Pennsylvania (Philadelphia), Windsor Locks, Connecticut (Hartford), and Palo Alto, California (San Francisco). New companies in the experimental or development stage included three in Philadelphia, two in Los Angeles, one in Danbury, Connecticut, and one in Wichita.

One new reciprocating engine company was reported in Los Angeles. In the field of jet engines several newcomers appeared, most of them with products still in the experimental stage. The great interest in jet engines toward the end of the war attracted many concerns, both

---

[11] In the following discussion, an attempt has been made to distinguish between the companies actually in production, regardless of how small the output, and those merely listed in periodical directories. As has been true throughout the history of the industry, anyone with an idea, an unused garage and a few tools and materials can claim to be a builder of airplanes. Many such companies with uncertain futures are listed in current directories as prominently as Lockheed or Consolidated Vultee. The writer has investigated several so-called aircraft companies whose names appear year after year and has found little or no evidence of activity to warrant their inclusion.

within and outside of the industry. Upsetting the industry's earlier pattern, a few airframe companies, Northrop, McDonnell, Boeing and Lockheed, heretofore uninvolved in engine manufacture, became interested in the jet engine field. Most of them soon sold their designs, however, and by 1950 only Boeing was listed as active. A few nonaircraft companies, including Packard, Allis-Chalmers and Willys-Overland were engaged in jet research and development for a time. Two new jet companies were listed in Los Angeles and one in Buffalo.

Two aircraft companies entered the propeller field for the first time, Beech Aircraft Corporation in Wichita, and Continental Aviation and Engineering Corporation in Muskegon. Other new propeller companies were located in Fort Worth, Wichita, New York, and Pasadena, California (Los Angeles). Also introducing the manufacture of propellers was one nonaircraft company, Koppers Company, Inc., which established the Aeromatic Propeller Department within its Metal Products Division in Baltimore.

New Branch Plants
General Electric Corporation, expanding beyond its facilities in the Boston area, leased a large amount of space in the former Wright Aero plant at Cincinnati for the production of jet engine sub-assemblies.

Changes of Location
A few companies moved their major manufacturing activities from the location occupied in 1944. In four instances interregional shifts were involved.

Inter-Regional Moves
Among these changes was that of the Curtiss Airplane Division of the Curtiss-Wright Corporation which abandoned its original site in Buffalo to concentrate its operations in the wartime branch plant at Columbus, Ohio.

One of the smaller companies, Luscombe Airplane Corporation, Trenton, New Jersey, left its former West Trenton site to occupy a newly built plant and airfield at Garland, Texas, a suburb of Dallas. Another light plane producer, Stinson Aircraft Division of Consolidated Vultee, gave up its properties in Wayne, Michigan (Detroit), and planned to continue all activities in the San Diego plant of the parent company.[12]

[12] Before production was started in San Diego, the Stinson Division was purchased by the Piper Aircraft Corporation of Lock Haven, Pennsylvania, and is now operating as the Stinson Division of Piper Aircraft in Lock Haven.

One of the most spectacular migrations in recent industrial history was the move of the Chance Vought Division of United Aircraft Corporation from Bridgeport to Dallas to occupy the former North American plant at Grand Prairie. Fifteen hundred key employees and their families were involved in the move, as were some 2,000 machines and 50 million pounds of equipment comprising approximately 1,000 carloads. The change was made gradually, requiring better than a year, and was so planned that disruption of the flow of work was kept to a minimum.

Local Moves
A number of other moves took place involving no change of metropolitan district and consisting of either shifts from one community to another within the district, or merely change of building site within a community. Among those were the moves of Wright Aeronautical from Paterson to Wood Ridge, New Jersey (New York); of Curtiss Propeller Division from Clifton to Caldwell, New Jersey (New York); of Kellett Aircraft from Philadelphia to North Wales, Pennsylvania, and later back to Camden, New Jersey (Philadelphia); and of Bell from Buffalo to Niagara Falls.

In the Los Angeles area, North American Aviation, expanding sufficiently in early 1948 to require facilities beyond those of its own plant in Inglewood, occupied the former Consolidated Vultee plant in Downey and a portion of the Douglas Long Beach plant.

The industry resulting from these many developments may be described as follows:

Size and Structure of the Industry in 1950
The Bureau of Labor Statistics reports 224,900 employees in aircraft, engine and propeller factories for January, 1950. This figure represents about one-sixth of that reported for January, 1944, and almost three times that of January, 1940.[13] Aircraft manufacture, accounting for approximately 1.8 per cent of all employees in manufacturing for the month, represented the nation's fifteenth largest industry.[14]

[13] 1950 figures from *Monthly Labor Review,* April, 1950, p. 445; 1944 and 1940 figures from *Aviation Facts and Figures, 1945,* pp. 20–21.
[14] Based on the Bureau of Labor Statistics figure for the total Aircraft and Parts Industry including "Other Aircraft Parts and Equipment." The January, 1950, employment was equal to only 12 per cent of the grand total reported at the peak of wartime employment in November, 1943.

During the preceding year, 1949, the industry produced 3,409 personal planes, 151 transports, and an unspecified number of military planes (probably around 2,600), with a total airframe weight of 36,496,500 pounds, and a total value of $1,100,000,000. Engine plants turned out 3,987 civil aircraft engines and an unspecified number of military aircraft engines, with a total horsepower of 46,389,100, and a total value of $508,000,000. Propeller shipments, including 11,343 for civil planes, were valued at $57,600,000. This output, although equal to only one tenth the value of the 1944 production, was six times as great as the value of the industry's output in 1939.[15]

In spite of the numerous changes that attended four years of expansion followed by a period of contraction, the basic structure of the aircraft industry differed but little from that of 1940. Although new companies appeared and disappeared with amazing rapidity (fifty-nine new names appeared in 1950; forty-nine of those on record in 1944 and forty of those in 1940 failed to appear in 1950) the bulk of the industry's output was the product of the same few companies that constituted the industry's leaders before the war.

The President's Air Policy Commission has selected fifteen firms which it describes as the major airframe companies (1948).[16] Each of the fifteen, with two exceptions, were major components of the industry in 1940. These two, McDonnell Aircraft Corporation and Northrop Aircraft, Inc., recently established and barely under way in 1940, have risen to prominence since that date. And of the major companies in 1940, only three, Vega Airplane Company, absorbed by Lockheed; Vultee Aircraft, Inc., now part of Consolidated Vultee; and Brewster Aeronautical Corporation, fail to appear on the 1950 list.

The Commission also lists nine major makers of personal planes. Comparison with the 1940 situation reveals only one newcomer, the Texas Engineering and Manufacturing Company, and only three omissions of the major 1940 personal plane companies, Culver Aircraft Corporation, Waco Aircraft Company, and Stinson Division of Aviation Corporation (absorbed by Piper Aircraft Corporation in 1948).

It appears that the airframe segment of the aircraft industry with its low birth rate and mortality rate as far as major producers are

---

[15] The number of airplanes produced was approximately one-sixteenth of the number produced in 1944; airframe weight was one-twenty-sixth as great; and engine horsepower one-ninth that of 1944.

[16] *Survival in the Air Age*, a Report of the President's Air Policy Commission (Washington: Government Printing Office, 1948), p. 51.

concerned, shows recently a stability and maturity, possibly comparable to that of the automobile industry.

In like manner reciprocating engine and propeller manufacture are still dominated by the same companies operating in essentially the same locations.

It is in the turbo-jet engine field that the earlier patterns of the industry have been most disturbed. Nonaircraft companies, General Electric and Westinghouse, familiar with the manufacture of turbines, were granted government funds for research and development of turbo-jets during the war while the established aircraft engine companies were required to concentrate on reciprocating engines. Consequently the former took an early lead in jet engine production and for a time theirs were the only models in quantity production. The aircraft engine companies, limited to privately financed research, have only recently begun to compete and seem destined to continue to share this segment of the industry with the electric companies.

The Companies and Their Products[17]

Models, orders, and production schedules change rapidly in the aircraft industry, but in January, 1950, the major companies in operation and the principal types of products in which they specialized could be described as follows:

Military and Commercial Airplane Companies

The Boeing Airplane Company in its Seattle plant was producing transports and medium bombers for the Air Force, as well as a commercial transport model. The entire output of the company's plant in Wichita consisted of jet bombers for the Air Force. Lockheed Aircraft Corporation in Burbank, California (Los Angeles), included among its products a 4-engine commercial transport, jet fighters and trainers for the Air Force, and patrol bombers for the Navy. Northrop Aircraft, Inc., Hawthorne, California (Los Angeles), was engaged in the production of Air Force fighters and transports.

Douglas Aircraft Company operated three plants in the Los Angeles area, producing 2- and 4-engine commercial transports at Santa Monica; Navy attack and fighter planes at El Segundo; and Air Force transports at Long Beach. North American Aviation, Inc., likewise operated three

---

[17] The following section was compiled from information in the annual directory issue of *Aviation Week*, February 27, 1950, and the *Aircraft Yearbook for 1949*.

plants in the Los Angeles area, specializing in fighters and trainers for
the Air Force at Inglewood; attack planes for the Navy at Downey;
and jet bombers for the Air Force at Long Beach.

Consolidated Vultee Aircraft Corporation produced 2-engine
commercial transports and Air Force trainers at the San Diego plant, and
the 6-engine, B-36 bomber for the Air Force in its Fort Worth plant.
Both Chance Vought Division of United Aircraft Corporation in Dallas
and McDonnell Aircraft Corporation in St. Louis were producing fighters
for the Navy. The Curtiss Aeroplane Division of Curtiss-Wright
Corporation in Columbus had no models in production but was engaged
in modification and experimental work for the Air Force.

The Glenn L. Martin Company in Baltimore produced patrol and
attack planes for the Navy. Transports for the Air Force were the
principal products of Fairchild Engine and Aircraft Corporation in
Hagerstown, Maryland. Grumman Aircraft Engineering Corporation in
Bethpage, Long Island (New York), was building fighter, attack, and
rescue planes for the Navy, and a 12-place amphibian for commercial
use. Republic Aviation, Inc., Farmingdale, Long Island (New York),
produced jet fighters for the Air Force. Chase Aircraft Company, Inc., in
West Trenton, had under development an assault transport for the Air
Force.

Helicopter Companies
Several models of both military and commercial helicopters were in
production at the plants of Bell Aircraft Corporation in Buffalo and the
Sikorsky Aircraft Division of United Aircraft Corporation in Bridgeport.
The Piasecki Helicopter Corporation in Morton, Pennsylvania
(Philadelphia), produced military models for the Air Force and the
Navy. Many companies had commercial helicopters in limited production
or in the development stage, but significant production came only from
Hiller Helicopters, Palo Alto, California (San Francisco).

Personal Plane Companies
As has nearly always been true during the history of the aircraft
industry, dozens of companies in all parts of the country claimed to be
manufacturers of light planes for private flying. Producers in quantity,
however, were limited in number and included only Piper Aircraft
Corporation in Lock Haven, Pennsylvania; Cessna Aircraft Company,
Wichita; Aeronca Aircraft Corporation, Middletown, Ohio; Beech

Aircraft Corporation, Wichita; Ryan Aeronautical Company, San Diego; and Luscombe Airplane Corporation, Garland, Texas (Dallas). Smaller outputs originated in the plants of Bellanca Aircraft Corporation, New Castle, Delaware (Wilmington); Engineering and Research Corporation, Riverdale, Maryland (Washington); Mooney Aircraft, Inc., Wichita; Taylorcraft, Inc., Conway, Pennsylvania; and the Texas Engineering and Manufacturing Company, Inc., Dallas.

Engine Companies
Pratt & Whitney Division of United Aircraft Corporation in East Hartford, Connecticut, produced the conventional air-cooled radial engines with horsepower ratings from 450 to 3,500, but was also producing turbo-jet and turbo-prop engines with increasing emphasis on these types. Wright Aeronautical Corporation, Wood Ridge, New Jersey (New York), likewise produced the air-cooled radial engines, horsepower 700–3,350, but was becoming interested in turbo-jets and turbo-props. Allison Division of General Motors Corporation in Indianapolis was engaged exclusively in the production of turbo-jet and turbo-prop engines for military planes. Turbo-jets were the products of the Aviation Gas Turbine Division of Westinghouse Electric Corporation in Philadelphia, and the Aircraft Gas Turbine Division of General Electric Company in West Lynn, Massachusetts (Boston).

Smaller engines with horsepower (65–565) were produced by Air-cooled Motors, Inc., Syracuse; Continental Motors Corporation, Muskegon, Michigan; Jacobs Aircraft Engine Corporation, Pottstown, Pennsylvania; Lycoming-Spencer Division of AVCO Manufacturing Corporation, Williamsport, Pennsylvania; and Ranger Engines Division of Fairchild Engine and Aircraft Corporation, Farmingdale, Long Island (New York).

Propeller Companies
Propellers for high horsepower engines (500 to 3,000 and above) were produced by three companies only, Hamilton Standard Propeller Division of United Aircraft Corporation in East Hartford; Curtiss Propeller Division of Curtiss-Wright Corporation in Caldwell, New Jersey (New York); and Aeroproducts Division of General Motors Corporation in Dayton.

Propellers for engines of lower horsepower (50–500) came largely from the plants of Aeromatic Propeller Department of Koppers

Company, Inc., Baltimore; Sensenich Corporation, Lancaster, Pennsylvania; Hartzell Propeller Company, Piqua, Ohio; G. B. Lewis Company, Watertown, Wisconsin; Flottrop Manufacturing Company, Grand Rapids, Michigan; and McCauley Corporation, Dayton.[18]

A more specific treatment of the location of the aircraft industry in the postwar year of 1950 follows.

II. *Location of the Industry in 1950*

In contrast to earlier periods, factory floorspace could not be accepted as a satisfactory measure of the industry in 1950. Unlike the periods of expansion, full utilization of capacity was not to be assumed. The existence of excess capacity, some of it idle, some semi-idle, created a problem of measurement. Nearly all companies were operating in plants with space that exceeded their needs and much space was used for storage and other unproductive purposes. The space in productive use was producing at far less than capacity and little relation existed between capacity and output. Many large plants were employing two or three thousand men where 25,000 worked during the war. Any measurement of the industry by means of floorspace alone becomes quite meaningless.[19]

Current employment, then, in spite of being subject to sudden fluctuations, becomes the most satisfactory measure. Figures for

---

[18] As has been noted earlier, it is impossible to treat of the many manufacturers of parts, instruments, and accessories, indeed it would be impossible even to list all the producers of these vital components. Among the more important ones that warrant mention, however, were the following: Bendix Aviation Corporation, Sperry Corporation, Air Associates, Inc., Kollsman Instrument Division of the Square D Company, General Electric Company, Westinghouse Electric Corporation, Cannon Electrical Development Company, Thompson Products, Inc., The B. F. Goodrich Company, The Goodyear Tire and Rubber Company, Inc., Jack and Heintz Precision Industries, Inc., Leach Relay Company, Micro-Switch Division of First Industrial Corporation, Parker Appliance Company, Vickers, Inc., AiResearch Manufacturing Company, Thomas A. Edison, Inc., Adel Precision Products Corporation, Lear Incorporated, Minneapolis-Honeywell Regulator Company, Rohr Aircraft Corporation, Eaton Manufacturing Company, Solar Aircraft Company and several divisions of General Motors Corporation.

Location of these companies was influenced primarily by the need for labor skills. The industrial northeastern part of the country, consequently, could claim the majority. Within this area no significant distribution is noted except for the concentration of a large part of the aircraft instrument production in or near Metropolitan New York. Aircraft manufacturing centers outside of the industrial belt, notably Los Angeles, attracted a number of these producers, in some instances the main plant of the company being located therein, in other instances division or branch plants of Eastern concerns were so located.

[19] Total floorspace of the prime contractors for the services (except General Electric Corporation and Westinghouse Electric Corporation) was reported to be 56,406,752 square feet, distributed as follows: airframe, 45,536,752; engines, 9,570,000; propellers, 1,300,000. *Aviation Week,* February 27, 1950, p. 25.

individual plants, are available for January, 1950.[20] Although a few small companies are omitted in the tabulation, the bulk of the industry is represented and resulting errors will be slight. The total, 212,360, compares favorably with the figure 211,746, reported by the Department of Commerce[21] and the figure 224,900 reported by the Bureau of Labor Statistics[22] for the same month.

Distribution of Employment
With this as a basis, the following observations may be made. Airframe manufacture is found in eleven states, eight of which have as much as 1 per cent of the total. Leading is California with 40.0 per cent of the total, followed by Texas with 14.4 per cent; Washington, 11.7 per cent; New York, 10.9 per cent; Maryland, 7.8 per cent; and Kansas, 7.6 per cent....

Eleven metropolitan districts have 1 per cent or more of the total with the larger shares in Los Angeles, 35.2 per cent; Seattle, 11.7 per cent; Fort Worth, 10.4 per cent; New York, 8.1 per cent; and Wichita, 7.5 per cent....

The manufacture of aircraft engines is somewhat more restricted, with only eight states and seven cities in position to claim 1 per cent of the total. The leading states are Connecticut with 34.5 per cent; Indiana, 19.9 per cent; New Jersey, 14.5 per cent; and Massachusetts, 11.4 per cent.... Outstanding among the metropolitan districts are Hartford, 34.5 per cent; Indianapolis, 19.9 per cent; New York, 18.0 per cent; and Boston, 11.4 per cent....

Still more limited in extent is the manufacture of propellers with practically all production originating in three centers in three different states. Leading are the metropolitan districts of New York (Caldwell, New Jersey), Hartford and Dayton, and consequently New Jersey, Connecticut and Ohio, with 52.7, 29.9, and 15.9 per cent of the total respectively....

For the "total industry" fourteen states are represented. Eight

---

[20] These figures were obtained from several sources including the Western Regional Office of the Aircraft Industries Association, *Aviation Week*'s Seventeenth Annual Inventory of Air Power, February 27, 1950, p. 25, and reports from the companies directly. In a very few cases for which data were unavailable, estimates were made, based on earlier employment figures and current production rates.
[21] U.S. Department of Commerce, *Facts for Industry, Complete Aircraft and Aircraft Engines,* January, 1950, p. 4, and *Aircraft Propellers,* 1950, p. 2.
[22] *Monthly Labor Review*, April, 1950, p. 445.

leading states, together containing 85.2 per cent of the total, are California, 30.4 per cent; Texas, 10.9 per cent; New York, 9.0 per cent; Washington, 8.9 per cent; Connecticut, 8.8 per cent; Maryland, 5.9 per cent; Kansas, 5.7 per cent; and New Jersey, 5.6 per cent. An additional six states each have 1 per cent or more of the nation's aircraft industry . . . .

The more important metropolitan districts include those of Los Angeles with 26.7 per cent of the total; New York, 11.9 per cent; Seattle, 8.9 per cent; Hartford, 8.3 per cent; Fort Worth, 7.9 per cent; and Wichita, 5.7 per cent. Nine other cities each have more than 1 per cent of the total . . . .

Once again it is on the regional basis that the uneven distribution is most apparent. In airframe production the Pacific region, containing the leading states and two leading metropolitan districts, holds an outstanding place with 51.7 per cent of the total. It is followed by the West South Central region with 14.4 per cent; Middle Atlantic, 12.5 per cent; West North Central, 11.7 per cent; South Atlantic, 7.8 per cent; East North Central, 1.0 per cent; and New England, 0.7 per cent . . . .

Engine manufacture is confined to three regions; New England, 45.9 per cent; East North Central, 32.3 per cent; and Middle Atlantic, 21.6 per cent . . . .

The total industry is distributed among the regions as follows: Pacific, 39.4 per cent; Middle Atlantic, 16.0 per cent; New England, 11.2 per cent; West South Central, 10.9 per cent; West North Central, 8.8 per cent; East North Central, 8.0 per cent; and South Atlantic, 5.9 per cent . . . .

Comparison with 1944 Pattern of Location
The 1950 industry, after shrinking to about one-eighth the size of the 1944 industry, necessarily displayed a greatly altered pattern of distribution. Fewer regions, states, and metropolitan districts as producing units, greater concentration, and reduced rank of most of the interior areas, summarize the principle variations.

The East North Central Region, undisputed leader during the war, is reduced to sixth place among the regions represented. The East South Central and Mountain Regions fail to appear as aircraft producers.

Only fourteen states are represented as against thirty in 1944. Several important wartime producing states have disappeared from the list; Illinois, Georgia, Oklahoma, Wisconsin, Kentucky, and Tennessee. The states of Ohio and Michigan, ranking third and fourth in 1944, are reduced in rank to twelfth and thirteenth, respectively.

On the other hand the relative importance of a few is increased, Texas rising from seventh to second place, Connecticut from eighth to fifth place, Washington from twelfth to fourth and Maryland from tenth to sixth. Massachusetts appears on the list as a significant producing state.

In contrast to 1944 when twenty-six metropolitan districts each had at least one per cent of the total aircraft employment, only fifteen can now make such a claim and such important war centers as Chicago, Detroit, Atlanta, Kansas City, Flint, Tulsa, and Oklahoma City now play no part. Altogether fifteen of the major centers in 1944 and thirty-one of the minor centers fail to appear.[23] First and second place are still held by Los Angeles and New York; Buffalo falls from fourth to fourteenth. Substantial gains in relative importance are made by Seattle, Hartford and Fort Worth, and Boston appears as a new center of significance.

Also on the credit side is the appearance of a few smaller centers that did not qualify in 1944, among them, Elmira, New York; and Palo Alto, California (San Francisco).[24]

The existence of fewer producing areas implies a greater concentration than existed in 1944, a result that is expressed by the reduced coefficient of scatter. The figure, 10 for 1944, falls to 7 for 1950, as the seven leading states together contain 80.1 per cent of the nation's total aircraft wage earners. Further indication of the intensified concentration is seen in the percentages of the total found in the leading state and metropolitan district for the two periods. In 1944, California had but 18.9 per cent of the total. By 1950 this had increased to 30.4 per cent. The share of Los Angeles over the same period rose from 15.4 per cent to 26.7 per cent.

The above paragraphs suggest that the greatest losses were suffered by the states and cities of the interior regions; most of the larger gains made by those on the coasts. As a final product of these changes, 1950

[23] A more complete coverage of the smaller aircraft companies would have resulted in the retention of the war centers of Washington, Wilmington, Akron, and Grand Rapids.
[24] Again a more complete coverage would lengthen the list of producing centers. Actual production of C. A. A. approved and certificated aircraft (although often on a very small scale) is taking place in Afton, Wyoming; Coffeeville, Kansas; Melbourne, Florida, and Conway, Pennsylvania. Small propellers for light planes originate in Piqua, Ohio, and Watertown, Wisconsin.

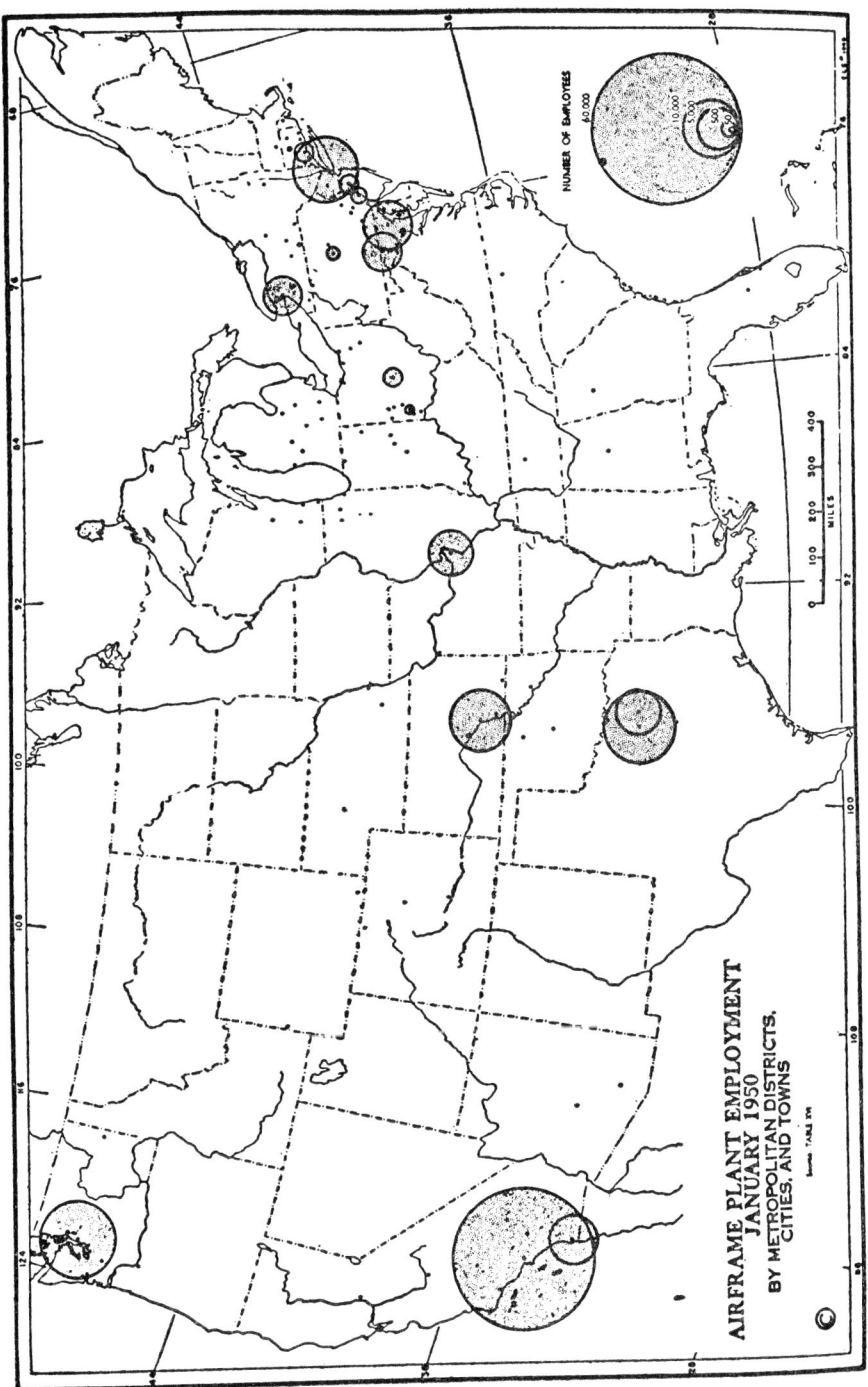

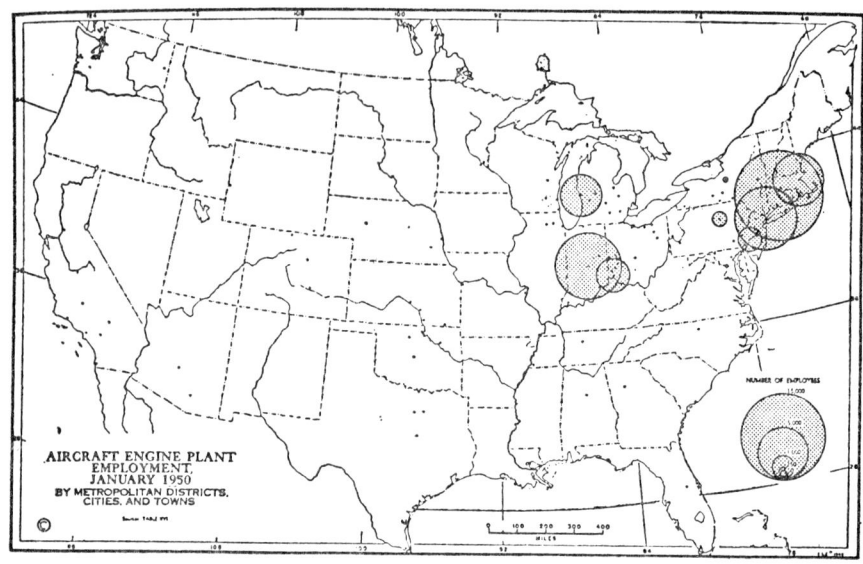

(Fig. 13)

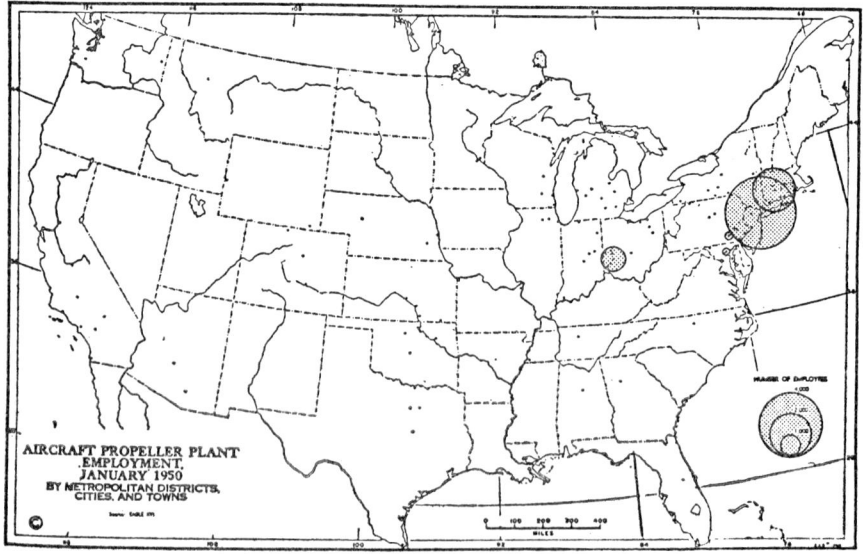

(Fig. 14)

finds only 27.7 per cent of the industry located in the interior of the country in contrast to 57.7 per cent in 1944.[25]

The most conspicuous phase of this shift is found in the relocation of engine and propeller production, most of which was located in the interior during the war, but which has largely returned to the prewar coastal locations.

The correspondence, noted in 1944, between the distribution of aircraft manufacture and the distribution of all manufacturing, is lessened considerably by the reduction in the importance of aircraft in the East Central region and the heavy emphasis in the Pacific region. However, a slightly heavier concentration in the thirty-three Industrial Areas (73.7 per cent in 1950; 63.4 per cent in 1944) has followed the elimination of several nonindustrial aircraft centers such as Atlanta, Omaha, Tulsa, Oklahoma City, and New Orleans, and the further concentration in the industrial areas of Los Angeles, Seattle, Baltimore, Hartford, Indianapolis and New York.

In a similar fashion, correspondence of the distribution of the aircraft industry with the distribution of the nation's population has lessened with the withdrawal of the industry from many states, especially the populous states of the East North Central region, and its concentration in certain less populous states such as Washington, Maryland and Connecticut.

Comparison with 1940 Pattern of Location

Elimination of the wartime centers that resulted from the temporary occupance of branch plants and converted facilities is an expected product of the return to normalcy. Of far more significance than a comparison with the abnormal situation of 1944 is a comparison of the 1950 situation with that of 1940, both representing periods of aircraft manufacture in a peacetime economy.[26] Any variations noted are much more apt to be indicative of significant trends.

In summary, the distribution of the aircraft industry in 1950 can be described as essentially a return to the prewar pattern. In degree of concentration, in the states and cities of heaviest concentration, and even

---

[25] The 1944 percentage is based on floorspace capacity; the 1950 figure on number of employees.

[26] It is recognized that the two periods, one preceding and one following a world war, are far from identical in all respects, and that "peacetime" itself is a relative term, possibly not strictly applicable to either year. Nevertheless the emergency factors that dominated in 1944 were largely absent in 1940 and in 1950 (January).

in the relative rank in importance of producing areas, resemblances are more prominent than was true in the comparison with 1944. Differences do exist, however, and are frequently significant.

The industry is located in the same seven regions as in 1940 but they appear in somewhat shuffled order except for the Pacific region, in first place in both years. The South Atlantic has fallen from third to seventh. New England has risen from fourth to third, and the West South Central from seventh to fourth.

The fourteen states listed as containing units of the industry represent a gain of three over the 1940 list. Oklahoma, appearing in 1940, is missing in 1950, while the new states of Massachusetts, Ohio, Missouri and Texas are added.[27] Only eight states in 1940 had one per cent or more of the total. This is increased to thirteen in 1950 with the addition of Pennsylvania, Massachusetts, Ohio, Missouri and Texas.

The principal changes occurring in the order of importance of these states consist of the rise in rank of Washington from sixth to fourth, and the appearance of Texas in second place; and the fall in rank of Maryland from second to sixth, of Connecticut from third to fifth and of New Jersey from fifth to eighth.

The list of ten metropolitan districts containing as much as one per cent of the total, loses Bridgeport but is augmented by the addition of six, St. Louis, Muskegon and Hagerstown, which claimed small units of the 1940 industry, and the entirely "new" cities of Fort Worth, Dallas and Boston.

Los Angeles and New York remain in first and second place although with reduced percentages in each case. Seattle has jumped from seventh to second place, Wichita from ninth to sixth, and Fort Worth appears as fourth. Changes in the opposite direction include that of Baltimore from third to ninth, Buffalo from fifth to fourteenth, and Bridgeport from eighth to nineteenth.

The greatest changes have occurred in the airframe segment of the industry, and the major changes noted in the total industry can largely be attributed to shifts in the airframe plants. Such changes account for the introduction of Texas and Missouri, and the cities of Fort Worth, St. Louis, and Dallas to the ranks of major aircraft areas; and for the increase in the relative importance of the West South Central region, of the state of Washington, and the cities of Seattle, Wichita and Hagerstown.

[27] Except for Massachusetts, the omission of these states in 1940 is a product of incomplete coverage as all contained small units of the industry.

Changes in the distribution of airframe manufacture also resulted in the elimination of Tulsa, the state of Oklahoma, and the East South Central region; and the relative decline of the South Atlantic region, of Connecticut and Maryland, and of Baltimore, Buffalo and Bridgeport.

In the engine field, change in the relative position of the three major companies has resulted in a change of rank in engine manufacture by the three leading regions, states and metropolitan districts. In first place are New England, Connecticut and Hartford, followed by the East North Central region, Indiana and Indianapolis, and finally by the Middle Atlantic region, New Jersey and metropolitan New York— the opposite of the situation in 1940. Expansion of engine manufacture has added the states of Massachusetts and Ohio and the cities of Boston, Cincinnati, and Philadelphia to the major aircraft producers. Syracuse also appears as an engine center of minor importance.[28] The relative decline of New Jersey is attributable to shifts in aircraft engine labor.

The increase in the number of significant states and cities indicates a somewhat lessened degree of concentration over the 1940 situation. This is expressed by the revised coefficient of scatter: 4 in 1940 with the four leading states containing 79.1 per cent of the total employment; 7 in 1950 with the seven leading states containing 80.1 per cent.

The share attributable to California, the leading state in both years, is reduced slightly from 38.9 per cent in 1940 to 30.4 per cent in 1950. The share of the leading metropolitan district, that of Los Angeles, falls from 33.2 per cent to 26.7 per cent.

The creation of a few new inland aircraft centers has resulted in a decrease in the industry's concentration on the two coasts, 72.3 per cent being so located in 1950; 88.0 per cent in 1940. This again is largely the result of shifts in airframe manufacture. The production of engines and propellers remains rather concentrated in the prewar and new centers near the North Atlantic coast.

A lighter concentration in the Industrial Areas of the country, 73.7 per cent in 1950 compared to 90.7 per cent in 1940[29] followed the establishment of important aircraft centers in the nonindustrial cities of Fort Worth, Dallas and Columbus and the additional concentration in Wichita and Hagerstown.

[28] Philadelphia and Syracuse were small scale producers of aircraft engines in 1940.
[29] The *Census of Manufactures* figure of 88.1 per cent, quoted earlier, was for the year 1939. The above figure, 90.7, was computed from the same sources as the other tabulations in this chapter and applies to February, 1940.

Interpretation of Postwar Location

Aside from the highly important question as to why the prewar companies, with large, modern plants available in interior locations, chose to return to their prewar coastal sites, the variations of the 1950 pattern of distribution from that of 1944 seem to require little in the way of interpretation. It seems adequate to make the very simple observation that the temporary wartime centers were eliminated with the closing of unnecessary modification centers, of emergency-operated branch plants, and with the reconversion of the properties of nonaircraft facilities.

On the other hand, the variations from the 1940 pattern call for the explanation of the selection of sites new to the industry—by new companies and by old companies changing location.[30]

Developments Affecting the 1950 Locational Pattern

Return to Prewar Locations

The most prominent of the industry's developments affecting location in the postwar period was the prompt closing of branch plants with the falling off of military orders. With the few exceptions noted, the airframe, engine, and propeller companies that had expanded by means of establishing branch factories, withdrew from the new sites and concentrated all activities in their prewar centers.

Suggestions to the contrary had been made. Undersecretary of War Patterson, in July, 1944, contended before the War Contracts Subcommittee of the Senate Military Affairs Committee that postwar plants should be scattered among inland plants.[31]

An immediate answer forecast the industry's unwillingness to comply and summarized the opposing arguments of the companies.

---

[30] A great many of the apparent shifts in the industry resulting in changes in the relative rank of cities, states, and regions, are often due to nothing more than the differing rates of expansion (or contraction) of individual companies. It should be observed that the cities of Seattle, St. Louis, Boston, Baltimore, Hartford, Buffalo, Bridgeport, and Fort Worth are single-company cities. The same may be said of the states of Washington, Missouri, and Massachusetts. As the fortunes of these companies fluctuate, so do the relative positions of the areas involved. Unless it can be determined that the change in rank of producing areas is the product of actual shift of a portion of the industry—removal or addition of a company—the change has been ignored in this discussion. It does not appear to be within the scope of this study to explain the success or failure of individual firms.

[31] "Industry Studies Patterson Plan to Decentralize Aircraft Plants," *Aviation News,* July 24, 1944, p. 25.

The early aircraft plants were built in their present locations for eminently practical reasons, and the same reasons will apply with equal force in the postwar period .... Restricted operations will require that the companies utilize their plants least expensive to maintain in areas where the proper labor supply is located, where tax problems have been stabilized, where good peacetime housing is available, and where climate is particularly suited to aircraft production.

Truly inland and southern manufacturing plants such as Omaha, Wichita, Fort Worth, and Marietta facilities, still are dependent upon the vulnerable mid-northern industrial section for materials, parts, and supplies.

It remains to be seen whether the Army and Navy in peacetime will have sufficient political influence to locate production strategically ....[32]

Apparently this influence failed to materialize during the period of demobilization. The Bureau of Aeronautics recognized the fact that the advantages of the companies' home locations outweighed those of the new sites and made no attempt to influence the companies that had chosen to return to their original sites.[33]

A specific example was provided on a later occasion. When the Wright Aeronautical Corporation announced plans to move from Paterson to nearby Wood Ridge, New Jersey (New York), it was approached by the Air Coordinating Committee with the idea of moving to the Cincinnati plant instead. The company agreed if the Government should pay the expenses of the move, but submitted costs so high that the Committee failed to request the appropriation.[34]

Reasons for Return.
The subcommittee on Demobilization of the Aircraft Industry, in preparing its report of October, 1945, to the Air Coordinating Committee, obtained from the companies their reasons for planning to return to prewar locations. These were summarized as follows:

(1) Prewar locations offer natural advantages as a result of climate, weather conditions, availability of skilled labor, and so forth.
(2) The companies in many cases have substantial investments in their home plants and experimental facilities.
(3) Executive, key personnel, engineers, and production workers have

---

[32] *Ibid.,* pp. 25–26.
[33] Interview with Capt. R. J. H. Conn, U.S.N., Industrial Planning Branch, Procurement Division, Bureau of Aeronautics, Washington, D. C., August 1, 1947.
[34] Interview with Col. John C. Vaughn, Industrial Planning Branch, Procurement and Industrial Planning Division, War Department, Washington, D. C., August 4, 1947.

family ties, including home ownership, in their prewar localities. As a result, they would be reluctant to move and in moving a company valuable people might be lost.[35]

Subsequent questioning of the companies disclosed essentially the same reasons for the return to early locations as those suggested before the moves took place, although an occasional additional influencing factor is offered . . . .

Developments in 1950

With the invasion of South Korea in June, 1950, and the threat of World War III, the aircraft industry began its third round of expansion. Although civil plane output dropped during 1950, military plane production was considerably above that of 1949. Total employment in the industry had increased to 292,000 by January, 1951.

Congress had appropriated $8,000,000,000 for aircraft by the end of the year, a sum expected to permit the production of from 12,000 to 15,000 planes. The heavier, more complicated planes of 1951 required about four times the effort of those produced during World War II, and it was estimated that the capacity for 50,000 a year, asked for by President Truman, would require an industrial base approximately equal to that of 1944.[36]

The necessary expansion soon began to follow the familiar pattern of the early 1940's. Home plants added to their payrolls and extensive subcontracting was undertaken by many companies, notably Boeing, Lockheed and Grumman. Nonaircraft companies re-entered the field.

Of greater interest in its effect on location of the industry was the re-use of idle plants by aircraft and nonaircraft companies. During the last part of 1950 and the first months of 1951, the following were accomplished or announced for early realization: Douglas Aircraft re-opened its Tulsa plant in order to build the Boeing B-47 bomber. Lockheed occupied the Atlanta plant for the modification of B-29 Superforts and the production of medium bombers. Bell leased the former Globe Aircraft plant at Fort Worth to produce jet engine nacelles for Boeing and Consolidated. North American Aircraft was scheduled to occupy the Columbus plant as soon as it was vacated by the Curtiss

---

[35] *War Plants Disposal—Aircraft Plants, Hearing*, p. 48. See *infra*, p. 180 for identification of the Air Coordinating Committee.
[36] *Aviation Week*, January 15, 1951, p. 12.

Airplane Division which had withdrawn from active airplane manufacture. Chase Aircraft, rapidly expanding to become one of the major producers, leased a portion of the Birmingham modification plant, moving most of its operations there from Trenton. Goodyear was scheduled to re-activate its Phoenix plant for the production of plane components.

Similar developments took place in the aircraft engine industry with Pratt and Whitney re-opening its Southington, Connecticut, plant for sub-assemblies; and General Electric occupying more of the Cincinnati plant in which it was planned to consolidate most of its turbo-jet production. Lycoming Division of AVCO Corporation was licensed to manufacture the Wright R-1820 engine in Stratford, Connecticut (Bridgeport).

Other wartime plants were occupied by nonaircraft companies licensed to manufacture the models of aircraft or engine companies. General Motors, utilizing the Kansas City aircraft plant for Pontiac automobile assembly, converted to build the Republic F-84F Thunderjet fighter. Wings for this plane were to be produced in Republic's wartime Evansville plant by Servel, Inc. (gas refrigerators). Kaiser-Frazer, occupying the Willow Run plant, was licensed to produce the Fairchild C-119 Packet. Ford took over the Dodge Chicago plant to build the Pratt and Whitney R-4360 engine.

The established automobile centers also re-entered the picture as automobile companies, licensed to manufacture aircraft engines, chose to do so in their own properties. Another heavy concentration of activity in the Detroit area seemed inevitable as Ford prepared for the production of Pratt and Whitney's R-4360 in Dearborn; Packard for the General Electric J-48 jet; Kaiser-Frazer for the Wright R-1300; and Chrysler for the Pratt and Whitney J-48 jet in a new plant planned for the Detroit area.

Elsewhere in the established automobile centers, Studebaker was licensed to produce General Electric's J-47 jet in South Bend; Chevrolet, the Allison J-35 jet in Tonowanda, New York (Buffalo); Buick, the Wright J-65 jet in Flint; and Nash, the Pratt and Whitney R-2800 in Kenosha, Wisconsin (Milwaukee).

Thus, another ten of the major wartime aircraft centers, as well as a few of the minor centers, had been, or were soon to be re-activated. Of the major ones, only Cleveland, Akron, New Orleans, Omaha and Oklahoma City were not included, and it seemed unlikely that the last two named, Defense Department-owned, would long remain idle.

8. The Korean War Expansion

The depressed state of the aircraft industry in 1947 led to studies by the President's Air Policy Commission and the Congressional Air Policy Board. Both groups recommended that immediate action be taken to increase appropriations for aircraft procurement. Action was taken in 1948 and 1949, although not to an impressive extent, but in 1950 the Secretary of Defense, Louis Johnson, opened the year with an all-out economy drive. The economy drive gave way to the necessity for a sharp increase in procurement with the advent of the Korean War in June, 1950. Between 1949 and 1953, the year that the Korean War was terminated, annual production of military aircraft expanded from 2,592 units to 10,626 units and the floorspace utilized was doubled. During the same period, profits increased from approximately 11 per cent of net worth to 29 per cent.

The expansion was characteristically different from that of World War II. Even though the maximum production attained during the Korean War was much less than that of World War II, aircraft firms spent more for facilities expansion than they did during World War II when the government was the principal investor. The Department of Defense was reluctant to finance new investments when it already possessed much idle floorspace and equipment that it considered useful. Aircraft producers, in many cases, found World War II facilities poorly suited for current production. The decrease in government assistance resulted in larger private investment. Private investment was significantly facilitated by the passage of the Defense Production Act of 1950, which allowed producers to amortize a new investment over a five-year period for tax purposes. Even with this legislation, however, producers felt restrained to limit their expansion to what could be profitably utilized during anticipated low swings of future procurement cycles.

Expansion was largely achieved by using the branch plants of the prime contractors and by subcontracting work that could not be handled by prime contractors' facilities. There was little need for licensing in view of the extent of the expansion required. Producers were naturally less willing to share the market with subcontractors and licensees when they were able to expand production themselves.

In the selection that follows, John S. Day, in a study prepared for the Harvard Business School, describes the nature of the aircraft industry's expansion during the Korean War and provides an interesting contrast between this expansion and that during World War II.

Accelerating Aircraft Production in the Korean War*
John S. Day

The Need to Expand Airframe Production Facilities During the Korean War

After the outbreak of the Korean War, as in World War II, the airframe companies and the Defense Department were faced with numerous instances where increased production schedules required facilities in addition to those already in operation in the industry. There was, however, a major difference between the two periods.

During World War II most of the airframes were constructed in buildings erected during the war years; i.e., 1939 to 1944. On June 25, 1950, the airframe manufacturers found present structures, either their own or government plants, more nearly sufficient to handle the tremendous increase in orders. Though the equipment was for a while extremely critical, with shortages developing for a number of long lead-time machine tools, the wait for new plants was never a major factor limiting the acceleration of airframe production during the Korean War.

What then were the reasons for the construction program[1] which did take place? Despite the generally favorable "bricks and mortar" situation, not all World War II facilities still in existence in 1950 were immediately usable and some additional structures were erected. Some of the buildings constructed 8 or 10 years earlier were found to be partially obsolete.

One reason for such obsolescence was the increase in size and weight of some of the airplanes. Bomber airframe assembly in 1953, in particular, required high ceiling space, balcony overhead area, traveling cranes, and wide bays. The need for spacious areas both in height and in breadth was spectacularly illustrated at Boeing's Seattle plant. Though the B-52 assembly is, perhaps, an extreme example, it represents the kind of space problem experienced to a somewhat lesser degree by all manufacturers of large airframes. In Seattle, assembly jigs towered up from the main floor with their height graphically accentuated by the red lights glowing atop each jig as a warning to the overhead crane operators.

Former temporary subcontractors expecting to recommence airframe

---

* Reprinted by permission of the publishers from John S. Day: *Subcontracting Policy in the Airframe Industry* (Boston: Division of Research, Harvard Business School, 1956), pp. 43–57, 68–69. The title supplied by the editor.

[1] See Exhibit 1 for the comparative sizes of the World War II and Korean War construction programs.

production sometimes discovered their older multistoried plants an important factor limiting efficient production. One temporary subcontractor was forced to remove an entire section of the rear wall of his multistoried plant to enable the construction of doors and an elevator large enough to handle the relatively small assemblies he was manufacturing. In turn, this remodeling created the need for replanning the production flow on each floor so that it would commence and end at this one elevator, the only entrance and exit sufficiently large to handle the assemblies. Yet this plant had successfully produced a similar subcontracted airframe unit during World War II.

The need for additional land around a plant is a requirement which developed with the jet airplane. In several cases, company runways long enough for propeller-driven aircraft, were found to be inadequate for jets. Extending the old runways was often impracticable because of the population growth which had taken place around the plant. Relocating the runway was usually the most economical and satisfactory answer.

The relocation of a runway to an area some distance from the final assembly line raised the question of whether it might not be wise to transfer the final assembly operation to a new building alongside the runway. This reasoning was based on the assumption that it would be easier to transport a subassembly over the road than to move the complete airframe.

Another problem which required new locations and subsequent facilities was the need for test areas where the jet engine noise would not bother the town's residents. In one instance a company had faced up to this problem early in the Korean War and had built a facility in a small town some distance from the city. All went well for a time. The company continued to hire additional workers many of whom moved to be near their work. As residential and business areas developed to supply these workers, some of the local citizenry, who had at first been delighted with the idea of a new employer moving into their town, began to protest strenuously about the noise and threatened legal action against the manufacturer.

The Size of the Prime Contractor Expansion

At the outbreak of the Korean War, more than 60,000,000 square feet of floor space were being used for aircraft manufacture as compared with the 9,500,000 square feet in operation in 1939 when European orders started the industry expansion.[2] In addition there were several large government-owned plants which were either on a so-called standby basis or had been leased to other kinds of businesses with the provision that they would be quickly returned to the government in time of need. The adjective "so-called" is used advisedly since these plants were not equipped to any degree with the highly specialized (and expensive) machine tools needed for modern aircraft production.

The large airframe plants originally proposed as a government reserve at the end of World War II would have provided approximately 23,000,000 square feet of new space in the event of a new emergency.[3] By 1947 the President's Air Policy Commission listed available reserve airframe space as being 21,200,000 square feet.[4] By 1949–1950 increased orders had made it possible to employ a portion of this plant reserve. Thus, by the outbreak of war in Korea, the plants in Fort Worth, Columbus, Dallas, and St. Louis were actively occupied, at least in part, by various airframe companies.[5] The remaining reserve plant area probably equaled at least 10,000,000 square feet, an amount which still provided opportunity for a sizable expansion without building a new plant.

The requirements of the Armed Services, however, soon made it apparent that something other than the reserve capacity would be needed to fulfill all the needs of the new airpower program. New plants plus the employment of de-mothballed government plants and the conversion of former airframe plants to their original use increased the industry floor area from 63,000,000 square feet in productive use in 1950 to more than 126,000,000 square feet by the end of 1953.[6]

Exhibit 1 shows that nearly all airframe companies paid more dollars for general expansion in 1950–1953 than they did during World War II. In addition, "structures" under Exhibit 2 makes it clear that the airframe industry as a whole spent or intended to spend far more of its own dollars on "brick and mortar" than it did during World War II years.

[2] R. Modley and T. S. Cawley, *Aviation Facts and Figures, 1953* (Washington, Lincoln Press, 1953), p. 8.
[3] Report of the Surplus Property Administration to the Congress, *Aircraft Plants and Facilities* (Washington, Government Printing Office, 1946), p. 51.
[4] A Report by the President's Air Policy Commission, *Survival in the Air Age* (Washington, Government Printing Office, 1948), p. 68.
[5] W. G. Cunningham, *The Aircraft Industry: A Study in Industrial Location* (Los Angeles, Lorin L. Morrison, 1951), p. 183.
[6] "New Doctrine Aims to Stabilize Industry," *Aviation Week*, March 15, 1954, p. 105.

EXHIBIT 1. *Company Expenditures for Airframe Facilities Expansion, World War II and Korean War (Millions of Dollars)*

NAME OF COMPANY	1940–1944[1]	1950–1953[2]
Bell Aircraft Corp.	$ 5.8	$ 6.2
Boeing Airplane Co.	10.8	15.3
Consolidated Vultee Aircraft Corp.	27.5	13.0
Douglas Aircraft Co., Inc.	15.1	18.1
Fairchild Engine and Airplane Corp.	1.4	6.9
Lockheed Aircraft Corp.	25.1	25.4
Glenn L. Martin Co.	3.9	4.0
McDonnell Aircraft Corp.	—	20.8
North American Aviation, Inc.	5.0	12.9
Republic Aviation Corp.	.6	9.9

[1] Value of facilities authorized.
[2] Value of requests for tax authorization received by the Aircraft Division of National Production Authority as of March 1953.

Source: R. Modley and T. S. Cawley, *Aviation Facts and Figures,* 1953 (Washington, Lincoln Press, Inc., 1953), p. 12.

EXHIBIT 2. *Cost of Emergency Facilities Expansion, Aircraft Industry World War II and Korean War (Millions of Dollars)*

	TOTAL	PRIVATELY FINANCED	FEDERALLY FINANCED
TOTAL EXPANSION			
1940–1945*	$3,894	$ 420	$3,474
1950–1953	3,528[1]	1,204[2]	2,324[1]
STRUCTURES			
1940–1945	1,556	212	1,344
1950–1953	1,085[1]	805[3]	280[1]
EQUIPMENT			
1940–1945	2,338	208	2,130
1950–1953	2,443[1]	399[4]	2,044[1]

* Cost of manufacturing facilities authorized July 1940–June 1945.
[1] Estimate by Aircraft Industries Association of Air Force and Navy obligations since Korea (excludes funds for guided missiles, electronics, and Air Force Heavy Press Program).
[2] Total Tax Amortization Certificates processed by the National Production Authority Aircraft Division as of March 1, 1953.
[3] Totals of Tax Amortization Certificates for land, building, facilities, and miscellaneous processed by National Production Authority Aircraft Division as of March 1, 1953.
[4] Total of Tax Amortization Certificates for plant equipment, machine tools, etc., processed by National Production Authority Aircraft Division as of March 1, 1953.

Source: R. Modley and T. S. Cawley, *Aviation Facts and Figures,* 1953 (Washington, Lincoln Press, Inc., 1953), p. 11.

There appear to be three reasons for industry's investing its own funds in buildings rather than waiting for the Defense Department to provide money for new construction. First, the Defense Department refused to supply construction funds in any large amount so long as usable floor space existed either in government plants or in plants owned by the permanent subcontractors and probably temporary subcontractors.

Second, there was also a tremendous need for new and larger types of machine tools. Some of these machines were in an early stage of development. With the general availability of funds increasing or decreasing as Congress read the headlines, the Armed Services preferred to employ their facility contracts to further machine tool development, to procure machine tools many of which were very expensive, and to pay for the installation of some of this special equipment. As a direct result of these policies the government supplied the bulk of the new machinery during the Korean War, making it possible for the industry to concentrate its spending on housing for the equipment.

Third, the government offered tax amortization privileges during the Korean War as it did during World War II. This was a powerful incentive for the investment of a company's own funds, although the straight five-year amortization period was not quite as attractive as the World War II period of five years or the duration of the emergency, whichever was shorter.

The Korean Expansion Policies of Several Airframe Manufacturers

Faced with a lack of Armed Services funds for building expansion, but conversely spurred on by the fast write-off tax provisions and the idea that requirements in the foreseeable future were bound to be greater than in the 1945–1949 period, most airframe companies undertook a limited expansion of floor space. Each airframe manufacturer's policies on the amount of expansion were different.

As soon as Company A's management realized that the exigencies of the Korean War demanded an appreciable amount of new floor space at its plant, the board of directors voted funds for a multimillion dollar plant expansion in the belief that the most efficient way to produce their type of airframe was in their own plant. As schedules continued to speed up and the backlog of orders continued to mount, it became apparent to Company A's management that even with the new facilities the company could not hope to meet the load thrust upon it. This time the board of directors considered the several millions of dollars already invested in new plant and equipment as the maximum and refused to authorize additional large capital expenditures. Since the Armed Services would not provide an appreciable amount of new floor space, the next step for the company was a major subcontracting effort.

In World War II Company B received comparatively little aid from government facility contracts and to a great extent matched government expenditures with its own funds. After Korea Company B spent double the amount of its own funds on facilities as compared with Company A. Company B claims, however, that it did so under the definite policy that it would not expand its over-all production ability beyond the sales point that it hopes it can maintain in the post-Korea market. Company B's management further claims that even though its dollar spending was twice that of Company A, this spending was not primarily for facilities to increase production but rather to modernize and round out certain kinds of production to provide a balanced production potential. Company B's plant and buildings are generally older and less desirable for aircraft production than Company A's which had purchased much of the modern plant built in its immediate area by the government during World War II. Company B immediately engaged in a subcontracting program at the outbreak of the Korean War.

Company C spent small amounts of its own funds on facilities in World War II and was one of the smaller recipients of government funds for facility expansion during that period. Although its facilities expenditures during the Korean War were many times those of World War II days, it still invested less in facilities than did many of its competitors. Company C had for one of its models *the largest subcontracting percentage by weight* of any airframe manufacturer.

The general government policy of "no bricks and mortar if they are available from a subcontractor" did much to limit expansion of prime contractor facilities. It is true that this policy of "no bricks and mortar" in some cases irked the prime contractors. In one instance, a member of company management remarked that the policy made little sense to him when the government refused his firm's request for a new facility on the basis that you should "use available subcontractor brick and mortar" and then authorized a multimillion dollar construction program for a subcontractor who had just received a wing contract from another airframe company. Another prime contractor representative pointed out that the government's position was sometimes unrealistic. A subcontractor needed more than just available floor space; he had to possess a wide bay and, more particularly, high bay area. This representative told of traveling almost the entire Pacific coast trying to find a subcontractor with such high bay space available or one that could be talked into making room for an aircraft order at the expense of his commercial production. Although there were cases in which the Armed Services increased a subcontractor's floor area, the majority of facilities expenditures in the subcontractor plants were also for machine tools, installing equipment, and modification of existing buildings.

The Air Force had available a large supply of stored machine tools and the standby buildings previously mentioned. The tools, those that were usable, were made available to companies which requested them. But the standby buildings were planned to increase total over-all assembly potential without taking into account the demand which would be created for subassemblies, fabrication, and minor assemblies. The activation of these standby plants created an additional demand in many respects competitive with the parent organization.

Most companies were not in the position of Company D which had once used a World War II government facility located only a few miles from its main plant. At the conclusion of the war, the government plant was sold to a private real estate operator who leased various sections of it to different firms. With the outbreak of the Korean conflict, the Air Force repurchased the plant from the real estate operator and turned it over to Company D to operate. As a result, Company D ended with a usable floor space about equal to that of any company in the industry which, when coupled with moderate sales, resulted in a subcontracting program of only minor size.

The Importance of Government Policy to Airframe Plant Expansion

Current Defense Department policies regarding the investment of government funds in assets for airframe manufacturing are highly important to the expansion of prime contractor facilities. Unless the government is willing to supply such fixed assets, the airframe industry must maintain adequate capital, credit, or plants in being to meet the tremendous cyclical production requirements generated by the historically spasmodic needs of national defense. Such a capital structure would be a costly burden during future prolonged periods of low sales volume similar to those which occurred in the 1920's and 1930's.

Traditionally, airframe managements have been extremely cautious about expanding facilities beyond the point they can be profitably employed during the low swings of the aircraft procurement cycle. From Exhibit 3 it can be seen that before World War II and the Korean War the sales dollar tended to increase somewhat proportionately to each dollar invested in facilities. During both wars, however, sales increased at a much faster rate than did company purchases of new facilities

EXHIBIT 3. NET BOOK VALUE OF FACILITIES AND SALES OF 12 MAJOR AIRFRAME COMPANIES, 1937-1954

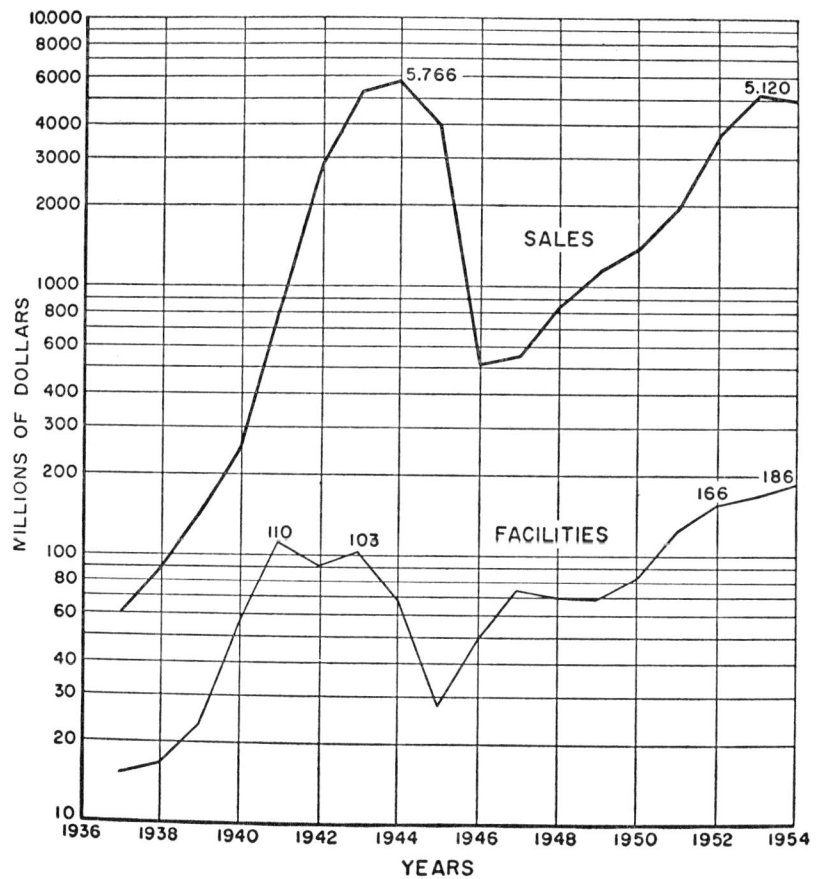

Source: *Aviation Facts and Figures, 1955.*

because of the tremendous investment by the government in airframe-producing assets.

In addition to airframe management's natural reluctance to invest funds in assets which might be idle more often than they are in production, there is the belief held throughout the industry that present-day earnings are much too low to justify any such risky investment. Exhibit 4 shows that earnings as a percentage of sales for 12 major airframe companies have ranged from almost nothing in 1948 to a high of over 4% in 1950.[7] On the other hand, earnings as a percentage of net worth climbed by 1954 to almost 30% because of the wide employment of government-owned facilities, particularly new equipment, during the Korean War and post-Korean War period. Exhibit 5 indicates clearly the heavy investment by the United States Government in the airframe industry even though the figures may not be strictly comparable because of varying depreciation policies.

High-level management personnel stated to the author and have since made it clear before the House Armed Services Committee that unless airframe companies can retain a larger percentage of earnings, it will be increasingly difficult for them to buy more and more plant and equipment to meet the needs of emergency defense. Conversely, the plane makers are probably planning sufficient investment to provide the new capacity required to fulfill normal sales forecasts. For example, the House hearings disclosed that Douglas, Boeing, and Convair planned to invest a total of about $65,000,000 in new facilities in 1956–1957 and North American, $30,000,000. Significantly, the first three firms have commercial airliner programs underway and North American is developing new interests in the atomic reactor, rocket, and electronics fields.

The airframe industry, which has paid out as much as 50% of its earnings in dividends,[8] currently is in no position to tie up funds in nonproductive plants and equipment. Even if the government were disposed to allow higher profits, the author believes present-day management would employ such increased earnings to expand working capital and to further research and development. Again this is borne out by the statements made before the House Armed Services Committee.

---

[7] Current renegotiation proceedings may reduce even these low percentages of profit. For example, the renegotiation board ruling that the Boeing Airplane Company must return $9,800,000 of its 1952 profits, unless set aside by higher court decision, will lower the over-all percentage of profit shown in Exhibit 4 for 1952.

[8] *The Wall Street Journal,* February 21, 1956.

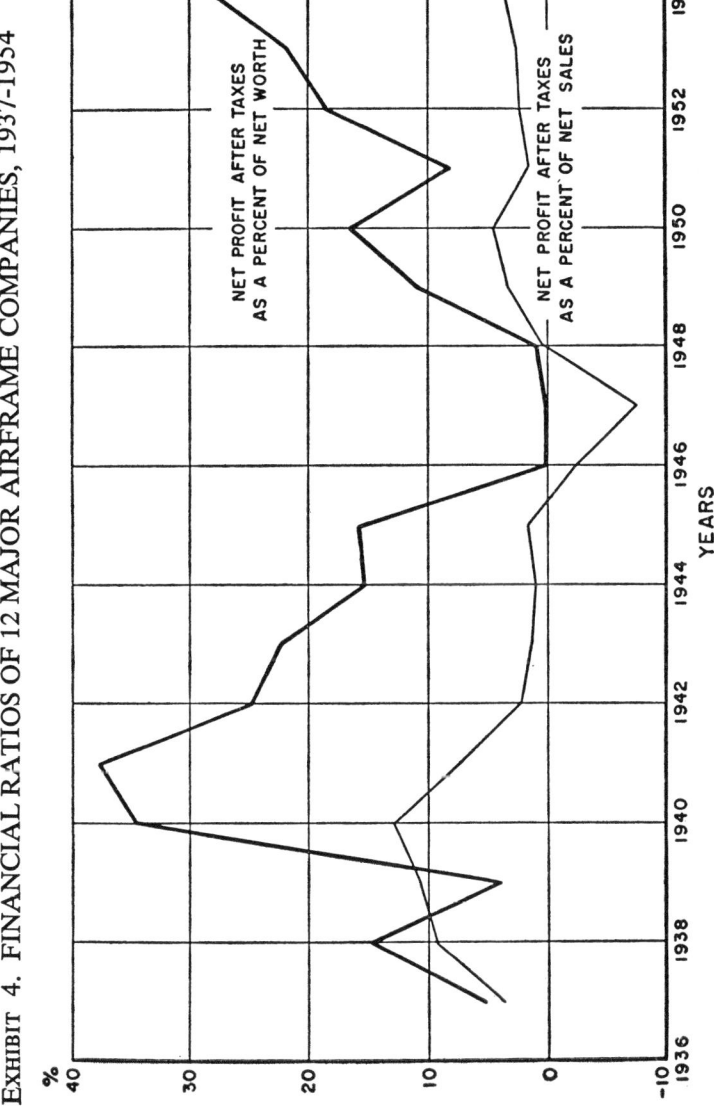

EXHIBIT 4. FINANCIAL RATIOS OF 12 MAJOR AIRFRAME COMPANIES, 1937–1954

Source: *Aviation Facts and Figures, 1955.*

For example, Lockheed officials claimed they required at least $100,000,000 in short-term loans and perhaps as much as $30,000,000 from new stock issues to finance working capital needs.[9] The executive vice president of McDonnell Aircraft stated that the airframe industry needed increased earnings to buy more research facilities.[10] And in a statement to his stockholders, J. L. Atwood, President of North American Aviation, Inc., pointed out that the $66,000,000 worth of capital improvements made or planned since 1950 were insufficient since "requirements are pyramiding on us."

It appears that even if the government allowed profit margins to increase, the airframe manufacturers would still require, in the foreseeable future, large expenditures of taxpayer funds to meet expanded production needs during a defense period or any period when a sharp, sudden increase in airframe output is needed. This single, important factor provides government planners with an extremely potent control over the amounts of work which will be processed in prime contractor controlled facilities during an emergency.

Several Air Force officers at Wright Field frankly admitted that this control factor was recognized and used during the Korean War. This was evidenced by the previously discussed policy of no funds for prime contractor "brick and mortar" as a means of suggesting to the prime contractors that subcontracting should be employed in lieu of new plant construction. Admittedly, the real power in the refusal to supply construction funds stems from the nature of the airframe industry since nothing in the Defense Department's Korean War decision prevented, or could even remotely be construed to prevent, the prime contractor from spending his own funds for expansion. The economic strength inherent in the Defense Department's ability to force subcontracting by the refusal to advance funds for facilities can only be employed beyond the point where current industry plant capacity will no longer handle the production load.

The Use of Branch Plants

Though the Defense Department effectively prevented the prime contractors from obtaining government funds to construct new airframe facilities, the outputs of the individual manufacturers continued to rise during the early 1950's. In part, this was due to subcontracting and, in

[9] *Ibid.*, March 8, 1956.
[10] *Ibid.*, February 29, 1956.

EXHIBIT 5. TOTAL INVESTMENT OF GOVERNMENT AND PRIVATE FUNDS IN FACILITIES USED BY CERTAIN COMPANIES DURING 1955

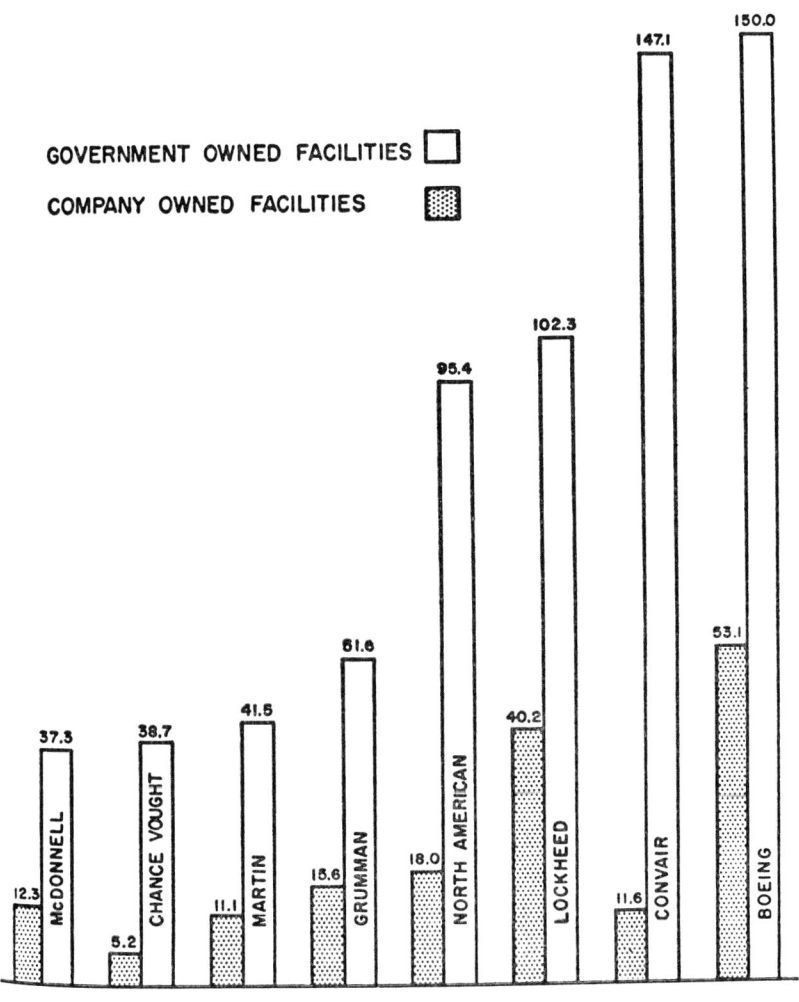

Source: Testimony before the House Armed Services Committee, as reported in the *Wall Street Journal,* February 20, 1956, to March 8, 1956.

part, it was the result of the assignment of government reserve plants to specific airframe companies as branch plants.

The use of large branch plants in the airframe industry commenced with the influx of sizable Army, Navy, and European orders prior to Pearl Harbor. For example, Douglas, with its parent plant in Santa Monica, had a big prewar branch facility at El Segundo where it built plants to be located at a great distance from the parent plant. For the famous SBD. As the defense planners continued to emphasize the need for dispersion[11] and the ability of widely spaced plants to tap new labor markets, the tendency was for the newer, government-constructed example, North American, though it expanded its basic Inglewood plant eleven times, opened a Dallas plant to produce the AT-6 trainer and then a midwestern branch at Kansas City to increase B-25 output.[12]

The branch plants constructed during World War II were designed as complete airframe manufacturing facilities. If a company has sufficient orders for a new model so that the operation of two production lines is economical, or is producing several different models, then a branch plant becomes of great value to the parent corporation. Although at least one of the major airframe producers has "subcontracted" work to a branch plant, the problems of distance, transportation, and space utilization make branch facilities expensive to operate unless a reasonably large output is required. Thus, the branch plants in operation in 1954 were administered as separate divisions of their parent corporations and produced what was essentially a complete airframe in their own right. For example, Lockheed manufactured the B-47 at Marietta, Boeing the B-47 at Wichita,[13] North American the FJ-2 and specific models of the F-86 at Columbus.

Branch plants obviously add to the total airframe production potential. Since such facilities often operate almost as separate companies hundreds of miles from the parent plant, they tend to create their own outside manufacturing requirements rather than to support the "bits and pieces" needed of the parent plant. Thus the manufacturer faced with the task of increasing the output of a particular model would not consider branch plant operation unless forecasts of future requirements were so great that it appeared there would be a continuing need for the relatively large potential of such a plant . . . .

[11] See Chapter 7 for a discussion of dispersion and its effect on subcontractor selection.
[12] F. J. Taylor and L. Wright, *Democracy's Air Arsenal* (New York, Duell, Sloan & Pearce, 1947), p. 79.
[13] Upon the implementation of the increased B-52 program, Boeing-Wichita phased out of B-47 production and commenced work on the B-52.

The Lack of Licensing During the Korean War

Though a domestic airframe license is almost never granted by a design manufacturer in peacetime, the World War I and II situations were vastly different. With a temporarily assured market, wartime patriotism at work, and all companies operating at peak capacity, there was no economic reason for not licensing. A reasonable assumption, then, is that the Korean War would have resulted in a number of license arrangements. Actually the only two instances of major licensing were the formation of the B-47 pool with Boeing as the "design prime" and Lockheed and Douglas as the other prime contractors; and the Republic Aviation–General Motors agreement.[14]

There were two major reasons for this lack of licensing. First, the over-all airframe requirements never reached the proportions of World War II days; whereas the maximum airframe poundage delivered in 1944 equaled 962,000,000 pounds, the Korean crisis by 1953 had developed an estimated output of slightly more than 150,000,000 pounds per year.[15]

Second, as has been stated earlier in this chapter, the 1939 expansion commenced with only about 9,500,000 square feet of floor space in being whereas the Korean requirements were supported by an initial operating plant of over 60,000,000 square feet plus the several government-owned reserve plants. With this amount of standby facility available and the country engaged in a "guns and butter" effort, subcontracting with its greater flexibility had more appeal for both the airframe manufacturer and the producer of civilian goods.

[14] By 1956 several airframe manufacturers had licensed foreign firms to produce certain models of their aircraft.
[15] Modley and Cawley, *op. cit.,* p. 26.

Part V
The Aircraft Industry in Transformation
1956–1965

9. The Missiles Impact

There are four distinctive features of the aircraft industry's history in the period following the Korean War. Two of them pertain to developments in the civilian market for the industry's products and are of lesser importance from the standpoint of dollar sales; the other two relate to changes in government procurement.

In the civilian market, a sharp increase in demand for utility aircraft for personal and business uses took place. Between 1955 and 1963 utility aircraft sales more than doubled. Although this growth seems impressive, utility aircraft sales comprised less than 3 per cent of the dollar sales for the entire aircraft industry.

The second development in the civilian market was a changeover to commercial jet transports, starting in 1958, by Boeing, Convair, Douglas, Fairchild, Grumman, and Lockheed. The Boeing 707 and 720, Douglas DC-8, and Lockheed Electra accounted for the largest percentage of the dollar sales in this market up to 1964. The military market, however, still vastly overshadowed the commercial transport market sector.

The changes in government procurement and their effects on the aircraft industry were much more revolutionary. The first change was caused by guided missiles. Because of their superior speed in delivery of destructive power, missiles were considered a superior substitute for most types of manned military aircraft. Commencing in 1950, the missiles market grew to comprise one quarter of the total aerospace industry sales by 1958. As more missiles have been procured, military aircraft procurement has declined. The impact of this change has been pervasive in terms of the phenomenal adaptation that the aircraft industry has had to make in the composition and technology of its production.

The second major change in government procurement that significantly affected the industry has been in space program procurement, which is an even more recent development than missiles. The impact of the space program is discussed by Leonard S. Silk in the final selection in this book.

In the following article, G. R. Simonson, an economist, analyzes the dynamic influence that guided missiles have had on the aircraft industry. In the decade after the Korean War, the industry, which once was thought of as strictly a producer of aircraft, was being transformed as a consequence of technological innovation.

Missiles and Creative Destruction in the American Aircraft Industry, 1956–1961[1*]
G. R. Simonson

Missiles are known to most of us as aerial vehicles capable of delivering enormous destructive power. Their influence in a business competitive sense already has been almost as devastating. According to the celebrated thesis of the late Joseph A. Schumpeter, the competition that really matters comes from ". . . the new commodity, the new technology, the new source of supply, the new type of organization (the largest-scale unit of control for instance)—competition which commands a decisive cost or quality advantage . . ."[2] It is such stimuli, he said, that ". . . incessantly revolutionizes the economic structure from within, incessantly destroying the old one, incessantly creating a new one."[3] This historic process by which a business firm, or indeed an entire industry, may also become unexpectedly obsolete because of such innovations is what Schumpeter so aptly described as "creative destruction." The "creation" of a new and superior product may form the basis for growth and success of the business involved in its production and sale, while at the same time "destroying" in part or totally those businesses whose products have been surpassed.

In recent years the American aircraft industry, the nation's second largest industrial employer,[4] has had its position of eminence seriously threatened by such a "new product" with a decisive "quality advantage." The new product, in this instance, is the guided missile and the quality advantage it possesses to a remarkable extent is superior speed in aerial weaponry.[5]

[1*] Reprinted by permission of the publishers from *The Business History Review*, XXXVIII, No. 3 (Autumn, 1964), pp. 302–314. Figure 1 has been substituted by the author for Table 3 of the original version.

[1] I am particularly grateful to the Directorate for Statistical Services, Office of the Secretary of Defense, for making available much of the statistical data used in this study.

[2] Joseph A. Schumpeter, *Capitalism, Socialism, and Democracy* (3rd ed., New York, 1950), p. 84.

[3] *Ibid.*, p. 83.

[4] Of all the manufacturing industries within major industrial groupings, as classified by the Department of Labor, the aircraft and parts industry ranked second largest with 701,600 employees in June, 1961. It was exceeded by the first-ranking, motor vehicles and equipment, with 715,800 employees. As recently as 1959, the aircraft and parts industry was the largest employer in the United States. U.S. Department of Labor, *Monthly Labor Review*, vol. 85 (May, 1962), pp. 573–575.

The aircraft industry is usually broken down into four subgroups: airframes; aircraft engines and parts; aircraft propellers and parts; and other aircraft parts and equipment. The concern herein is with the principal segment of the industry, that of airframe manufacturing. Airframe producers are those who assemble the aircraft components, which they may or may not produce themselves, and produce the finished aircraft.

[5] By the time the final versions of the Atlas ICBM are produced, it is expected

Questions concerning the impact which this technological innovation in aerial vehicles has had on the airframe industry, in this already dynamic industrial atmosphere, heretofore have not been sufficiently answered. The purpose of this paper is to suggest the extent to which missiles, the creative innovation, have had a "destructive" effect on the military airframe industry in the United States, and to denote how the industry has responded in these circumstances. The first part of the paper discusses the factors which have conditioned the outcome of the force of creative destruction introduced by missiles and the nature of the change which it has induced in military airframe industry. In the second part, the consequences of this force are measured, denoting particularly the extent of the destructive effects on the military market of airframe producers, and the "creative response"[6] of airframe producers by their entry into the missiles market.

I

The recent missiles innovation in aerial vehicles presented a tremendous challenge to the American airframe industry. The speed at which missiles could travel seemed to provide no effective defense against them. They demonstrated that they were a superior substitute for most military aircraft. A United States Air Force policy statement, for example, noted: "As readily as missiles become operationally suitable, they will be placed into units either to completely or partially substitute for manned aircraft according to military requirements."[7]

The military business of the aircraft industry was thus very much in jeopardy. To quote the observations of one study: "What has put it in jeopardy is the change that missiles have brought to the industry. They not only promise the end of manned military bombers and fighters, but have brought such other lightning changes that huge projects, calling for hundreds of millions of dollars, can be obsolete almost overnight. To

---

to exceed a speed of Mach 15. Wayne Proell and Norman J. Bowman, *A Handbook of Space Flight* (2nd ed., Chicago, 1958), p. 293. This speed vastly exceeds the 650 miles-per-hour speed of the advanced versions of the B-52 which is our principal long range striking force. Aerospace Industries Association, *Aerospace Yearbook* (Washington, D. C., 1962), p. 312.

[6] Schumpeter used this descriptive term when referring to the reaction of the economy, or firms or industries within it, in adapting to a change in ways that are "outside the range of existing practice." See Joseph A. Schumpeter, "The Creative Response in Economic History," *Journal of Economic History*, vol. VII (November, 1947), p. 150.

[7] U.S. Air Force, "The Guided Missile," *The Air Reservist*, vol. IX (December, 1957), p. 4.

meet the challenge, the plane and enginemakers are well aware that their industry must undergo the fastest and most radical change in its history— or die."[8]

No doubt there would continue to be a military demand for transports, trainers, and several other classes of military aircraft; but the demand for fighters and bombers, which accounted for approximately 80 per cent of military aircraft expenditure, was going to decrease. It was apparent that the military aircraft market was going to contract abruptly while the missiles market was going to expand sharply. If the airframe producers were to continue to maintain a high dollar volume of sales, it was obvious that it would not be in producing military aircraft.

One alternative for the industry was to expand its civil aircraft market. Indeed, the industry did increase its civil aircraft market sales absolutely and also relatively to military aircraft sales. Between 1956 and 1960, civil aircraft dollar sales increased by almost 90 per cent while military aircraft dollar sales dropped by approximately 34 per cent.[9] In fact, military aircraft production declined from 5,203 units in 1956 to an estimated 2,700 units in 1960.[10] But the big market for aircraft, of course, was and always had been the military market; and producers fully realized prospects for a sufficiently conpensating growing civil market were decidedly unrealistic.

Diversification in the production of other than aerial vehicles was another alternative. Lockheed, for example, engaged in producing plastic products, municipal refuse disposal systems, shipbuilding, and several other items not related to aerial vehicles. Even though it was one of the more diversified of the airframe producers, this type of production accounted for only around 3 per cent of Lockheed's sales in 1960.[11]

Such diversification by airframe producers, for the most part, evidently was not too appealing. The largely unsuccessful attempts of airframe producers to diversify after World War II undoubtedly had some effect of discouraging efforts in this direction. Moreover, diversification meant entering new and unfamiliar fields of production which presented countless obstacles to be overcome. Perhaps even more deterring was the adjustment, which would be necessary with diversifica-

[8] "Aviation," *Time*, vol. 74 (September 14, 1959), p. 92.
[9] Ben S. Lee (ed.), *Aerospace Facts and Figures, 1962* (Washington, D. C., 1962), p. 14.
[10] *Ibid.*, p. 7.
[11] Moody's Investors Service, *Moody's Industrial Manual*, 1961 (New York, 1961), p. 604.

tion, to dealing with the mass market. Even in peacetime more than 80 per cent of the industry's sales had been to one customer—the Department of Defense. A large part of the balance had been to the airlines which represented a very limited number of customers. Diversification, therefore, in many instances presented a large number of new problems in the areas of production and product distribution which were mostly outside the experience of the industry.

There remained really only one plausible alternative for airframe producers, under the circumstances, if they hoped to maintain a high volume of sales—they had to adapt their production to the missiles demand. Although missiles differed markedly from airplanes, in at least one respect they were alike. The guided missile was made up of the same basic systems as an airplane, namely, the airframe, guidance system, and powerplant. This was one basis for the claim by members of the airframe industry that they were the best qualified by experience to produce missiles.[12] The fact that the relatively small number of airframe producers had 20,000 of the 90,000 professional research engineers and scientists in the United States in their employment in 1952[13] (when missiles procurement was just getting under way) was an added advantage in that a large part of government contracts in the missiles field was of a research and development nature. Also, who had more experience and better established reputations in doing business with the government? Government procurement had accounted for by far the larger part of the sales of most of these companies for over thirty years. These three factors—related production experience, highly technically qualified personnel, and customer-producer familiarity were the primary reasons why the airframe producers were prepared to enter the missiles market.

Despite the impressions of the airframe producers that they were best qualified to produce missiles, they were in for more competition from a larger number of producers than they had experienced for thirty years. Prior to the missiles breakthrough, years of successful experience in airframe production was a necessary condition before a firm would even be invited by the government to compete for such a government contract award. This experience, of course, offered the government some assurance of successful contract performance on the part of the producer.

---

[12] Ben S. Lee (ed.), *Aerospace Facts and Figures, '61* (Washington, D. C., 1961), p. 39.
[13] U.S. Congress, House Committee on Armed Services, *Aircraft Production Costs and Profits* (Washington, D. C., 1956), p. 2583.

Consequently, the market was reserved for the existing producers because experience could not be gained without production, and production depended on previous product sales to the government. But now, as far as the government was concerned, the introduction of missiles to the aerial weapons field had altered the technology of production so immeasurably that the experience factor of airframe producers no longer provided such an insuperable barrier to new competition. Non-airframe producers, particularly those in the electronics field, in some respects were considered technologically better qualified to produce missiles than those with years of experience in aircraft manufacture.

According to Boeing's president, William M. Allen, this new competition was very much in evidence: "Five or six years ago, a competition for Air Force business might have drawn 10 or 12 firms; today when we go to Wright Field or the space agencies, we find upward of 30 to 40 firms competing for major and minor contracts. Included in that group will be the auto producers, the major electrical firms, the principals in the electronics industry, and of course, the principals in the aircraft business.[14] In 1956, non-airframe producers were prime contractors on 10 out of 26 missiles projects which were under way in various stages of development.[15] Missiles, the new product, had broken down the experience barrier to market entry in aerial vehicles production. As a result of this force of creative destruction, airframe producers were experiencing new competition which seriously threatened their hold on the military aerial vehicles market.

Not only did the new technology in missilery sweep aside the most important barrier to entry in the production of military aerial vehicles, which previously meant airplanes almost exclusively, but also it destroyed capitalized values in production facilities. Airframe production facilities were, for the most part, technologically obsolete for missiles production. An extensive amount of investment had to be undertaken by the airframe companies to produce missiles. From 1956 to 1961 the industry spent in the neighborhood of $2,000,000,000 on facilities geared to the development and production of missiles and associated space products.[16] Paradoxically, the industry was building new facilities at a time when it

[14] William H. Gregory, "Write-Offs Swell as Industry Diversifies," *Aviation Week*, vol. 73 (March 7, 1960), pp. 208–209.
[15] Ben S. Lee (ed.), *Aviation Facts and Figures, 1957* (Washington, D. C., 1957), p. 37.
[16] Lee (ed.), *Aerospace Facts and Figures, '61*, p. 42.

had a large amount of excess floor space. To quote a statement by an official of the Aerospace Industries Association:[17]

> Although quite a bit of the productive know-how the industry had acquired in building aircraft was applicable to missilery, manufacturing methods underwent a revolutionary change. Missile parts had to be assembled in dust-free, vibration-free plants under rigid temperature and humidity control. These devices had to be continuously tested and retested while they were actually on the production line. Computer operated tools were required for the high precision machining needed for missiles parts.
> The industry found that its old aircraft plants were not suitable for conversion to missile manufacture; missile facilities had to be built from the ground up. So, while industry was retiring its old plants for lack of plane production, it had to provide new facilities for missiles.

The old airframe facilities were, in many instances, obsolete for the development and production of the new product. In other words, because guided missiles were extremely different from aircraft, so was their technology of production. Technological obsolescence of facilities in the airframe industry and the coincident requirements for new investment were further consequences of the creative destruction caused by missiles.

In addition, missiles brought about drastic change in the composition of labor force in the industry.[18] Jobs were destroyed and new ones created as new skills and technical abilities were required to produce missiles. Between 1954 and 1962 the percentage of hourly production workers in the industry dropped sharply from 71.6 per cent to approximately 40 per cent as the number of technical jobs required to produce the more complex product increased at an astounding rate.[19]

II

The most striking feature about the airframe industry's history during this period was its remarkable success in adapting to the circumstances imposed by the new product and the new technology. Rather than being destroyed, what was so outstanding was the industry's "creative response." The data and discussion below suggest the extent to which the traditional

---

[17] Lee (ed.), *Aerospace Facts and Figures, 1962*, p. 21.
[18] This is not meant to minimize the fact that the advance in aircraft technology has also played an important part in bringing about this change.
[19] Lee (ed.), *Aerospace Facts and Figures, 1962*, pp. 61–66.

airframe producers were successful in adapting to the reduced demand for aircraft and to the new demand for missiles.

Table 1 indicates the principal airframe producers, their military

TABLE 1 *Military Sales, Missile Sales, and Missiles Market Shares, Fourteen American Airframe Producers, Fiscal Years, 1956–1961*[a] (*in thousands of dollars*)

FIRM[b]	FISCAL YEAR	TOTAL MILITARY SALES	MISSILES SALES	PER CENT MISSILES OF MILITARY SALES	MISSILES MARKET SHARE (PER CENT)[c]
Beech[d]	1956	$ 17,863	—	—	—
	1957	33,368	—	—	—
	1958	24,723	—	—	—
	1959	12,398	—	—	—
	1960	18,125	3,165	17.46	.08
	1961	7,951	5,365	67.48	.14
Boeing	1956	779,344	—	—	—
	1957	1,205,770	—	—	—
	1958	1,494,087	11,176	7.48	.41
	1959	1,356,675	108,315	7.98	3.24
	1960	1,208,355	369,022	30.54	9.74
	1961	1,173,317	432,276	36.84	11.09
Cessna	1956	100	—	—	—
	1957	749	—	—	—
	1958	13,435	—	—	—
	1959	23,153	—	—	—
	1960	15,850	—	—	—
	1961	12,605	—	—	—
Chance-Vought	1956	107,211	40,394	37.68	3.46
	1957	225,194	51,141	22.71	2.44
	1958	325,769	59,528	18.27	2.17
	1959	231,213	15,269	6.60	.46
	1960	138,683	9,144	6.59	.24
	1961	102,714	3,971	3.87	.10
Convair	1956	515,769	106,320	20.61	9.10
	1957	995,796	195,261	19.61	9.32
	1958	1,032,813	218,962	21.20	8.00
	1959	1,034,186	305,321	29.52	9.14
	1960	1,265,246	485,653	38.38	12.81
	1961	1,309,524	603,384	46.08	15.47

TABLE 1 (*Continued*)

FIRM[b]	FISCAL YEAR	TOTAL MILITARY SALES	MISSILES SALES	PER CENT MISSILES OF MILITARY SALES	MISSILES MARKET SHARES (PER CENT)[c]
Douglas	1956	797,504	11,331	1.42	.97
	1957	681,967	17,082	2.50	.82
	1958	622,273	162,245	26.07	5.93
	1959	672,723	265,018	39.39	7.94
	1960	470,542	128,261	27.26	3.38
	1961	343,363	135,081	39.34	3.47
Fairchild	1956	77,840	5	.006	—
	1957	76,966	45	.058	—
	1958	63,971	—	.003	—
	1959	36,695	—	—	—
	1960	24,415	—	—	—
	1961	29,402	—	—	—
Grumman	1956	195,027	—	—	—
	1957	177,859	—	—	—
	1958	171,446	—	—	—
	1959	215,909	—	—	—
	1960	251,908	—	—	—
	1961	228,799	12	—	—
Lockheed	1956	574,044	—	—	—
	1957	652,994	14,426	2.21	.68
	1958	639,289	102,370	16.01	3.74
	1959	719,673	391,098	54.34	11.88
	1960	740,868	577,347	77.93	15.23
	1961	973,238	675,833	69.44	17.34
Martin	1956	271,890	26,448	9.73	2.26
	1957	366,451	44,199	12.06	2.11
	1958	439,222	207,602	47.27	7.59
	1959	470,023	320,554	68.20	9.60
	1960	512,352	411,696	80.35	10.86
	1961	606,600	530,894	87.52	13.61
McDonnell	1956	161,973	4,449	2.75	.38
	1957	294,154	16,029	5.45	.77
	1958	415,297	24,774	5.97	.91
	1959	423,667	24,036	5.67	.79
	1960	365,622	8,762	2.40	.23
	1961	296,457	56,151	18.94	1.44

TABLE 1 (*Continued*)

FIRM[b]	FISCAL YEAR	TOTAL MILITARY SALES	MISSILES SALES	PER CENT MISSILES OF MILITARY SALES	MISSILES MARKET SHARES (PER CENT)[c]
North American	1956	743,179	100	.013	—
	1957	1,032,750	9,952	.96	.48
	1958	582,083	14,411	2.48	.53
	1959	735,734	91,886	12.49	2.75
	1960	908,700	165,767	18.24	4.37
	1961	1,046,476	422,138	40.34	10.83
Northrop	1956	252,969	85,347	33.74	7.31
	1957	215,748	74,800	34.67	3.57
	1958	165,277	63,698	38.54	2.33
	1959	142,386	71,545	50.25	2.14
	1960	161,932	103,403	63.86	2.73
	1961	134,550	47,749	35.49	1.22
Republic	1956	306,148	—	—	—
	1957	452,231	—	—	—
	1958	236,786	—	—	—
	1959	952,050	—	—	—
	1960	460,232	—	—	—
	1961	302,662	124	.04	—

[a] Expenditure data apply only to those contracts which the military departments placed directly with each contractor. Additional amounts which may have been paid indirectly to these companies, when serving as subcontractors to prime contractors, are not available. Data shown represent net expenditures for each fiscal year after credits against prior year expenditures have been deducted.
[b] These companies account for all but a very small percentage of total domestic production of completed aircraft. All had military aircraft in production or development as recently as 1959, but in 1961 Fairchild and Martin were no longer engaged in producing completed aircraft.
[c] Obtained by dividing the missiles sales of the company by the total Department of Defense missiles procurement, for that year.
[d] Navy data included in the fiscal-year totals shown for Beech cover the twelve-month period, October 1–September 30.
Sources: *Statistical Abstract of the United States*, 1959, 1960, 1961; Directorate for Statistical Services, Office of the Secretary of Defense.

sales, their missiles sales, and their missiles market shares for the fiscal years 1956–1961. As is observable from the table, the industry's structure was decidedly oligopolistic as it had been since well before World War II.[20] The fourteen firms listed in Table 1 were considered

[20] For an account of the industry's structure both before and during World War II,

the principal airframe producers during the period and produced all but a very small part of the output value of the airframe industry. All had military aircraft in development or production for all of the years except Fairchild and Martin, but they traditionally have been important producers. Stroukoff, Temco, Aero Design, and Piper each had military aircraft in production or development for one or two years during this period; but because their output was neither continuous nor relatively significant in value, they have not been listed in Table 1. All companies indicated had substantial military sales although Beech and Cessna, small producers by comparison, were mostly dependent on the civilian light plane market. Only Cessna was not engaged in missiles production, but that of Grumman, Fairchild, and Republic was relatively insignificant.

Convair, Lockheed, Martin, and North American were the only producers which had higher military sales at the end of the period in 1961 than for earlier years. Missiles sales increased over the period for Beech, Boeing, Convair, Lockheed, Martin, McDonnell, and North American. The change in the composition of military sales was drastic, particularly for Lockheed, which jumped from a ratio of missiles to military sales of 2.21 per cent in 1957 to 77.93 per cent in 1960. Martin's missiles to military sales ratio increase was similarly spectacular, with a rise from 9.73 per cent in 1956 to 87.52 per cent in 1961. Both Lockheed and Martin had increasing military and increasing missiles sales during the period. The remaining companies had missiles to military sales ratios ranging up to Convair's 46.08 per cent at the conclusion of the period.[21]

The six firms having the largest military sales were understandably the six firms having the largest missiles sales at the close of the period as the emphasis shifted from aircraft to missiles. Maintaining or increasing military sales depended more and more on capturing missiles contracts. For example, Convair rose from a rank of fifth in military sales to number one largely as a result of its successful missiles program; whereas Douglas fell from number one to the sixth position with correspondingly less success in securing missiles contracts.

Success in securing missiles contracts depended foremost on the

---

see G. R. Simonson, "The Demand for Aircraft and the Aircraft Industry, 1907–1958," *Journal of Economic History,* vol. XX (September, 1960), pp. 367, 375.

[21] Beech, in fact, had a ratio of missiles to military sales of 67.48 per cent but the high ratio was the result of a severe contraction in military sales value relative to a low value of missiles sales, rather than a rapidly expanding missiles demand.

ability to submit superior design proposals. This is apparent from viewing the usual steps in the competitive government procurement process which were frequently four in number:[22]

(1) Invitation by the government to qualified producers to submit product design proposals capable of fulfilling general performances specifications;
(2) Phase I contract award authorizing the selected producer to proceed with further design work and construction of mock-ups;
(3) Phase II contract award for the completion of engineering and construction of prototypes;
(4) Phase III contract for production of a specified number of units of the product.

The producer submitting the missile design proposal most capable of performing the task specified by the Department of Defense was the one which was awarded the initial and subsequent contracts for development and production. Cost and other factors were considerations governing contract awards but design was by far the most important consideration.[23]

Those airframe producers which were successful in securing missiles contracts are revealed in Table 2. Only 8 of the 14 airframe producers were engaged, to any notable extent, in missiles production. Ratios of individual airframe company missiles procurement to that of the airframe industry and to total missiles procurement reveal that there was notable concentration of missiles production among five producers by fiscal year 1961. Attesting to the considerable degree of concentration of missiles production within the airframe industry, the top five—Lockheed, Convair, Martin, Boeing, and North American—accounted for 91.46 per cent of missiles output value produced within the airframe industry, and 68.34 per cent of the entire missiles production value.

Concentration was an outgrowth of success in winning design competitions which led to missiles contracts. To be specific, the winning design of what came to be the Polaris missile put Lockheed on

[22] J. Stefan Dupré and W. Eric Gustafson, "Contracting for Defense: Private Firms and the Public Interest," *Political Science Quarterly*, vol. LXXVII (June, 1962), p. 166.

[23] *Ibid.*, and J. Fred Weston (ed.), *Procurement and Profit Renegotiation* (San Francisco, 1960), p. 86.

TABLE 2 *Concentration in Missiles Production of American Airframe Producers, by Rank, Fiscal Year, 1961*

RANK	FIRM	PER CENT FIRM MISSILES SALES OF AIRFRAME INDUSTRY MISSILES SALES		TOTAL MISSILES MARKET SHARES	
		FIRM'S PER CENT SHARE	CUMULATIVE PER CENT OF TOTAL	FIRM'S PER CENT SHARE	CUMULATIVE PER CENT OF TOTAL
1	Lockheed	23.20	23.20	17.34	17.34
2	Convair	20.71	43.91	15.47	32.81
3	Martin	18.22	62.13	13.61	46.42
4	Boeing	14.84	76.97	11.09	57.51
5	North American	14.49	91.46	10.83	68.34
6	Douglas	4.64	96.10	3.47	71.81
7	McDonnell	1.93	98.03	1.44	73.25
8	Northrop	1.64	99.67	1.22	74.47
9	All others	.33	100.00	.27	74.74

Sources: *Statistical Abstract of the United States,* 1959, 1960, 1961; Directorate for Statistical Services, Office of the Secretary of Defense.

top. Convair was successful in its Atlas design as well as several lesser missiles projects including the Terrior, Mauler, Tartar, and Typhon missiles. Martin owed its success largely to the Titan program but also to its contracts for the LaCrosse, Pershing, Mace, and Bullpup missiles. Boeing's growing missiles sales were an outgrowth of its Bomarc and Minuteman designs while North American was a recipient of contracts for the Hounddog missiles and the Minuteman guidance system.[24]

The extent of this consequential change by the airframe industry as a whole is portrayed in Figure 1. For the airframe industry there were sharp fluctuations of military sales between the fiscal years of 1956 and 1961. Despite this, the yearly trend of missiles sales by the industry was steeply upward. The product-mix of the industry changed significantly during the period with missiles making up 44.35 per cent of the output value in 1961 in contrast to 5.71 per cent in 1956. Department of Defense missiles expenditures more than tripled between 1956 and 1961 while missiles sales receipts of the airframe industry exceeded a tenfold increase. The ratio of airframe industry missiles sales to total missiles sales increased from 23.46 per cent in 1956 to

[24] For a listing of the American missiles programs and the firms engaged in them, see Lee (ed.), *Aerospace Facts and Figures, 1962,* pp. 30–31.

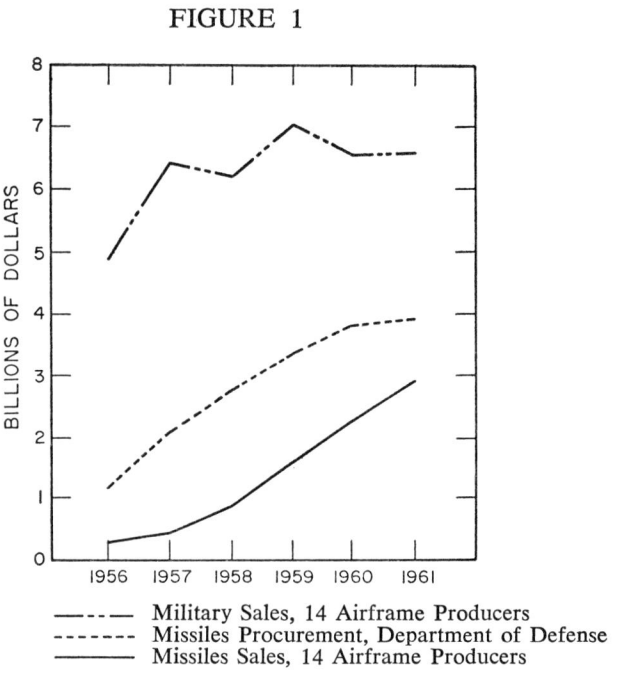

FIGURE 1

—·—·— Military Sales, 14 Airframe Producers
------- Missiles Procurement, Department of Defense
——— Missiles Sales, 14 Airframe Producers

Sources: *Statistical Abstract of the United States,* 1959, 1960, 1961 editions; Directorate for Statistical Services, Office of the Secretary of Defense.

74.74 per cent in 1961 disclosing the startling extent to which the airframe industry was increasing its hold on the growing missiles market.

III

To conclude, the Schumpeterian process of creative destruction has been very much in evidence in America's military airframe industry since the innovation of the guided missile. Because of technological superiority in important aspects of aerial weaponry, the innovation of the guided missile created a growing new market for missiles while destroying, in significant measure, the market for military aircraft. The product innovation caused a new technology of production to be created to produce the vastly different product while rendering obsolete, for this purpose, many old productive techniques of the aircraft industry. Creation of new plant and equipment was necessary to produce missiles and was accompanied by the destruction of capitalized values of obsolete producers' goods in the aircraft industry. Countless new skills and jobs were created while old ones were being destroyed. In short, the American aircraft industry was and is being revolutionized by the process of creative destruction as its old economic structure is being destroyed and a new one created.

The industry's success in missiles can be attributed in part to its somewhat related past production experience, its having at the outset a large proportion of the country's research and engineering personnel, and its established position in handling government business. Individual producer success depended significantly on demonstrated ability to produce missiles of superior design and winning design competitions for government contracts. As the emphasis switched from aircraft to missiles, at the close of the period the top six military aircraft producers were understandably also the top six missiles producers. Producers which were not notably successful in the missiles market in general were experiencing declining military sales as aircraft sales declined.

Unquestionably, the most striking feature of the American military aircraft industry's history from 1956 to 1961 was its extremely successful "creative response." The adaptation of the important airframe producers to the missiles innovation was such that not only were they not destroyed by the new competition, but they sharply increased the industry's share of the growing missiles market. Even with the drastic reduction in aircraft sales and the new competition, the industry's total military sales expanded significantly over the period as a result of the successful adaptation. In sum, the viability of producers of the historic aircraft industry in a changing world has been indeed remarkable.

10. The Space Age Opportunity

The most outstanding recent development affecting the aircraft industry has been its participation in government-sponsored space programs. Aircraft manufacturers have been responsible for producing space vehicles and countless other related products.

Since 1948 the expenditures on space vehicles have risen to represent slightly less than one-fourth of the total sales of the aerospace industry. One study estimated that by 1970 the outlays for space may be upwards of $20,000,000,000 a year. As the demand for military aircraft continues to decline and the demand for missiles is expected to level off or decrease, it appears likely that the future of the aircraft industry will depend on its success in competing with other producers for government space contracts. As in the case of missiles, space programs have caused a drastic change in the composition and technology of the production of the traditional aircraft industry.

In the following article, Leonard S. Silk, an economist and Senior Editor of Business Week *magazine, discusses the influence that space programs have on the economy and the important prospects for industry that future space endeavors are expected to offer.*

Outer Space: The Impact on the American Economy*
Leonard S. Silk

The Cost Factor

Even if space programs were nothing more than an industrial civilization's equivalent of pyramid-building, the magnitude of the present effort would be impressive. And we are just at the beginning of really massive financial outlays for outer space.

From fiscal year 1955 through fiscal 1961 the United States government appropriated some $4½ billion for various space programs of the National Aeronautics and Space Administration (NASA), the Department of Defense, the Atomic Energy Commission, the National Science Foundation, and the Weather Bureau. In fiscal 1962 those appropriations increased by an additional $3 billion, to bring the cumulative total to about $7½ billion through July of 1962.

These figures are based on the minimal definition used by the Department of Defense to measure its own space activities—a definition which includes only those amounts spent by the military services for certain designated space and space-related projects (such as *Vanguard, Explorer, Discoverer, Midas, Samos, Transit, Advent, Courier, Space Track, Spasur, Blue Scout,* and the *X-15*). They do not include substantial amounts for construction and operation of the national missile ranges for use in the space programs; the cost of developing missiles, such as *Thor* and *Atlas,* which are also used in space programs; or supporting research and development (such as bio-medical research) which is more or less mutually applicable to other programs also.

If adequate account is taken of those excluded—but essential—Defense expenditures, the total outlay on space by the Defense Department would be increased from the fiscal year 1962 level of $1 billion to a figure double, or possibly treble, that amount. Some analysts place the true Defense Department space outlay at approximately $2.3 billion for fiscal 1962. This more realistic figure, when added to NASA's fiscal $1.7 billion and other agencies' smaller expenditures, implies that in fiscal 1962 we shall spend about $4.2 billion on all military and civilian space programs. (See Appendix A.)

It is extremely difficult to project how high space expenditures will go from here, given all the political, military, and scientific complexities. Even before the Soviets' successful earth orbit by Majors Gagarin

---

* Reprinted by permission of the publishers from Lincoln P. Bloomfield (ed.): *Outer Space: Prospects for Man and Society,* The American Assembly, Columbia University (Prentice-Hall, Inc., Englewood Cliffs, N.J., 1962), pp. 65–78, 83.

and Titov and America's successful suborbital flights by Commander Shepard and Captain Grissom—and President Kennedy's decision to step up the United States space effort—it appeared to many observers that substantial increases in space spending would occur throughout the 1960's. On October 7, 1960 one experienced industrial economist, Murray L. Weidenbaum, estimated that total NASA expenditures for the 10-year period through 1970 would amount to $17½ billion, mainly for big booster programs such as Saturn and Nova and vehicle and payload development.[1] Weidenbaum estimated that NASA expenditures would rise from about $500 million in 1960 to $2.2 billion by 1967 and thereafter level off. His NASA estimates now look too conservative. Although he did not break out projections of military expenditures on space and space-related programs, Weidenbaum was clearly expecting a continuing rise in that area of defense expenditures.

In January of 1961 another industrial analyst, D. C. Eaton, estimated that major military procurement for space would rise from an annual rate of about $900 million in 1960 to $4 billion in 1965 and to $6.5 billion in 1970. Eaton's estimates imply that major procurement for space programs in the decade will amount to $40 or $50 billion. From the military standpoint, Eaton argued, "our whole defense will rest upon the improved ability of our space systems. . . ." Over and above the strict military requirements for space systems, he assumed growing outlays on space exploration and the development of navigation, communication, and weather systems. "Should there be favorable changes in the international situation," Eaton predicted, "the proportion of monies devoted to the exploration of space will be even greater by 1970."

NASA has no official estimate of the cost of space programs for the next ten years; the rush of events has made earlier guesses obsolete. Before the Kennedy decision on the moon mission some NASA officials were talking in terms of a 10-year program costing $25 to $30 billion—"although $40 billion could be right." These estimates were admittedly very rough—and stated in terms of what 1961 dollars could buy in this area. But NASA officials have themselves estimated the cost of a three-man mission to the moon alone at $20 to $40

---

[1] M. L. Weidenbaum, "The Changing Structure of the Military Market," Conference on Space Age Technology, American Management Association, New York, October 7, 1960.

billion. An acceleration of that program would obviously swell the bill for the 1960's.

Some analysts believe actual space outlays are likely greatly to outrun any predictions government officials have thus far been willing to make. James Williams, of United Research, Inc., notes that major research and development efforts conducted by the Defense Department and NASA and other agencies have typically overrun original estimates by a factor of 2–3 times. Williams therefore takes such projections as the recently-anticipated $20 billion outlay by NASA in the 1960's plus the $30 billion which some consider reasonable projections of Defense Department outlays on space in the next ten years and multiplies them by 2 or 3 to get a total of $100 billion to $150 billion for the outlay on space programs over the next decade. This sum may sound unbelievably high. Williams notes, however, on the assumption that total defense outlays over that period amounted to $400 to $500 billion (assuming that the cold war continued in something resembling its recent state, and that defense spending continued at its present level, or increased only moderately), that outlays of this magnitude would constitute only about a fifth to a third of total defense expenditures over the next ten years. A greater emphasis on conventional or paramilitary defense, which the Kennedy administration has advocated and which some observers anticipate, would push the total defense bill up markedly higher. So, obviously, would price inflation.

Admittedly, there is some possibility that such projections for NASA and Defense Department space programs over the next ten years may be too high. There may be heating up of the cold war and a diversion of funds (and of human and physical resources) away from space programs to more immediate military uses; or a shift in Soviet "competitive coexistence" strategy away from the space area to some other area which we might be moved to follow. We may have a national election in which a political party with a highly conservative budget and fiscal policy receives a national mandate to cut back federal outlays. Such developments could cause the actual expenditure on space during the next decade to drop well below the totals presently foreseen by industrial or government economists in the space field, whose vision may conceivably be distorted by their organizational interest in seeing space programs expand.

Moreover, although there is certainly a considerable degree of public enthusiasm for a space effort of some size, and a desire "to beat the Russians," it is far from clear how large an outlay for space the taxpayers would be willing to support. The first Gallup poll on this subject, published May 31, 1961, found that only 33 per cent of those polled said *Yes* to spending $40 billion to get a man on the moon, 58 per cent said *No,* and 9 per cent had *no opinion.* There are also signs that some scientists and other informed observers consider that expenditures of the magnitudes presently contemplated would be an unwise use of resources compared to other scientific, welfare, military, or foreign aid programs that could be undertaken. For example:

Rather let us make a balanced scientific effort, including research, but informing the world that we are more interested in other things than racing to the moon. Let us improve our medical research and make it available to the world. Let us put more effort into social, economic and political research, to be used to ameliorate and improve the human condition at home and abroad.

Let us encourage cultural development—literature, the arts, music—at home and abroad, as evidence that we do not subscribe to the Communist idea that man is essentially an economic automation. Let us improve our foreign aid. Let us keep up our defenses. Let us improve our educational system for all our citizens.

Let us strive harder to realize our ideals of human rights and equality under democracy.

These are the things on which we could well spend $20 to $40 billion instead of shooting it to the moon.[2]

But even the skeptics rarely go so far as to suggest junking space research or neglecting programs for the military utilization of the space environment for defensive or arms control purposes. And there is such evidence in favor of increased expenditures as that furnished by the *Harvard Business Review* poll[3] of business executives, who declared that they preferred expanded space programs even to tax reduction, and by Congressional and press reaction both to the successful suborbital *Mercury* shots and to Mr. Kennedy's space message.

Thus, although the crystal ball is very clouded as one peers into space, it appears probable that the American people are likely to favor and to back with their tax dollars a greatly increased space effort

[2] Letter to *The New York Times,* May 28, 1961, by Herbert S. Bailey, Jr.
[3] Issue of September–October, 1960.

in the decade ahead. It seems safe to predict that space programs running into the tens of billions of dollars over the next decade will reach into nearly every channel of American business, and that space will constitute a market which no businessman or investor will want to ignore.

The Complexity of Industry's Role

To get some notion of the widely-ramifying effects of the space effort on American business, consider the contract structure of a single past venture, the U.S. Navy-directed *Vanguard* project for orbiting a four-pound six-inch diameter, "sophisticated" (a lovely space-age term of technical approbation) satellite. *Vanguard* had a miserably black day on December 8, 1957, when it was supposed to provide America's first answer to the big Soviet *Sputniks I* and *II*, both already in orbit. That day—at 11:44.559 in the morning—the *Vanguard* space vehicle blew up on its pad, and the sophisticated grapefruit, still beeping away, fell into the flames. But *Vanguard* went on to achieve some brilliant successes which contributed much to the discovery of the Van Allen radiation belts and gave the United States its first tracking system.

Who had a hand in *Vanguard?* The Martin Co. was the prime contractor and was itself responsible for the background *Viking* project, the airframe of the first stage, the nose cone, the third stage support, spin and bearing, and certain ground support equipment. The General Electric Co. provided the first stage propulsion; Aerojet General Corp. handled the second stage propulsion; and Grand Central Rocket Co. and Hercules Powder Co. the third stage propulsion. Atlantic Research Corp. built the spin and retro rockets and the igniter. Air Associates, Inc. made the accelerometers, the Empire Devices Corp. the noise intensity meter, and Hoover Electronics Co. the frequency converters. Henry O. Berman, Inc. made and installed the control equipment. Designers for Industry, Inc. did the programmers. And Minneapolis-Honeywell Co. built the three-axis gyro reference system.

The Behnson-Lehner Co. supplied the data reduction section equipment for the Martin Co.; and Reeves Instrument provided the computers for the *Vanguard* section. The Ludwig Henald Mfg. Co. built the instrumentation and transportation trucks for the ground handling of data; and Polarad Electronics supplied the ground handling test equipment. Loewy Hydropress built the static firing and launching structure, Derby Steel Co. the test stands and related tools, and William T. Lyons Co., Inc. the test stand for vertical assembly at the Martin Co.

Dian Laboratory, Inc. computed the longitudinal vibration of the vehicle; and the University of Maryland handled the wind tunnel tests (to determine from small models what air drag and air pressure and heat the vehicle would feel along its skin as it moved through the atmosphere). Bendix Radio was responsible for the Minitrack system for spotting the satellite's orbit. Radiation, Inc. supplied the data recording and reduction equipment. Elsin Electronics constructed the telemetering ground stations. International Business Machines handled the orbit computations.

Brooks & Perkins Co. built the shell and braces of the satellite's structure. The Raymond Engineering Co. made the satellite's separation mechanism. The Connecticut Telephone & Electric Co. made the transistorized decoder. And dozens of other companies and nonprofit institutions—such as General Radio, Fruehauf, Hewlett-Packard, Tektronix, Melpar, Hazeltine Electronics, New Mexico College—supplied beacons, antennas, and miscellaneous units and equipment.

Moreover, a full accounting of U.S. industry's contribution to *Vanguard* would also have to include many other companies that supplied materials or equipment or transportation or other services to the project's prime contractor and subcontractors and also to the Navy (especially through the Naval Research Laboratory, which managed the entire venture) and to the Army and Air Force, both of which were ultimately involved—the Army by building and operating the South American Minitrack stations and the Air Force by contributing the missile firing range and by plotting and relaying some of the *Vanguard* satellite's data.

The national effort behind that four-pound, six-inch, long-lived grapefruit-in-space (the *Vanguard I,* with its high orbit, is expected to continue swinging around the earth for a thousand years) is fantastic to contemplate.

Yet the *Vanguard* project was a small venture compared with the total space program today, and even smaller compared with the billion-dollar programs that lie ahead. When *Vanguard* was first announced back in 1955, it was estimated to cost $20-$30 million.

The project wound up costing (as of January 1959) $111,085,000, or roughly four times the original estimates. The *Mercury* project, originally estimated to cost $200 million, will probably wind up costing about $500 by the end of 1961.

Some Social Perspectives

It is difficult enough to maintain perspective on outlays amounting to $100 million, let alone on outlays in the many-billions class. *Vanguard* alone involved expenditures greater than many large industries will spend on their research and development programs in 1961—stone, clay, and glass ($111 million), rubber products ($109 million), paper and allied products ($93 million), textiles and apparel ($47 million). One hundred million dollars would pay for half a million air-conditioning units. It would cover the annual college tuition fees of a hundred thousand students. *Vanguard* cost more than 25 times as much as the estimated costs of such other highly regarded research projects as Table Mountain in Colorado for studying the earth's atmosphere. If the marginal value for the nation of space expenditures in the $100 million class requires strong justification when measured against the types of alternate uses of funds suggested above, consider the difficulty of providing the justification for space outlays in the $50 billion class.

Let us not ignore the possibility that in a somewhat sated, high-consumption society such huge outlays might be justified simply for their employment or income effects—a form of sophisticated pyramid-building. Consciously or unconsciously, they might be favored as a means of providing a cure for economic stagnation or as an alternative use of resources should defense programs achieve levels of "overkill" capacity of "stable mutual deterrence" where military procurement could be markedly reduced.

The latter possibility—the reduction of military procurement, to the detriment of the industries involved—raises an issue worth noting here.

President Eisenhower in his Farewell Address suggested that some defense contractors were engaged in efforts to get the government to maintain military expenditures at extraordinarily and unnecessarily high levels for reasons of vested interest; he was apparently making the type of charge leveled by Lord Byron in the *Age of Bronze* against the landed English country gentlemen after the Napoleonic wars:

> The last to bid the cry of warfare cease,
> The first to make a malady of peace.

Can such charges be made against those who are advocating enormous expenditures on outer space projects? Certainly the charge that space is essentially a massive boondoggle would be bitterly resented by the companies involved. It would be countered by the contention that United States private industry, the most resourceful and inventive in the world, through its participation in both space and defense programs, is contributing enormously to the strength, security, prestige, welfare, and growth of the nation. Many companies heavily involved in defense programs refuse to grant the contention that their survival or growth depends upon a continuing supply of federal contracts, or to accept the implied charge that they are "merchants of death." One major diversified defense supplier states his company's philosophy this way:

> Reviewing the history of two almost disastrous wars and appraising the technological and ideological realities of this century, it is my conviction that defense must be a permanent business, a permanent way of life. And that in order to keep in being those aggregates of vital skills that underlie our capability not only to be strong but always to appear to be strong, the modern industrial corporation must, I believe, have a broader base. It must be strong in defense production, strong in civilian production . . .

Not all companies with a stake in the space or defense business, however, would be ready—or able—to survive a drastic reduction in defense or defense-type expenditures. Since very heavy space expenditures are justified by their proponents as essential to national prestige in the cold war, or, more directly, for their relation to defense or arms control, they may be regarded in large measure as defense-type expenditures.

The Prospects for Industry

However one evaluates the admixture of national and self-interest on the part of companies already involved or wanting to become involved in the space effort, the objective fact is that the venture into space looks extremely attractive to many areas of American industry. It will have significant effects upon profits and growth of the economy, upon the structure and skills of the labor force, upon the composition of national resource and capital equipment requirements, upon the level of research and development expenditures, and upon the geographical location of industry.

In our sketch of the contract structure of *Vanguard* we noted how that project cut across many industrial lines, involving dozens of widely scattered companies. A comprehensive view of the entire NASA program would of course fan the distribution of contracts out still more widely.[4] It may be noted that all of the companies with substantial NASA contracts also stand high on the list of Defense Department prime contractors for experimental, development, test, and research work. As space programs expand, it is safe to say that many other companies and nonprofit institutions heavily involved in Defense R & D will turn up on NASA's list of substantial contract holders, probably augmented by some companies that do not yet exist but which will come into being in order to tackle the formidable technological problems that lie ahead.

Though we are moving into a largely unknown area, one can get some notion of the impact of the expanding space program of the future on industry by considering the past impact of the missile programs of the Defense Department upon industry and the economy. An analysis of missile production in fiscal year 1959 shows that the total outlay of $3.5 billion was split up as follows: 38 per cent for the assembly and testing of missiles; 34 per cent for electronics work, both airborne and ground; 16 per cent for propulsion systems; 5 per cent for non-electronic ground support—mainly stationary launching platforms; 4 per cent for nose cones; and 3 per cent for missile structure work.

Clearly, the percentage distribution of funds going for a future major space program will differ markedly from those indicated above for missile production in fiscal 1959. The necessity of shooting far

---

[4] As of March 1961, companies with substantial NASA contracts included Aerojet-General Corp. (a subsidiary of the General Tire and Rubber Co.); Azusa of California; Ball Brothers Research Corp. of Boulder, Colorado; Bell Aerospace Corp. of Buffalo, N.Y.; Bendix Corp. of Detroit, Michigan; Brown Engineering Co. of Huntsville, Alabama; Chance Vought Aircraft, Inc. of Dallas, Texas; Chrysler Corp. of Detroit; Grumman Aircraft Engineering Corp. of Bethpage, N.Y.; Hayes Corp. of Birmingham, Alabama; Lockheed Aircraft Corp. of Burbank, California; McDonnell Aircraft Corp. of St. Louis, Missouri; North American Aviation, Inc. of Los Angeles, California; Radio Corporation of America, New York, N.Y.; Douglas Aircraft Co. of Santa Monica, California; General Dynamics Corp. of New York City; Thompson Ramo Woolridge, Inc. of Cleveland, Ohio; and Western Electric Co. Inc. of New York City.

greater weights far greater distances, and of keeping men alive in the hostile space and moon environment, will require tremendous outlays on a whole range of new things: the *Rover* nuclear motor, the *Saturn* series of motors, solid-fueled rockets, the *Nova,* new guidance and control systems, biological research, etc. It is obviously impossible at this point to predict the composition of outlays as compared with the pattern for the missile industry indicated above. However, the following table based on the guesses of space industry experts, may at least suggest the direction of change in components of the program through the 1960's:

Percentages of Total Expenditure

	MISSILE PROGRAM FY 1959	SPACE PROGRAM 1965	SPACE PROGRAM 1970
Assembly & Test	38	25	15
Electronic ground support & airborne guidance and control	34	50	65
Propulsion	16	20	15
Non-electronic ground support	5	2	2
Nose cone	4	—	—
Structure	3	3	3

What the table is meant to emphasize is that a marked shift will be occurring toward heavier outlays on electronics work, with an initial shift (through 1965) on heavy R & D spending for propulsion, then a relative reduction by 1970; and a continuing decline in the proportion of expenditures going for assembly and testing—which might be accelerated if recoverable boosters or second-stages can be designed.

These shifts, particularly the heavily increasing share of outlays for electronics, are going to produce a battle royal in which the character of the aerospace industry will undergo some major changes and in which the position of the former aircraft companies will be under continuing challenge from electrical and electronics firms. Former aircraft firms aiming to survive in the space age have of course already been diversifying heavily into electronics. As D. C. Eaton puts it, "The airframe manufacturer can no longer lay any claim to any special position in the industry. Companies whose experience and growth has been in electronics are and will be equally, if not better, qualified to perform major system development."

In 1959, of the 16 companies that dominated the missile business and accounted for 72 per cent of the sales, eight were originally aircraft companies, six were electrical and electronics manufacturers, one was an automobile manufacturer, and one a subsidiary of a rubber producer. But the six top spots were all occupied by aircraft firms.[5] In 1961, of NASA's 18 principal contractors,[6] only eight were originally aircraft firms. Spectacular rises—and declines—of particular companies in the space business are likely to occur in the decade ahead. Consider what has happened within the traditional aircraft industry since the end of World War II. Curtiss-Wright Corp., the largest producer of aircraft in that war (measured in terms of pounds of airframe manufactured),* had dropped to 53rd place in 1959; indeed, its production no longer included complete aircraft but was limited to engines and components. The Martin Co., which made a timely shift from aircraft to missiles, leaped from 23rd place on the list of defense contract holders in 1953 to eighth place in 1959. Defense is clearly a high-risk and unstable business; 21 of the 100 firms on the 1958 list of top defense contractors did not make the 1959 list.

Many industry observers foresee an intensifying battle for survival in the aerospace industry in the years ahead. Some believe that by 1970 the present number of close to fifty major companies in the aerospace industry will have shrunk perhaps to twenty or twenty-five; that the several hundred present medium-sized subcontractors will be markedly reduced as the prime contractors broaden their activities and pull in much present subsystem work; but that in 1970 there will still be thousands of small specialized companies providing specific and limited services at relatively low cost as there are today.

The Manpower Problem

Many people not close to the missile or space business have considered that space will be a low user of manpower. Nothing could be further from the truth. The *Mercury* project—costing in the neighborhood of $500 million by the end of 1961—has involved something like 4,000 companies which employed more than 200,000 people in the project. One cannot be sure how many manhours of labor

---

* Editor's Note: This statement is inconsistent with the data of the Harvard Study appearing above. Douglas was the largest while Curtiss-Wright ranked sixth. See Lilley *et al.*, Exhibit II, *supra*, p. 126–127.

[5] In order of rank, the top 16 missile companies were Convair, Boeing, Douglas, Martin, North American, Lockheed, General Electric, Aerojet-General (a division of General Tire), Raytheon, Hughes, General Motors, Western Electric, R.C.A., Northrop, Sperry Rand, and Arma.

[6] See footnote 4.

were actually involved in *Mercury* without a detailed survey of all those firms, but it is safe to say that tens of thousands of full-time jobs were created.

To obtain a rough idea of the employment effects of space, it may be noted that the somewhat similar missile industry is extremely labor-intensive. A study by the U.S. Department of Labor shows that during fiscal 1959, when the government was spending at a $3.5 billion annual rate on missiles, the number of persons directly employed in missile activity totaled 319,300.[7] This works out to a ratio of $10,893 in sales per worker in the missile industry, compared with $12,329 per worker in newspapers, $22,112 in construction equipment, and $99,566 in petroleum refining. The space industry is likely to be even more labor-intensive than missiles.

In the decade ahead space vehicles are not going to come off production lines with designs frozen for long runs over time; they are going to be jiggered and altered, almost item by item, both to incorporate continuously the results of scientific and technological progress and to design vehicles to accomplish different types of missions. All this implies a heavy use of manpower relative to the cost of the product. If the space program gets up to annual expenditure rates of $10 billion, and if the types of ratios indicated by recent experience hold, space will employ over a million workers directly—with important secondary employment effects on many other industries.[8] By comparison, automobile manufacturing in 1961 was directly employing about 800,000 and steel about 700,000.

Of course the manpower required for space programs will be in large measure highly specialized and skilled. The space programs appear certain to provide further momentum for the trend, so marked in recent years, for labor requirements to shift from low-skilled production workers to scientific, technical, and managerial occupations.

---

[7] U.S. Department of Labor, *Manpower in Missiles and Aircraft Production,* Industry Manpower Survey No. 93, August 1939. This study defined missile activity as including research, development, and production of rockets and missiles, launching devices, ground control and testing units, propulsion units, warheads, fuel, electronic components, and other parts designed for inclusion in the missile or in ground support equipment. It included government-owned and operated research, development, and production facilities, but not those segments of the military services or NASA engaged purely in administrative activities such as planning and procurement. Nor did it include construction activities involved in the building of missile launching bases or test sites.

[8] A more careful estimate of the total employment effects of a space program of some given size and composition would require use of a detailed Leontief-type input-output model.

The shift has resulted chiefly from the tremendous increase in expenditures for research and development. The R & D portion of the total cost of an intercontinental bomber was 20 per cent according to Weidenbaum's estimates; this share rose to 60 per cent for an intercontinental ballistic missile. For space systems the R & D proportion will go still higher; indeed, one might define space system work in the period that lies immediately ahead as virtually 100 per cent R & D. Companies which in the days of heavy aircraft production had two-thirds of their labor force made up of industrial workers will see that proportion decline to perhaps one-fourth as the proportion of scientific, technical, and managerial personnel keeps rising. These shifts will create great opportunities for those people who can handle the new jobs and serious strains and dislocations for those who cannot. The shifts will impose a growing responsibility upon the American educational system to increase and upgrade the national supply of brains, talents, and skills.

Economic Benefits—and Risks

There can be little doubt that the most important element in economic growth is the expansion of scientific and technological knowledge which culminates in new products, new techniques of production or communication, new resources. This assertion is not a novel statement: John Rae developed the theme of the impact of new technology on economic growth very competently in the early part of the nineteenth century, and Joseph Schumpeter handled it even more brilliantly in the twentieth century. In our own time some economists have reached the conclusion that technological advance has accounted for about 90 per cent of the rise in productivity—output per manhour—in the United States since the latter part of the 19th century. The implications of these findings are of outstanding importance for policy makers and economists; they mean that the greatest emphasis in any program for long-term economic growth must focus on technological progress and the factors that promote it or obstruct it.

Technological progress resulting from space programs will stimulate economic growth basically in three ways:

(1) Innovations emerging from space programs will lead to increases in the productivity of both labor and capital and, consequently, to higher real income, either as a result of reducing prices or by

permitting a rise in money incomes without an inflationary rise in prices. At the same time, from the standpoint of the firms that do the innovating, the savings in cost resulting from higher productivity will widen profit margins, making more funds available for expansion or research by the profit-making innovator, or will attract additional funds and resources from less profitable industries. Specifically, space programs will lead to the development of high-speed, lightweight computers which will replace the giant electronic brains of today; advances in "human engineering"; more efficient means of communication, through satellites; new and improved power sources—special types of batteries, smaller and safer nuclear motors, plasma power generated through the use of hot, ionized gas; cost-savings in many fields (such as agriculture and transportation) through better weather forecasting; better methods of preventing corrosion; better methods of adhesion; and progress in all areas of electronics which will have great relevance to advancing the efficiency of industrial production.

(2) By creating new products space research will stimulate demand, create new markets, necessitate additions to the stock of capital required to produce the new goods. Some space proponents have described as "space age" products such things as kitchenware made from ceramics that can stand extreme and sudden temperature changes; new battery-powered flashlights and radios that can be recharged by plugging them into a wall socket; remote control devices for opening garage doors, tuning radios or television sets, etc.; electronic wristwatches; heart stimulators, artificial larynxes, and other medical devices; monitoring systems for hospital patients which might both reduce hospital costs and save lives. Speedier and safer passenger travel may result from programs like the X-15 or *Dyna-Soar,* and from improved radar systems, engines, flight equipment, automatic pilots, improved weather forecasting. New "space" products also include such things as observation satellites or sensing devices, which increase the security and stability of the nation and the world and are fully as important to the firms that produce them as consumer goods.

(3) By making available new resources or by finding new uses for old resources space technology will increase the economic system's output and, through the price and profit mechanism, redirect resources to increase total production. Science and technology in our time have come to play the role that war and exploration formerly played

in expanding a nation's economic resources. Space research is leading to the development of many new materials; synthetics and composites of synthetics and metals; new and very durable fabrics; reinforced plastics—silicones, polyesters; epoxy resins and phenolics reinforced with a variety of materials—asbestos, quartz fibers, graphite cloth, glass fiber, etc. Some observers believe that space research will underlie major breakthroughs in increasing the world's supply of traditional resources: for efficiently getting fresh water from sea water; for extracting minerals from sea water; for drilling more deeply into the earth for taconite (as high-grade iron ore becomes an increasingly scarce resource) or for other minerals; for replacing traditional energy resources with new fuels, solar energy, etc. Observation and sensing satellites and improved seismological instruments may provide a valuable additional means for discovering new resources on earth—or, conceivably, in outer space.

Obviously it may not be essential to send men on long-distance space missions to achieve many of these earthly by-products. And not all of the by-products can be ascribed solely to space research rather than to earlier or other types of research programs. Nevertheless, there can be little doubt that a major space research effort would accelerate this by-product "fallout." As Hugh Dryden has put it, "Perhaps the greatest economic treasure is the advanced technology required for more and more difficult space missions. This new technology is advancing at a meteoric rate. Its benefits are spreading throughout our whole industrial and economic system." It is this great impetus which the space programs will give to scientific and technological advance in many fields—in electronics, metals, fuels, the life sciences, ceramics, machinery, plastics, instruments, textiles, thermals, cryogenics, and, most important, to basic research in all the sciences—that provides the reason one must consider the space effort not simply as an elaborate form of modern pyramid-building or pump-priming but, far more importantly, as a powerful ongoing force for innovation and economic growth.

The most striking economic development of the postwar period has been the way American businessmen and investors have caught on to the potency of research and development as a force for profits and growth; innovation—the celebrated elixir of capitalism—has become a widely recognized and increasingly diffused element in our system.

Competition among business firms to participate in the space program will therefore be intense. It will represent a real opportunity for companies to subsidize their own research programs. There are inherent excitement and challenge in the problems to be solved, and there will be prestige as well as profit accruing to the business firms that crack those problems. (After Commander Shepard's first successful *Mercury* suborbital flight, there was a great rash of newspaper and magazine advertising by companies that had had some share in the *Mercury* program.) There will be keen competition for the scientific talents that attract the government's funds. But, based as it is on the scientific imagination, space will be a rapidly-changing and high-risk business; the problems for business in this field are proportional to the tremendous opportunities ahead.

Appendix A

Space Activities of the United States Government
New Obligational Authority/Program Basis—in millions
Historical Summary and FY 1962 Recommendation and Congressional Adjustments

	NASA[1]	DEFENSE[2]	AEC[3]	NSF[4]	WB[5]	Total
FY 1955	$ 56.9	$ 3.0	$ —	$ —	$ —	$ 59.9
FY 1956	72.2	30.3	7.0	7.3	—	117.3
FY 1957	78.2	71.0	21.3	8.4	—	178.9
FY 1958	117.3	205.6	21.3	3.3	—	347.5
FY 1959	338.9	489.5	34.3	—	—	862.7
FY 1960	523.6	560.9	43.3	.1	—	1,127.9
FY 1961	964.0	751.7	62.7	.6	—	1,779.0
1962 Budget, 1/16/61	1,109.6	846.9	55.1	1.6	2.2	2,015.4
Increases recommended 3/28/61	125.7	159.0	23.5	—	—	308.2
Increases recommended 5/25/61	549.0	77.0	7.0	—	53.0	686.0
Total FY 1962 recommendation	1,784.3	1,082.9	85.6	1.6	55.2	3,009.6
Specific Congressional adjustments	—112.6	85.8	—	—	—5.0	—31.8
FY 1962 as approved by Congress	1,671.7	1,168.7	85.6	1.6	50.2	2,977.8

[1] National Aeronautics and Space Administration amounts are totals for all activities of NASA and include totals for NACA prior to establishment of NASA.
[2] Department of Defense amounts are based on identifiable Defense funding for space and space-related effort and do not include substantial amounts for (1) construction and operation of the national missile ranges with regard to space programs, (2) the cost of developing missiles such as *Thor* and *Atlas* which are also used in space programs, or (3) supporting research and development (such as bio-medical research) which is more or less mutually applicable to programs other than "space."
[3] Atomic Energy Commission amounts are those identifiable with ROVER nuclear rocket and SNAP atomic power source projects.
[4] National Science Foundation amounts are those identifiable with VANGUARD and with the NSF space telescope project.
[5] Weather Bureau amounts are those identifiable with the meteorological satellite program. Bureau of the Budget, October 30, 1961.

Bibliography

Books

Aircraft Industries Association of America, *Aviation Facts and Figures, 1945,* McGraw-Hill Book Co., New York, 1945.

The Aircraft Year Book, published since 1919 by the Aircraft Industries Association of America, Inc., Lincoln Press, Washington. Since 1960 known as *The Aerospace Year Book* and published by the Aerospace Industries Association of America, Inc.

Asher, Harold, *Cost-Quantity Relationships In The Airframe Industry,* Rand Project R-291, Rand Corp., Santa Monica, 1956.

Aviation Facts and Figures, prepared yearly since 1953 by the Aircraft Industries Association of America, Inc., Lincoln Press, Washington. Since 1959 known as *Aerospace Facts and Figures* and published by the Aerospace Industries Association of America, Inc.

Axe, W. W., and Co., *The Aviation Industry in the U. S.,* Axe-Houghton Economic Studies, Series B, no. 6, New York, 1938.

Bollinger, Lynn L., and Tom Lilley, *Financial Position of the Aircraft Industry,* Harvard Business School, Business Research Studies no. 28, Cambridge, Mass., 1943.

Bollinger, Lynn L., and Arthur H. Tully, Jr., *Personal Aircraft Business at Airports,* Division of Research, Harvard Business School, Boston, 1947.

Brooks, Peter W., *The Modern Airliner,* Putnam, London, 1961.

Cleveland, Reginald M. (ed.), *The Aviation Annual of 1947,* Harper & Bros., New York, 1947.

Cleveland, Reginald M., and Frederick P. Graham (eds.), *The Aviation Annual of 1945,* Doubleday, Doran & Co., Garden City, 1944.

Cleveland, Reginald M., and Frederick P. Graham (eds.), *The Aviation Annual of 1946,* Doubleday, Doran & Co., Garden City, 1946.

Collison, Thomas, *The Superfortress Is Born. The Story of The Boeing B-29,* Duell, Sloan & Pearce, New York, 1945.

Craven, Wesley F., and James L. Cate, *The Army Air Forces in World War II,* vol. 6, *Men and Planes,* University of Chicago Press, Chicago, 1955.

Crosby, Maynard (ed.), *Flight Plan for Tomorrow: The Douglas Story. A Condensed History,* Douglas Aircraft Co., Santa Monica, 1962.

Cunningham, Frank, *Sky Master, the Story of Donald Douglas,* Dorrance and Co., Philadelphia, 1943.

Cunningham, William Glenn, *The Aircraft Industry: A Study in Industrial Location,* Lorrin L. Morrison, Los Angeles, 1951.

Day, John S., *Subcontracting Policy in the Airframe Industry,* Division of Research, Harvard Business School, Boston, 1956.

de la Cierva, Juan, and Don Rose, *Wings of Tomorrow: The Story of the Autogiro,* Brewer, Warren and Putnam, London, 1931.

Fraser, Chelsea, *The Story of Aircraft,* Thomas Y. Crowell Co., New York, 1933.
Freudenthal, Elsbeth E., *The Aviation Business,* Vanguard Press, New York, 1940.

Goldberg, Alfred (ed.), *A History of the United States Air Force, 1907–1957,* D. Van Nostrand, New York, 1957.

Harlan, Neil E., *Management Control in Airframe Subcontracting,* Division of Research, Harvard Business School, Boston, 1956.
Hatch, Alden, *Glenn Curtiss: Pioneer of Naval Aviation,* Julian Messner, Inc., New York, 1942.
Hinton, Harold B., *Air Victory: The Men and Machines,* Harper & Bros., New York, 1948.
Holley, Irving B., Jr., *Ideas and Weapons,* Yale University Press, New Haven, 1953.
Hubler, Richard G., *Big Eight: A Biography of an Airplane* (DC-8), Duell, Sloan & Pearce, New York, 1960.

Jane's All the World's Aircraft, published yearly by the Trade Press Association, Ltd., London, and McGraw-Hill Book Co., New York.

Kelley, Fred C., *The Wright Brothers,* Harcourt, Brace, and Co., New York, 1943.

Lilley, Tom, et al., *Problems of Accelerating Aircraft Production During World War II,* Division of Research, Harvard Business School, Boston, 1947.
Loening, Grover, *Our Wings Grow Faster,* Doubleday, Doran & Co., Garden City, 1935.

Magoun, F. Alexander, and Eric Hodgins, *A History of Aircraft,* Whittlesey House: McGraw-Hill Book Co., New York, 1931.
Mansfield, Harold, *Vision* (Boeing); Duell, Sloan & Pearce, New York, 1956.
Mingos, Howard, *Birth of an Industry,* W. B. Conkey Co., New York, 1930.
Moore, Frederick T., *Military Procurement and Contracting: An Economic Analysis,* Rand Memorandum RM 2948-PR, Rand Corp., Santa Monica, 1962.
Morris, Lloyd, and Kendall Smith, *Ceiling Unlimited: The Story of American Aviation from Kitty Hawk to Supersonics,* Macmillan Co., New York, 1953.

National Planning Association, *National Policy for Aviation,* National Planning Association, Washington, 1946.

Peck, Merton J., and F. M. Scherer, *The Weapons Acquisition Process: An Economic Analysis,* Division of Research, Harvard University Press, Boston, 1962.

Reguero, Miguel A., *An Economic Study of the Military Airframe Industry,* Wright Patterson Air Force Base, Ohio, 1957.

Rolfe, Douglas, and Alexis Dawydoff, *Airplanes of the World from Pusher to Jet, 1940 to 1954,* Simon & Schuster, New York, 1954.

Schlaifer, R., *Development of Aircraft Engines,* School of Business Administration, Harvard University, Cambridge, Mass., 1950.

Shrader, Welman A., *Fifty Years of Flight, A Chronicle of the Aviation Industry in America, 1903–1953,* Eaton Manufacturing Co., Cleveland, 1953.

Simonson, G. R., *Economics of the Aircraft Industry,* unpublished Ph.D. dissertation, University of Washington, Seattle, 1959.

Smith, Henry Ladd, *Airways,* Alfred A. Knopf, New York, 1942.

Stekler, Herman O., *The Structure and Performance of the Aerospace Industry,* University of California Press, Berkeley, 1965.

Studer, Clara, *Sky Storming Yankee. The Life of Glenn Curtiss,* Stackpole Sons, New York, 1937.

Stout, Westley W., *Great Engines and Great Planes,* Chrysler Corp., Detroit, 1947.

Taylor, Frank J., *High Horizons* (United Airlines), McGraw-Hill Book Co., New York, 1951.

Weston, J. Fred (ed.), *Procurement and Profit Renegotiation,* Wadsworth Publishing Co., Inc., Belmont, Calif., 1960.

Wilson, Eugene E., *Slipstream,* 3rd ed., Literary Investment Guild, Palm Beach, Florida, 1967.

Wright, Orville, *How We Invented the Airplane,* Fred C. Kelley (ed.), David McKay Co., New York, 1953.

Government Publications

Air Coordinating Committee, *Air Coordinating Committee Report, 1947,* Government Printing Office, Washington, 1947.

Air Coordinating Committee, *Civil Air Policy,* Government Printing Office, Washington, 1954.

Loening, Grover, "Fifty Years of Flying Progress, 1955," *Smithsonian Institution Annual Report,* Government Printing Office, Washington, 1955.

Mixter, Col. G. W., and H. H. Emmons, *United States Army Aircraft Production Facts,* Government Printing Office, Washington, 1919.

Modernization of the National System of Aviation Facilities, Government Printing Office, Washington, 1957.

National Requirements for Aviation Facilities: 1956–1975, vol. 1, Government Printing Office, Washington, 1957.

Northrop, John K., *Aviation History, 1903 to 1960,* U.S. Library of Congress, Washington, 1949.

President's Air Policy Commission, *Survival in the Air Age,* Government Printing Office, Washington, 1948.

Statistical Handbook of Civil Aviation, published yearly by the United States Department of Commerce, Federal Aviation Agency, Government Printing Office, Washington.

U.S. Air Force, *The History of Military Flight,* U.S. Air Force, Washington, 1956.

U.S. Congress, House of Representatives, *Aircraft Production Costs and Profits,* Hearings before the Subcommittee for Special Investigations of the Committee on Armed Services, U.S. House of Representatives, 84th Cong., 2d Sess., under authority of H. Res. 112, Government Printing Office, Washington, 1956.

U.S. Congress, House of Representatives, *The Aircraft Industry,* Hearings before the Subcommittee no. 4 on Small Business, Pursuant to H. Res. 114, 84th Cong., 2d Sess., Government Printing Office, Washington, 1956.

U.S. Congress, House of Representatives, *Report of Aircraft Production Costs and Profits,* Subcommittee for Special Investigations for the Committee on Armed Services, under authority of H. Res. 112, 84th Cong., 2d Sess., Government Printing Office, Washington, 1956.

U.S. House Report 1121, Committee on Government Operations, *Organization and Management of Missile Programs,* 86th Cong., 2d Sess., Government Printing Office, Washington, 1959.

United States Surplus Property Administration, *Airplane Plants and Facilities, Report to Congress, January 14, 1946,* Government Printing Office, Washington, 1946.

Articles and Periodicals

Note: Only a select list of articles appears below. The aerospace periodicals noted are the sources of current developments in the industry.

Aerospace, published monthly by the Aerospace Industries Association of America, Inc.

Alchian, A., "Reliability of Progress Curves in Airframe Production," *Econometrica,* XXXI (October, 1963), 679–693.

Aviation Age, published monthly.

Aviation Week and Space Technology, published weekly.

Hartley, K., "The Learning Curve and Its Application to the Aircraft Industry," *The Journal of Industrial Economics,* XIII (March, 1965), 122–128.

Kupinsky, Mannie, "Growth of Aircraft and Parts Industry, 1939–1954," *Monthly Labor Review,* LXXI (December, 1954), 1320–1325.

Leach, W. Barton, "Obstacles to the Development of American Air Power," *The Annals of the American Academy of Political and Social Science,* CCXCIX (May, 1955), 67–75.

Levenson, Leonard G., "Wartime Development of the Aircraft Industry," *Monthly Labor Review,* LXI (November, 1944), 909–931.

Missiles and Rockets, published weekly.

Rae, John B., "Financial Problems of the American Aircraft Industry, 1906–1940," *The Business History Review,* XXXIX (Spring, 1965), 99–114.

Silk, Leonard S., "The Impact on the American Economy," *Outer Space: Prospects for Man and Society,* edited by Lincoln P. Bloomfield, Prentice-Hall, Inc., Englewood Cliffs, N.J., 1962.

Simonson, G. R., "Missiles and Creative Destruction in the American Aircraft Industry, 1956–1961," *The Business History Review,* XXXVIII (Autumn, 1964), 302–314.

Simonson, G. R., "The Demand for Aircraft and the Aircraft Industry, 1907–1958," *Journal of Economic History,* XX (September, 1960), 361–382.

Index

Aero Design, 237
Aerojet General Corp., 248, 252n, 254n
Aeromarine Airways, 56
Aeromarine Plane & Motor Company, 32
Aeronautical Chamber of Commerce, 24, 56, 57, 58, 59, 65, 66, 151
  officers of, 56
Aeronautical Society of America, 34
Aeronca Aircraft Corporation, 148, 184, 193
Aerospace Industries Association, 233
Air Associates, Inc., 248
Air Commerce Act of 1926, 23, 63, 64, 87, 170, 177
Air-cooled Motors, Inc., 194
Air Coordinating Committee, 205
Air Mail Act of 1925, 23
Air Mail Act of 1934, 73, 94, 97
  compliance with, 98
Air mail, first, 48, 58
  take-over by Army Air Corps, 93
Air policy recommendations after W.W. II
  Aircraft Industries Assoc. of America, 174, 175, 177
  Arnold, General H. H., 171, 173, 178
  Burden, William A. M., 175–176
  Harvard University study, 172
  Senate Military Affairs Committee, 183
  United Nations, 173
Aircraft engines
  Cyclone, 87
  Hornet, 87
  J-35, 207
  J-47, 207
  J-48, 207
  J-65, 207
  Liberty, 168
  OX, 36
  R-1300, 207
  R-1820, 123, 207
  R-1830, 123
  R-2600, 122, 124
  R-2800, 123, 124, 133, 207
  R-3350, 124
  R-4360, 207
  Ranger, 148
  Wright Whirlwind, 76, 123
Aircraft engine production, W.W. II, 121–127 *passim,* 133–135 *passim*
Aircraft facilities, value of, 1939–1944, 163

Aircraft
  invention of, 3
  first powered flight, 21, 22
Aircraft production
  contraction after W.W. II, 182
    companies affected, 184–185
    effects on locational pattern, 185, 186, 187
  expansion during Korean War, 210–223 *passim*
  1939, 171
  1940, 171
  1941, 171
  1944, 137–139 *passim*
  number of types, W.W. II, 165
  W.W. II, 128–133 *passim*
Aircraft Production Board, 32, 33
Aircraft production costs, W.W. II, 166
Aircraft production expansion after W.W. II
  companies and products, 1950, 192, 193, 194, 195
  industry size, 1950, 189, 190, 191
  location changes, 189, 190
  major airframe companies, 191
  new aircraft companies, 187, 188, 189
  new branch plants, 189
Aircraft supply contracts, 1940–1943, 144
"Aircraft trust," 34–35, 40, 50, 51, 61, 82
Aircraft types
  AT-6, 222
  Avenger, 167
  B-17 Flying Fortress, 150, 167
  B-24 Liberator, 146, 167, 184
  B-25, 131, 222
  B-29 Superfortress, 167, 175, 206
  B-32 Dominator, 166
  B-36, 193
  B-47, 206, 222, 223
  B-52, 210, 229n
  Bristol, 36
  C-119 Packet, 207
  Corsair, 150, 167, 184
  Curtiss Commando, 150
  DC-2, 3
  DC-8, 227
  DeHavilland, 36
  Electra, 227
  F-86, 222
  F-84F Thunderjet, 207
  FJ-2, 222
  Grasshopper, 168

267

Aircraft types (*continued*)
  Helldiver, 167
  1901 machine, 11, 12, 16, 17
  1902 machine, 16, 19–20, 21
  1903 machine, 21
  P-38 Lightning, 153, 167
  P-51 Mustang, 166
  P-61 Black Widow, 166
  707, 227
  720, 227
  Spad, 36
  Tempco Swift, 188
  Wildcat, 167
Aircraft War Production Council, W.W. II, 145, 146, 150, 151, 166
Aircraft Year Book
  first, 58
  for 1928, 64, 76, 77
  for 1935, 97
  for 1936, 100
Airframe builders, 1944, 147, 148
Airframe facilities expansion
  Korean War, 213, 218
  branch plant use, 220, 221, 222
  company policies for, 214–216 *passim*
  government and private investment, 221
  government policies toward, 216, 217, 218, 220
  reasons for private investment, 214
  W.W. II, 213
Airships, Incorporated, 56
Allard, John S., 104
Allen, William M., 232
Allis-Chalmers, 189
Allison Division, General Motors Corporation, 121–127 *passim*, 148
American Airlines, 98
American Airways, 82, 83, 98
American Aviation Corporation, 184, 186
American Aviation Mission, 46–47
  recommendations of, 47–48
American-Hawaiian Steamship Company, 81–82
American Radiator Company, 33
American Telephone and Telegraph Company, 33
Ames, Joseph S., 32
Amtorg Trading Company, 112
Amundsen, Roald, 75
Arma, 254n

Armistice, 45, 168
Arms Embargo Act, 171
Army Air Service, 59
Arnold, H. H., 171, 173, 178
Assembly-line method, 119
Atlantic Aircraft Corporation, 77
Atlantic Research Corp., 248
Atomic Energy Commission, 244, 260
Atwood, J. L., 220
Austin, Warren R., 102
AVCO Manufacturing Corporation, Lycoming-Spencer Division of, 194, 207
Aviation Corporation of Delaware, 81, 82, 83, 84, 98, 111, 112
Aviation Equipment and Export, 112

Baker, Newton D., 27, 35, 99, 101
Baker Board, 74, 99, 100, 101
Ball Brothers Research Corp., 252n
Bancamerica-Blair, 80
Bank of England, 25
Beach Aircraft Corporation, 148, 189, 193, 194, 234, 237
Behnson-Lehner Co., 248
Bell, Alexander Graham, 5
Bell Aircraft Corporation, 100n, 126, 167, 190, 193, 206, 213, 236n, 252n
Bellanca, 184, 194
Bendix Aviation Corporation, 79, 195, 252
Bendix Radio, 249
Bennett, Floyd, 75
Berliner-Joyce Aircraft, 79
Black, Hugo, 81, 91, 94
Black Hearings, 81n
Blair, James A., Jr., 46
Boeing, William E., 31, 59
Boeing Airplaine Co., 53, 77, 81, 88, 89, 93, 111, 126, 127, 147, 150, 167, 186, 189, 192, 206, 210, 213, 218, 223, 227, 232, 234, 237, 238, 239, 254n
Bradley, Samuel Stewart, 30–69 *passim*
Branch plants, closing of, 186
Brewster Aeronautical Corp., 111, 150, 167, 183, 184, 187, 191
Brinkley, W. C., 22
Brock, William S., 64, 75
Bronte, 64
Brooks & Perkins Co., 249
Brown, Donald L., 88

Brown, Walter F., 83n, 94
Brown Engineering Co., 252n
Browning, C. W., 85
Bruce, David K. E., 81
Brunswick-Balke-Collender, 184
Brush, Matthew C., 81
Budd, 184
"Buffalo plan," 157
Buick, 123, 167, 185
Burden, William A. M., 175, 176
Bureau of Aeronautics, 205
Bureau of Aircraft Production, 28
Burgess Company, 30
Byrd, Richard E., 64, 75

Canadian Car & Foundry, 167
"Cash-and-carry" system, 110
Cayley, Sir George, 5
Central Powers, 44
Century Airlines, 82
Cessna Aircraft Company, 148, 184, 193, 234, 237
Chaco war, 103
Chamberlin, Clarence, 64, 75, 96n
Chance Vought, 81, 93, 126, 167, 184, 193, 234, 252n
Chanute, Octave, 4, 5, 11
Chanute machine, 6, 9
Chase Aircraft Company, Inc., 188, 193, 207
Chevrolet, 123, 167, 185
Chrysler Corporation, Dodge Division of, 123, 252n
Civil Aeronautics Act of 1938, 98
Coffin, Howard E., 32, 46
Collier Trophy, 3
Columbia Aircraft Corporation, 186
Colvin, Charles H., 56
Competition, foreign, in airplane production, 51
Congress, 60, 61, 62, 63
Congressional Air Policy Board, 209
Connecticut Telephone & Electric Co., 249
Consolidated Aircraft Corp., 89, 93, 100, 101, 111, 119
Consolidated-Vultee Aircraft Corporation, 77, 126, 127, 146, 147, 148, 150, 166, 167, 184, 186, 188n, 189, 190, 191, 193, 206, 213
Continental Aviation and Engineering Corporation, 189

Continental Motors Corporation, 123, 148, 167, 194
Contracts
 cancellation of, after W.W. II, 167, 181
Controversy, aircraft vs. battleship, 52, 53
Convair, Division of General Dynamics, 148, 150, 156, 157, 218, 227, 234, 237, 238, 239, 254n
Coolidge, Calvin, 61, 63
Cord, E. L., 82–83
Council of National Defense, 28, 46
Cowdin, J. Cheever, 80
Crane Committee, 73, 93, 94
"Creative destruction"
 defined, 228
 missiles as a cause of, 232, 240, 241
"Creative response"
 of airframe producers, 233–241 *passim*
 defined, 229
Crisp, W. Benton, 32
Crowell, Benedict, 46
Culver Aircraft Corporation, 187, 191
Cummings, Homer S., 96
Curtiss, Glenn H., 8, 31, 80
Curtiss Aeroplane and Motor Co., 47, 80, 93
Curtiss Company, 31, 32, 53, 56
Curtiss J.N. 4, 36
Curtiss-Wright Corp., 78, 79, 80, 85, 87, 101, 104, 111, 126, 147, 148, 167, 184, 186, 189, 193, 206, 254
Curtiss-Wright Export, 104, 109

Daniels, John T., 22
Daniels, Josephus, 26, 35
David, Paul T., 97
Davis, Dwight F., 68
Davis, William V., 64
Davison, F. Trubee, 63
Dayton Wright Airplane Company, 32, 53, 78
Deeds, Edward A., 33, 80, 90, 101
Defense Production Act of 1950, 209
Delaney Hearings, 87n
Department of Commerce, 65
Department of Defense, 244, 246
Department of Justice, 40
Depression, 73
Derby Steel Co., 249
Designers for Industry, Inc., 248
Dian Laboratory, Inc., 249

Dodge, 167, 185
Dollar, Robert A., 82
Dollar Steamship Company, 82
Dough, W. S., 22
Douglas, Donald, 3, 92
Douglas Aircraft Co., 53, 77, 79, 89, 92, 93, 100, 110, 111, 112, 126, 127, 147, 166, 167, 184, 190, 192, 206, 213, 218, 222, 223, 227, 234, 237, 239, 253n, 254n
Dryden, Hugh, 258
Dunwoody, Halsey, 46
Durand, William F., 33

Earhart, Amelia, 75
Eastern Airlines, 98
Eastern Air Transport, 79, 98
Eaton, D. C., 245, 253
Eaton Manufacturing Company, 123
Edison, Thomas A., 5
Eielson, Carl B., 75
Eisenhower, Dwight David, 250
Ellsworth, Lincoln, 75
Elsin Electronics, 249
Emmons, Harold H., 33
Empire Devices Corp., 248
Engineering and Research Corporation, 194
Equilibrium, flight, 5, 19, 20
Etheridge, A. D., 22
Europe, competition with, 52
Exports, 73, 103–115 passim, 161
  control by National Munitions Control Board, 110, 112, 114
  limitation of, 103

Facilities financing
  by government, W.W. II, 169
Fairchild, Sherman M., 56, 59
Fairchild Aerial Surveys, 56
Fairchild Engine and Aircraft Corporation, 148, 150, 167, 184, 193, 194, 213, 227, 235, 236n, 237
Farley, E. P., 81
Farley, James A., 93
Fechet, James E., 63
Federal Aviation Commission, 100
  1935 report, 85
"Feeder plants," 123, 186
"Final run," 134
"Five-year programs," 23, 24, 63, 64, 65, 73, 74, 84, 99, 161, 170, 199

Fleet, R. H., 31
Fleetwings, Inc., 148, 184, 187
Flight records, 60, 64, 75
Flint, Albert H., 32
Fokker, Anthony H. G., 77, 78
Ford, Henry, 32
Ford Instrument Company, 79
Ford Motor Company, 62, 119, 123, 127, 150, 167, 185, 187, 207
Foss, Benjamin S., 32
Franklin, J. M., 81
Freudenthal, Elsbeth E., 74
Fritsche, Carl B., 61
Front rudder control, 10
Fruehauf, 249

Gagarin, Yuri, 244
General Aircraft, 148
General Aviation Corporation, 78
General Dynamics Corp., 252n
General Electric Company, 186, 192, 194, 195, 207, 248, 254n
General Motors Corporation, 167, 184, 195n, 207, 254n
  Allison Division of, 194
General Motors–North American Aviation Group, 78, 79, 80, 81, 98
General Radio, 249
Gerdner, Lester D., 61
Gladden Products, 187
Glider producers, 148
Globe Aircraft Corporation, 184, 186
Goebel, Arthur C., 64
Goering, Hermann, 162
Goethals, George W., 32
Goodyear Tire and Rubber Co., 127, 147, 150, 167, 184, 186, 207
Graham-Paige Motors Corporation, 123
Grand Central Rocket Co., 248
"Great aircraft scandal," 41
Great Lakes Aircraft Co., 93
"Green run," 134
Gregory, Thomas W., 35
Grissom, Virgil, 245
Grumman Aircraft Engineering Corporation, 89, 93, 111, 126, 147, 167, 193, 206, 227, 235, 237, 252n
Guaranty Trust Company of New York, 33
Guy-Lussac, Joseph Louis, 5

Hamilton, 81
Hanshue, Harris M., 59
Harriman-Lehman interests
  in Aviation Corporation, 82–83
  in Dollar Steamship Company, 82
Hayden, Stone, and Company, 77, 80
Hayes Corp., 252n
Hazeltine Electronics, 249
Hegenberger, Albert F., 64, 75
Helicopter producers, 188
  Bell, 188
  Hiller, 193
  McDonnell, 188
  Piasecki, 193
  Sikorsky, 188, 193
Henderson, Paul, 59
Henry O. Berman, Inc., 248
Hercules Powder Co., 248
Herring-Curtiss Company, 8
Hewlett-Packard, 249
Higgins, 150, 184
Hirohito, Emperor Showa, 162
Hitler, Adolph, 170
Holding companies, 73
Hoover, Herbert, 61
Hoover Electronics Co., 248
House Armed Services Committee, 218
House Naval Affairs Committee, 101
Houston, George H., 32, 47
Howard Aircraft Corporation, 184, 187
Howe, R. G., 33
Hoyt, Richard F., 31, 59, 80
Hudson Motor Car Company, 123
Huffaker, Edward C., 15
Hughes, 254n
Hughes, Charles Evans, 23, 43
Hughes investigations, 23, 42
Hull, Cordell, 108
Hunsaker, J. C., 174

Industrial concentration, 73, 76, 84, 85, 86, 88
  Aviation Corporation, 77
  Curtiss-Wright, 77, 79
  General Motors, 77, 78
  United Aircraft and Transport, 77, 78
Industry expansion, Korean War, 210–223 *passim*
Ingalls, David S., 87, 92
Ingersoll, Raymond V., 30
Injunction against imports, 52

Instrument producers
  Adel Precision Products, 195n
  Air Associates, 195n
  AiResearch Manufacturing, 195n
  B. F. Goodrich, 195n
  Bendix Aviation, 149, 195n
  Cannon Electrical Development, 195n
  Eaton Manufacturing, 195n
  General Electric, 149, 195n
  General Motors, 195n
  Goodyear Tire and Rubber, 195n
  Jack and Heintz Precision Industries, 195n
  Kollsman, 149, 195n
  Leach Relay, 195n
  Lear, 195n
  Minneapolis-Honeywell, 195n
  Parker Appliance, 195n
  Pioneer, 149
  RCA, 149
  Rohr Aircraft, 195n
  Solar Aircraft, 195n
  Sperry Gyroscope, 149, 195n
  Thomas A. Edison, 195n
  Thompson Products, 195n
  Western Electric, 149
International Harvester Company, 33
International Mercantile Marine, 81
Interstate Aircraft and Engineering Corporation, 187
Interstate Commerce Commission, 98

Jacobs Aircraft Engine Company, 123, 148, 167, 194
"Job shop" method, 119
  1940, 135–137 *passim*
Johnson, Birger, 75
Johnson, Louis, 209

Kaiser, 150
Kaiser-Frazer, 207
Kellett Aircraft, 190
Kennedy, John F., 245, 246, 247
Kesselring, Albert, 162
Kettering, Charles F., 80
Keys, C. M., 31, 46, 59, 78, 80
Keystone Aircraft Corp., 93
Kill Devil Hill, 10, 11, 14
King, Ernest J., 87, 91, 92
Kinners Motors, Inc., 187
Kitty Hawk, 7, 10, 11, 16, 20
Kluge, Gunther von, 162

Labor force
 employment of
  1917, 37
  1918, 37
  1943, 145
 layoffs after W.W. II, 167
  1939, 163
  1943, 163
 productivity of
  1941, 164
  1944, 164
 women, W.W. II, 164
Lampert, Florian, 61
Lampert Committee, 61
Landon, Archer A., 33
Langley, S. P., 4, 5
Lawrance, Charles L., 31, 57, 59, 61
Lehman Brothers, 82
Lend-Lease Act, 171
Levine, Charles A., 75
Licensing agreements
 lack of, in Korean War, 223
 W.W. II, 124, 167, 223
Lightplane producers, 148
Lilienthal, Otto, 4, 5, 11
Lilienthal tables, 7, 10, 11, 12
Lindbergh, Charles A., 23, 24, 64, 65, 75, 76, 96n
"Lindbergh Boom," 24, 73, 76, 78
"Line production," 137–139 passim
Location of industry, 1950, 195–207 passim
 comparison with 1940, 201, 202, 203
 comparison with 1944, 197, 198, 199, 200, 201
 developments affecting, 204, 205, 206, 207
 distribution of employment, 196, 197
 plan to decentralize, 204
"Locator points," 133
Lockheed Aircraft Corporation, 108, 110, 111, 112, 126, 147, 153, 154, 166, 167, 185, 188n, 189, 191, 192, 206, 213, 220, 223, 235, 237, 238, 239, 252n, 254n
"Lockheed plan," 154
Loening, Albert, 31, 53, 61
Loening, Grover, 31, 53, 56, 77
Loewy Hydropress, 249
"Lofting," 132
"Lot" production, 135, 136
Ludington Air Lines, 79

Ludwig Henald Mfg., 248
Luscombe Airplane Corporation, 189, 194
L.W.F. Engineering Corporation, 32
Lycoming, 148

MacCracken, William P., Jr., 63
McDonnell Aircraft Corporation, 184, 189, 191, 193, 213, 220, 235, 237, 239, 252n
McFarlane, William D., 85n, 87, 92, 94
McNab, Gavin, 41
McNary-Watres Act, 83, 94, 97
Maitland, Lester J., 64, 75
Man-hours per aircraft, W.W. II, 145, 146
Manpower problems, W.W. II, 156–159 passim
Manufacturers Aircraft Association, 23, 29, 31, 37, 46, 49, 57, 67, 85, 87
Marey, Étienne J., 4
Marshall, Snowden, H., 41, 42
Marshall investigation, 42
Martin, Glenn L., 31, 61
Glenn L. Martin Company, 53, 93, 100, 111, 126, 127, 147, 150, 167, 193, 213, 235, 236n, 237, 238, 239, 248, 249, 254n
"Master layout," 132
Maxim, Sir Hiram, 5
Mayo, William B., 80n
Mead, George, 80
Mellon, Andrew, 81
Mellon, R. K., 81
Melpar, 249
Melville, George W., 5
Mercury project, 247, 250, 254, 255, 259
Mingle, Harry Bowers, 32
Mingos, Howard, 23
Minneapolis-Honeywell Co., 248
Missiles
 airframe industry concentration in, 239
 as aircraft substitutes, 229
 airframe producers of, 234–240 passim
 as basis for new competition, 231, 232, 253
 as threat to aircraft industry, 229, 230
 basic systems of, 231
 expenditures breakdown, 1959, 252
 impact on aircraft sales, 230
 impact on barriers to entry, 232, 253, 254
 impact on capitalized values, 232, 233

impact on composition of labor force, 233
names of
  Atlas ICBM, 228, 239, 244, 260
  Bomarc, 239
  Bullpup, 239
  Hounddog, 239
  LaCrosse, 239
  Mace, 239
  Mauler, 239
  Minuteman, 239
  Pershing, 239
  Polaris, 238
  Tartar, 239
  Terrior, 239
  Thor, 244, 260
  Titan, 239
  Typhon, 239
sales of, 1956–1961, 234–240
why aircraft industry qualified to produce, 231
Mitchell, William, 62, 96, 63
"Mock-up," 132
Modification center, 185
Moffett, William A., 63
Montgomery, Robert L., 33
Mooney Aircraft, Inc., 188, 194
Moore, Johnny, 22
Morrow, Dwight W., 63
Morrow Board, 23, 63, 170, 177
Morse, Frank L., 32
Mustin, Henry C., 46

Nash, C. W., 33
Nash-Kelvinator, 167, 184
Nash Motors, 33, 123,
National Advisory Committee for Aeronautics, 26, 27, 28, 32, 33, 54, 62, 174, 260
National Aeronautic Association, 33
National Aeronautics and Space Administration, 244, 245, 246, 254, 255n, 260n
National Aircraft War Production Council, 150, 166
National Air Transport, 79
National City Bank, 80
National Industrial Recovery Act of 1933, 97
National Munitions Control Board, 103, 107
National Science Foundation, 244, 260

Naval Aircraft Factory, 92, 101, 187
Naval Research Laboratory, 249
Navy Bureau of Aeronautics, 59, 63
Neutrality Act, 104, 105, 107, 108, 109
New, Harry S., 81, 94
Newcomb, Simon, 5
New Mexico College, 249
Nobile, Umberto, 75
North American Aviation, Inc., 78, 79, 83, 98, 102, 110, 111, 112, 126, 127, 147, 166, 167, 190, 192, 206, 213, 218, 220, 222, 236, 237, 238, 239, 252n, 254n
Northrop Aircraft, Inc., 81, 147, 166, 189, 191, 192, 236, 239, 254n
Nye, Gerald P., 94
Nye Committee investigation, 94–95, 103, 105

Obsolescence of airframe production facilities, reasons for, 210, 233
Ohio Crankshaft Company, 123
Otis Elevator Company, 123

Packard, 125, 189, 207
Pan American Airways, 75, 79
Patents, 26, 28, 51
Patrick, Mason M., 63
Patterson Plan, 204n
"Penalty run," 134
Pennsylvania Forestry Commission, 48
Perkins, Randolph, 61
Phillips, Horatio, 5
Pilcher, Percy, 5
Pioneer Instrument Company, 56
Piper Aircraft Corporation, 148, 189n, 191, 193, 237
Pitcairn, Harold F., 59
Polarad Electronics, 248
Post Office Department, 40, 48, 49, 58
Potter, William C., 33
Praeger, Otto, 48
Pratt and Whitney Aircraft Company, 81, 85n, 86, 89, 92, 93, 121–127 passim, 148, 167, 194, 207
President's Air Policy Commission, 209, 212n
Procurement of contracts, steps in, 238
Production levels
  1914, 23
  1918, 23

Production levels (*continued*)
  1929, 73, 84
  1932, 73
  1940–1945, 163, 164
  1941–1943, 143
  1943, 143, 144
  1943–1946, 182–185
  post-W.W. I, 45
  W.W. I, 44
Profits, company
  on net worth, Korean War, 218, 319
  1929–1933, 88, 89, 91, 92
Propeller producers
  Aeroproducts, 148, 186, 194
  American Propeller, 148, 186
  Beech Aircraft, 189
  Curtiss Propeller, 190, 194
  Flottrop Manufacturing, 195
  Frigidaire, 167
  G. B. Lewis, 195
  Hamilton Standard, 148, 167, 194
  Hartzell Propeller, 195
  Koppers, 189, 194
  McCauley, 195
  Nash-Kelvinator, 167
  Remington-Rand, 167
  Sensenich, 195
Propellers, W.W. II
  Curtiss Electric, 148
  Hamilton Standard, 148

Radio Corporation of America, 252n, 254n
Rae, John, 256
Raymond Engineering Co., 249
Raytheon, 254n
Rear rudder control, 18
Reconversion problems after W.W. II, 177
Redden, Charles F., 56
Reeves Instrument, 248
Rentschler, Frederick B., 31, 56, 59, 80, 81, 90, 91
Rentschler, Gordon S., 80
Republic Aviation Corp., 111, 126, 147, 193, 207, 213, 223, 236, 237
Roosevelt, Franklin D., 95, 96, 104, 110, 115, 119, 141, 150, 163, 171
Royalties, 51
Rundstedt, Karl Rudolf Gerd von, 162
Russell, Frank H., 30, 31, 32, 56, 57, 59, 61

Ryan, John D., 33
Ryan Aeronautical Company, 148, 166, 194

St. Louis Aircraft Corporation, 184, 187
Sales, aircraft industry
  diversification of, 230, 231
  1918, 23
  1927, 24, 73
  1929, 24, 73
  1933, 73
  1934, 99
  1939, 99
  1940, 99
  1955–1963, utility aircraft, 227
  1956–1960, military, 230
  1958, commercial jet transports, 227
  1958, missiles, 227
  per cent of government sales, 1927–1933, 93
  W.W. II, 147, 148
Schlee, Edward F., 64, 75
Schulter, 64
Schumpeter, Joseph A., 228, 229n, 256
Shepard, Alan, 245, 259
Signal Corps, 42
Sikorsky, 81
Silliman, Harriet, 6
Smith, Charles Kingsford, 64
Smithsonian Institution, 4, 5, 33
Southern Aircraft, 187
Space budgets, United States, 1955–1962, 260
Space programs
  annual appropriations for 1955–1961, 1962, 244, 260
  complexity of, 248–250
  as an employer, 254–256 *passim*
  estimate of military procurement to 1970, 245, 246
  estimate of NASA expenditures to 1970, 245, 246
  estimated annual outlays for, 243
  opportunity cost of, 250, 251
  prospects for industry, 251–254 *passim*
  public support for, 247
  technological progress resulting from, 256
  Vanguard project, 248–250
Space projects
  Advent, 244
  Blue Scout, 244, 257

Courier, 244
Discoverer, 244
Dyna-Soar, 257
Explorer, 244
Midas, 244
Nova, 253
Rover, 253, 260
Samos, 244
Saturn, 253
SNAP, 260
Space Track, 244
Spasur, 244
Transit, 244
Vanguard, 244, 248–252 passim
Viking, 248
X-15, 244
Spanish-American War, 62
Spartan Aircraft Company, 187
Sperry, Lawrence, 56
Sperry Corporation, 79, 195n
Sperry Rand, 254n
Spoils Conference, 83, 84, 90, 94, 95, 96, 97
Spratt, George A., 15, 16
Sputniks I and II, 248
Squier, George O., 33
Standard Aircraft Corporation, 32
Standard Oil Company of California, 80n
Standard Statistics Company, 84
Stearman, 148
Stout, William B., 31
Stroukoff, 237
Studebaker Corporation, 123, 167, 185
Sturtevant Aeroplane Company, 32
Subcontracting
  Korean War, 209, 214–216 passim, 222
  W.W. II, 129, 152–156 passim
Surplus aircraft
  after W.W. I, 168
  after W.W. II, 167, 181
  effect on engine development, 168, 169, 170
  spares, W.W. I, 168
Surplus Property Board, 168

Talbot, Harold E., Jr., 32, 80
Tarbox, John P., 32
Taylor, D. W., 33
Taylorcraft, 148, 184, 194
Tektronix, 249
Temco, 237

Texas Engineering and Manufacturing Company, 188, 191, 194
Thayer, H. B., 33
Thomas-Morse Aircraft Corporation, 31, 32, 53
Thompson Ramo Woolridge, Inc., 252n
Timm Aircraft Corporation, 187
Titov, German Stepanovich, 245
"Tooling," 131
Training-plane producers, 148
Transcontinental Air Transport, 79
Transcontinental and Western Air, Inc., 79, 98
Truman, Harry S., 206
Tyler, Carrol L., 175

United Aircraft and Transport Corporation, 33, 79, 80, 81, 83, 85, 89, 90, 108, 111, 188, 190, 193, 194
United Airlines, 91, 98
United Kingdom, defense in W.W. I, 25
United Nations, 173
United States Aeronautical Board, 114
United States Employment Service, 158
University of Maryland, 249
Uppercu, Inglis M., 32
U.S. Federal Aviation Commission Report, January, 1935, 85

V-E Day, 182, 186
V-J Day, 167, 169, 183
Van Allen radiation belts, discovery of, 248
Vanguard project, 248–252 passim
Vega Aircraft Company, 147, 150, 191
Vinci, Leonardo da, 5
Vinson-Trammell Act of 1934, 74
  as procurement authorization, 100
  profit limitation of, 101, 102
Vought, Chance, 31, 53, 57
Vought Sikorsky, 147
Vultee Aircraft, Inc., 191

Waco Aircraft Company, 148, 191
Walcott, Charles D., 33
Waldon, Sidney D., 33
War Manpower Commission, 158
Warner, Edward P., 63
Warner Aircraft Engines, 176, 184
War Production Board, 144, 158
Watres Act, 94, 97
Weather Bureau, 244, 260

Webster, Clarence W., 104
Weidenbaum, Murray L., 245, 256
Western Air Express, 79, 98
Western Electric Co., Inc., 252n, 254n
Westinghouse Electric Corporation, 186, 192, 194
Wilbur, Curtis D., 68
Wilkins, Sir Hubert, 75
Willard, Charles F., 31
Willebrandt, Mabel Walker, 82
William T. Lyons Co., Inc., 249
Williams, James, 246
Willys-Overland, 189
Wilson, Woodrow, 41, 42

Wings
  how warped, 8
Witmer, Charles C., 56
World War I, 25
World War II, 119
  importance of air power in, 162
Wright, Orville, 3, 4, 31, 79, 80, 96n
Wright, Wilbur, 3, 4, 6, 8, 12n, 79
Wright Aeronautical Corporation, 47, 56, 80, 85, 87, 89, 91, 101, 121, 123, 148, 167, 190, 194, 205
Wright Company, 8, 32, 53
Wright-Martin Company, 31, 32
Wright patent, 17